Untold histories

Manchester University Press

Untold histories
Black people in England and Wales during the period of the British slave trade, c.1660–1807

KATHLEEN CHATER

Manchester University Press
Manchester and New York

distributed in the United States exclusively
by Palgrave Macmillan

Copyright © Kathleen Chater 2009

The right of Kathleen Chater to be identified as the author of this work has been asserted by her in accordance with the Copyright, Designs and Patents Act 1988.

Published by Manchester University Press
Oxford Road, Manchester M13 9NR, UK
and Room 400, 175 Fifth Avenue, New York, NY 10010, USA
www.manchesteruniversitypress.co.uk

Distributed in the United States exclusively by
Palgrave Macmillan, 175 Fifth Avenue,
New York, NY 10010, USA

Distributed in Canada exclusively by
UBC Press, University of British Columbia, 2029 West Mall,
Vancouver, BC, Canada V6T 1Z2

British Library Cataloguing-in-Publication Data is available

Library of Congress Cataloging-in-Publication Data is available

ISBN 978 0 7190 8597 0 paperback

First published by Manchester University Press in hardback 2009

This paperback edition first published 2011

The publisher has no responsibility for the persistence or accuracy of URLs for any external or third-party internet websites referred to in this book, and does not guarantee that any content on such websites is, or will remain, accurate or appropriate.

Printed by Lightning Source

Contents

List of tables and figures   *page* vii
List of illustrations   ix
List of abbreviations   xi

Introduction   1

Part I   Counting heads

1. The Black population of England and Wales   21
2. The Black population of London   35

Part II   Black people and the law

3. Free or enslaved?   77
4. Black people and the criminal justice system   102
5. Black people, settlement and the poor laws   136

Part III   Living and working in the wider community

6. Assimilation or integration?   159
7. Names and identities   176
8. Marriage and family   203
9. Working lives   222

Select bibliography   247
Index   265

List of tables and figures

Tables

1	Descriptions used for Black people 1660–1812	page 23
2	Baptisms of Black people in Wapping 1730–1812	51
3	Crimes for which Black people were tried at the Old Bailey, 1674–1812	110
4	Verdicts passed on Black and all defendants at the Old Bailey, 1674–1812	111
5	Sentences passed on Black people at the Old Bailey, 1674–1812	115
6	Verdicts passed on men committing crimes against Black men	124
7	Verdicts passed on women committing crimes against Black men	125
8	Most popular names of white and Black men, seventeenth to nineteenth centuries	188
9	Most popular names of white and Black women, seventeenth to nineteenth centuries	189
10	Most popular surnames of white and Black people, seventeenth to nineteenth centuries	190

Figures

1	Area of origin of Black people in England 1660–1812	64
2	Area of origin of Black people in Westminster 1660–1812	64
3	Area of origin of Black people in the City of London 1660–1812	65
4	Origins of the Black population of the City Without 1660–1812	65

List of illustrations

1	The slave trading ports of England	page 28
2	The areas of metropolitan London covered by the Bills of Mortality	36
3	The parish of St Giles in the Fields	43
4	Tom and Jerry in the Holy Land, from Pierce Egan's *Life in London*. Author's collection	47
5	Record in the vestry minutes of the parish of West Ham of 20*l* 1d collected for the redemption of white slaves in Algeria (1670/1). Newham Archives and Local Studies Library	80
6	The murder by John Sutherland of his cabin boy. Author's collection	82
7	A potential typical crime involving a Black person, attributed to Thomas Rowlandson (1756–1827). Author's collection	126
8	Family tree of George John Scipio Africanus	213
9	Family tree of John Cranbrook	215
10	Family tree of Peter George Florida	217
11	Elizabeth Keppel by Sir Joshua Reynolds, 1761. Reproduced by permission of His Grace the Duke of Bedford and the Trustees of the Bedford Estate	223
12	Bill Richmond acting as second to the Black boxer Tom Molineux by George Cruikshank, c.1820. Author's collection	230
13	William Davidson, engraving by Robert Cooper, 1820, from a portrait by Abraham Wivell. Collection of Richard Rose	239

List of abbreviations

AAGHS	Afro-American Historical and Genealogical Society
bap.	baptised
BASA	Black & Asian Studies Association
bur.	buried
CLRO	Corporation of London Record Office (now part of LMA)
CWA	City of Westminster Archives
FFHS	Federation of Family History Societies (publications now produced by The Family History Partnership)
FHS	Family History Society
GHC	Greenwich Heritage Centre
GL	Guildhall Library
GLC	Greater London Council (now defunct)
HMSO	Her Majesty's Stationery Office
HS	Harleian Society
IGI	International Genealogical Index
LMA	London Metropolitan Archives
mar.	married
NMM	National Maritime Museum, Greenwich
NY	New York
Proceedings	*Proceedings of the Sessions of Oyez and Terminer held at the Old Bailey*
RO	Record Office
SoG	Society of Genealogists
TNA	The National Archives (formerly the Public Record Office), Kew

Introduction

Around the year 2000 I began researching the lives of Black people in eighteenth-century England because, in the course of tracing my own family history (which I have been doing for some thirty years), I began to suspect that one of my ancestors might be Black. He was born about 1803 and worked first as a coachman, then as a publican in an area where there were a number of people born in the West Indies, but there was no record of his origins in any official records. In the hope of discovering other sources which would confirm or refute my suspicions, I read books on the history of Black people in England. The picture that emerged was not one I entirely recognised. Most historians made the assumption that Black people in Britain were mainly slaves and regarded as subhuman. However, in the course of my genealogical research, both personal and professional, I had come across a number of references that suggested otherwise. Black people were baptised and buried in the same churches as the white population: there was no segregation.[1] Inquests were as carefully carried out on them, as on the white population, and eighteenth-century newspaper reports mentioned their involvement in events without any racialised comments on their colour or ethnicity. At that time I had seen no parish records, nor inquests nor newspaper accounts where a Black person either was called a slave or had died at the hands of a master. I also knew that the white majority left behind few traces of their own creation and that many people in the Victorian era regarded the poor, whatever their colour, as subhuman.

Historiography

> When we attempt to answer the question 'What is history?', our answer consciously or unconsciously, reflects our own position in time and forms part of our answer to the broader question what view we take of the society in which we live.[2]

E.H. Carr drew this conclusion from considering the differences in approaches to historical interpretation between two historians, Lord Acton and Sir George Clark, writing in periods sixty years apart. As John Tosh wrote, 'history is a political battleground. The sanction of the past is sought by those committed to upholding authority and by those intent on subverting it.'[3] In the seven years between the first and second editions of his book, Tosh noted three new methods of historical interpretation which had gained influence in that time. Each generation (approximately thirty years) reacts against the previous generation in a number of ways, including interpreting the past. Interpretations of the past both help to create and are created by current theories. Race has been one of the most contentious issues in public life since the late 1950s, so it follows that the history of Black people in both England and its ex-colonies is problematic and discussion of it is inevitably influenced by current concerns and beliefs.

When I read works on Black British history, I was, therefore, not surprised to see that there seemed to be three distinct phases in writing about Black people in Britain: the first covered the period up to the 1960s, the second the thirty-odd years up to the 1990s and the third continues into the early twenty-first century These three correlated to what might be called intellectual fashions in historical interpretation. To oversimplify, the first phase was the product of a period of relative social stability. After the Second World War, the political and social landscape changed dramatically. From the 1960s onwards, the theories of socialism became more dominant, until the late 1980s saw a change from collectivity to individualism. Why these changes happened is for debate elsewhere. What is clear is how they affected works on the history of Black people in Britain.

M. Dorothy George seems to have been the first modern historian to mention the presence of Black people in London in the eighteenth century. *London Life in the Eighteenth Century*, first published in 1925, contained six pages on the subject, one of which was devoted to lascars (sailors from the Indian subcontinent and China).[4] J. Jean Hecht's monograph, *Continental and Colonial Servants in Eighteenth Century England* appeared in 1954.[5] These early references treated Black people as part of the general population, not separate from it. There seem to be no other scholarly works dealing with Black people in Britain until 1948, when Kenneth Little's *Negroes in Britain* appeared. This was the first book to look at the history of Black people as a distinct group. Its publication came in the same year as the arrival of the SS *Empire Windrush*, the first of many ships bringing Black people from the West Indies to Britain when labour was needed to rebuild in the post-war period, although the work must have been written earlier. Although Little's book mainly detailed the results of a sociological and anthropological survey into the contemporary Black community in Cardiff, there was a chapter containing a brief history of Black people in Britain from AD 1600 to the present, i.e. 1948, which contained a section on the development of English racial attitudes. He seems to have been the first to explore the development of racial prejudice, which he dates from the middle of the nineteenth century. His sources for this part of the book were largely secondary, so Little mainly concentrated on those who were obviously slaves, using advertisements for sales and runaways and detailing the Somerset case and the Mansfield Judgment. There was little about ordinary Black people. This book had a great influence on subsequent studies, not least in its emphasis on slavery. Most subsequent works have followed the same pattern: a historical survey, a description of the events leading up to the Mansfield Judgment of 1772, the effect scientific racism in the nineteenth century had on the development of prejudice and discrimination, and much more detailed work on the involvement of Black people in political movements of the late nineteenth and the twentieth centuries.

At the time that the second edition of Little's book appeared in 1972, Edward Scobie's book *Black Britannia* (Chicago, 1972) was published and developed Little's historical chapters with considerably more research. The first third of the book was taken up with Black people, or more precisely Black men, in Britain before the early nineteenth century and the abolition of slavery in England. The rest dealt with the period up to 1969. Like Little, he wrote perceptively about the change in attitude and growth of 'scientific racism' that occurred after emancipation. Scobie, born in 1918 in Dominica, also came to the subject from a background in which the legacy of slavery was strong.

What is called 'Black history' developed in America from the 1960s onwards. It was part of the growing interest in the history of various minority groups or sections of the population, like women and the working classes, which had previously received scant attention from historians. James Walvin's books *The Black Presence* and *Black and White: the Negro and English Society 1555–1945* (1973) covered the same ground as Little and Scobie, but reproduced selected passages from contemporary documents. *The Black Presence* was largely a collection of transcripts of extracts from books and legal documents, linked by a commentary. It was part of a series edited by Laurence F. Orbach of Queens College, City University of New York and the influence of American Black history was strong. Walvin came to look at Black people in Britain after writing, with Michael Craton, *A Jamaican Plantation: the History of Worthy Park 1670–1970* (1970), which must also have influenced his emphasis on slavery.

The 1960s and 1970s were also a time of great civil unrest, in both the USA and Britain, when anger and contempt for authority seemed to be the prevailing emotions.[6] The next historian to look at the history of Black people in Britain admitted that his works were agitprop, then regarded in some academic circles as acceptable, even laudable. The Nigerian Folarin Shyllon's books *Black Slaves in Britain* (Oxford, 1974) and *Black People in Britain 1555–1833* (Oxford, 1977) had a very different tone from previous works on the subject. The dates of publication and the fact that these books were published for the Institute of Race Relations, at that time heavily influenced by Marxism, were also significant. In his preface to *Black People*, Shyllon admitted that this book was propaganda and in the epilogue demanded 'Black power in Africa, America, and Britain'.[7] He made claims about the experiences of Black people in Britain which depended on American writers like W.E.B. Du Bois, Calvin C. Hernton and John Howard Griffin, a white writer who travelled through the Southern States of the USA disguised as a Black man. Shyllon used a quotation from W.E.B. Du Bois' *The Souls of Black Folk* as an epigraph. As a preface to the list of the secondary sources used, he stated, 'Before writing anything on any aspect of Black History it is obligatory that the novice Black historian reads *The Autobiography of Malcolm X* and George Jackson's *Soledad Brother: the Prison Letters of George Jackson*, and goes back to them from time to time for a renewal of faith.' These writers were part of the American Black Power movement, one of the anti-establishment political movements that characterised the 1970s. It had followers in Britain. It is significant that Shyllon wrote 'faith', which is something that cannot be proved by evidence. Shyllon exemplifies the tendency among some historians of Black people to see them as an undifferentiated mass of victims rather than as individuals with the complete range of human qualities, individual personalities and experiences. Reducing Black people to passive symbols of oppression diminishes their humanity. However, intellectual honesty occasionally prompted Shyllon to undermine his own arguments by adding the odd sentence, such as the almost throw-away admissions that advertisements for runaway servants were less about their colour than about the authority men had over all members of their household; that most domestics were taught to read and write and that some were apprenticed.[8] These were all things that George had observed more than forty years before.

As well as those who saw Black people as a distinct sub-section of the British population, there were some who regarded them as part of the working class. One of the writers whose work concentrated on the political aspects of the Black presence was Ron Ramdin. *The Making of the Black Working Class in Britain* (Gower, 1987) concentrated on the period after 1830, but described the lives of three early Black political activists, Robert Wedderburn, William Davidson and William Cuffay. In *Reimaging Britain: 500 Years of Black and Asian History* (1999), Ramdin expanded and re-examined the work done for his previous publication about Black working-class people in Britain. Peter Linebaugh and Maurice Redeker's works, *The London Hanged* and *The Many-Headed Hydra*,[9] mentioned Black people, but saw them as part of the oppressed underclass, whose 'struggle' (a key word for socialists) was paramount. Those who lived quiet, unremarkable lives were of no interest, even though they were the majority. Michael Craton took issue with this concentration on resistance of those:

> bowled over by Herbert Aptheker's dictim that 'history is the story of resistance, not acquiescence' (which on reflection simply seemed to be another way of saying that 'since only resistance is important, we'll ignore all other types of subjects' behaviour').[10]

Slavery itself, particularly in the British Empire, continued to receive most attention. James Pope-Hennessy had published *Sins of the Fathers: a Study of the Atlantic Slave Traders 1441–1807* in 1967. After his publications mentioned above, Walvin's work largely concentrated on the British slave trade. In 1976 he produced *Slavery, Abolition and Emancipation*. Walvin, Craton and David Wright edited *Slavery and British Society 1776–1846* (1982), gathering together a number of essays on various aspects of slavery, most of which fall outside the scope of this work. Walvin's next book on the subject was *Slavery and British Society* (1982). His *Passage to Britain* (1984) was written to accompany a Channel 4 series made by TVS, although it was an autonomous study, and concentrated on Black immigrants after 1880. There were, however, chapters on immigrants in general, in which the presence of Black people in England from 1560 was mentioned. *England, Slaves and Freedom 1776–1838* (Basingstoke, 1986) was his next publication.

Interest in the slave trade remained strong the 1990s. In 1992, Walvin produced *Slaves and Slavery: the British Colonial Experience* (Manchester) and *Black Ivory: A History of British Slavery*. In *The Slave Trade* (1997), Hugh Thomas explored the European slave trade with the New World.

S.I. Martin's *Britain's Slave Trade* (1999) grew out of a series of television programmes on Channel 4, broadcast in 2000. It was aimed at a mass audience, and so simplified previous work on the slave trade. What the book did add that was new – and this was much more prominent in the television programmes – was present-day descendants of Black people, including Dennis Barber, a descendant of Francis Barber, Dr Johnson's servant and heir.[11] Not all those featured in the programmes were included in the book, but their emotional responses covered a wide range from anger to mild pride. The programmes were, therefore, much more valuable to an understanding of the legacy of slavery than the book produced from it. James Walvin's *The Slave Trade* (Stroud, 1999) and *Britain's Slave Empire* (2000) continued his work on the subject of the British slave trade. Walvin and Ged Heuman edited *The Slavery Reader* (2003). There were also a number of books on individual slave traders or ports from which the trade operated.[12]

The bicentenary of the abolition of the British slave trade brought more publications.[13] Like most of the works previously mentioned, they took the institution of slavery as their starting point, which was understandable, given the event they were commemorating. The majority of works have been issue driven: individuals appeared primarily to illustrate arguments. Black people were seen only in relation to their white masters or the traders who shipped them. The books thus reinforced the view that white people were in control, that they instigated the trade and directed the lives of the slaves. This, of course, is partly true but the African involvement in the trade was largely ignored or minimised. The following books and articles took an alternative approach. They focused on individuals: issues still emerged but were secondary to the people whose lives were affected by them. It is perhaps not a coincidence that many of these works are by women. There is a marked difference in the way men and women in general (there are always individual differences) approach a subject. Men are much more concerned with power and the obvious manifestations of it through laws and economic factors. This must be one of the reasons why it was a woman, M. Dorothy George, who was the first to notice the presence of Black people, poor, powerless and apparently uninfluential, in London.

This focus on individuals seems to be the result of the latest shift in the *zeitgeist*. Elizabeth Lasch-Quinn's *Race Experts: How Racial Etiquette, Sensitivity Training and New Age Therapy Hijacked the Civil Rights Revolution* (NY, 2001) explored how the mass demands for political reform in the 1960s and 1970s turned into individual quests for self-esteem in the 1980s and 1990s. It is an excellent overview of how current concerns shifted from the political to the personal. However, it was a man, Peter Fryer, who began this move to look at individuals. Fryer came to the history of Black people through journalism and his background was reflected in the style and content of his book *Staying Power: the History of Black People in Britain* (1984). The structure of his book was similar to those of previous writers but he adduced much more factual evidence, reporting rather than developing theories. He also took a wider view of the subject than had previous historians, who looked at Black people in Britain as if slavery and poverty were the only things that defined them. Although Fryer wrote a great deal about slavery, he looked beyond it to see how Black people were not stigmatised outsiders but were woven into English society as servants, workers and founders of families. He did this largely through a formidable list of sources, both primary and secondary.[14]

Stephen J. Braidwood's *Black Poor and White Philanthropists: London's Blacks and the Foundation of the Sierra Leone Settlement 1786–1791* (Liverpool, 1994) looked in detail at the project to create a colony of Black people in Sierra Leone, sparked by the influx of poor Blacks who came to England following the American War of Independence. Previous historians who covered the subject regarded it as, to quote Shyllon, the British government's 'patriotic enthusiasm to preserve the purity of the English bloodstream by expelling from England "the lesser breeds without the law".'[15] Braidwood looked at the individuals, both Black and white, involved in the planning and execution of the project, to reveal more complex personal agendas in which Black people were not passive victims but actively wanted to go to Africa.

Gretchen Gerzina's *Black England* (1995) and *Black London* (NJ, 1995) examined the period up to emancipation. The two books concentrated on individuals. They were populist works which mainly collected together and added details to material covered in previous publications. Although she added very little to what was already known, she made two important contributions. The first was to realise that in eighteenth-century England class (or, as it would have been called then, rank) seemed to be the determining factor in how Black people were perceived, not colour or race. The second was to look at people as human beings, not pieces of evidence in abstract arguments. Although others mentioned Dido Elizabeth Belle, Lord Mansfield's illegitimate grand-niece, who was of mixed race, Gerzina appears to be the first to have asked what making his judgement meant to him in personal terms.[16]

Individual lives

Only a few Black individuals in Britain before the nineteenth century have been written about at any length. Some produced autobiographies. Briton Hammon appears to have been the first, in 1760,[17] followed by Ukawsaw Gronniosaw (1770?);[18] Ignatius Sancho (1782);[19] John Marrant (1785);[20] Ottobah Cugoano (1787);[21] Olaudah Equiano (1789);[22] Boston King (1798)[23] and John Jea (c.1811).[24] Those about whom most secondary material has been written are Olaudah Equiano and Ignatius Sancho. This is partly because they are the ones about whom most is known, but Equiano's prominence in the abolitionist movement contributed greatly to the interest in him. His seafaring background, though extensively covered in his autobiography, was not much written about until the growth of interest in the personal, as opposed to political, experiences of Black people. Briton Hammon also spent time at sea. Between them, they cast interesting light on mariners' experiences, and the lack of prejudice encountered from shipmates, but Hammon is rarely mentioned. This may be because there is some dispute about whether he was a slave or a servant. He was ecstatic to be reunited with his old master after being kidnapped in America, but the focus of historians has been largely on the enslaved and the oppressed.

There have been several editions of Equiano's work. *Equiano's Travels* (1967) was an abridged edition, edited by Paul Edwards. The most recent and fullest edition of the *Narrative* is Vincent Carretta's edition of 2003. It includes additional ephemeral writings. Walvin wrote *An African's Life: The Life and Times of Olaudah Equiano* (2000). Carretta published a biography, *Equiano, the African* (Athens, GA, 2005) which contained much new material. His major discovery was evidence that suggests Equiano was not, as he claimed, born in Africa but in America.

Ignatius Sancho apparently exemplifies the life of a Black man in service and this is how he is still generally regarded. He formed the focus of an exhibition in the National Portrait Gallery, London in 1996. In the collection of essays that accompanied the exhibition Suhkdev Sandhu remarked that, when Black writers were rediscovered in the 1960s, 'Sancho seemed too well-fed, too affluent and self-assured to serve as an early dissident prophet', especially during the 1970s and early 1980s.[25] This may be why there is no full-length biography of him. Gronniosaw, too, encountered little or no prejudice based on his colour. His life was hard and he was possibly the first poor person to describe the desperate attempts such people had to make to keep themselves and their families.

There are ample references in his autobiography to enable a fuller biography to be put together, which could be used as an example of how many poor people, both Black and white, lived at the time, yet no one has undertaken this. John Marrant, Boston King and John Jea were all preachers, and therefore their experiences are of value in understanding the place of Black people in the religious life of the eighteenth century. But they are absent from the mainstream agenda, even though religion was one of the major factors shaping life in this period. *Black Voices: the Shaping of our Christian Experience* by David Killingray and Joel Edwards (Nottingham, 2007) has made a preliminary attempt to look at this neglected area.

I concluded that the literature on Black people during the period of the British slave trade concentrated on a limited number of issues and mainly those individuals who illustrated the issues. Black people were rarely put into the context of their age.[26] It is as if, in two hundred years' time, some future historian were to look at Black people in early twenty-first-century Britain using only newspaper reports and official publications detailing educational failure. Certainly the picture that emerged would reflect a small section of the population but it is always more interesting and representative to look at what is so ordinary that it is not considered worth reporting. I thought I might write an article on this. To my surprise, I found there was no central database of references to Black people, so I began to search parish registers and other parish records. Within a few months I had some six hundred references, mainly baptisms but also a few burials. I had also found the will of the Black servant of a slave trader and realised why colour or origin were not consistently recorded in parish records. These formed the basis of two articles.[27] At this point, I registered to do a thesis, realising that my work so far had raised a large number of questions that no one had yet considered. I did not at this stage have any particular theory but was just curious to confirm or refute the assertions made by some historians that Black people were treated differently from the white population.

Research methodology

The database I set up now numbers over 4,500 entries, including references from both before and after the period covered by the thesis, and is still growing. It is the first of its kind, although increasing interest in the subject has meant that in the last few years most record offices have been collecting entries relating to Black and other ethnic minorities in their localities. The entries on the database are largely drawn from parish registers but also from other parish records (like settlement and bastardy examinations and workhouse minutes), newspaper reports, inquest records, the printed *Proceedings* of trials at the Old Bailey, private diaries and letters, etc. At first I used index cards to note those I found and when I reviewed the initial six hundred or so references I had gathered I noticed that there was common information in many of them that would allow some preliminary demographic data to be produced. For the majority of entries, unfortunately, there was little beyond the date and place of the event, name and colour/ethnic origin. Sometimes place of origin was given. A comparatively small number also included names of masters and baptismal sponsors. The latter, I thought, might help to establish occupations and the social milieu in which the individual lived but, because this information was rarely recorded, it did not prove to be very useful.

There are two main databases. The larger consists of Black people whose colour or ethnic origin is stated or can be surmised from other evidence. The fields are:

Surname
First name
Additional names
Sex
Type of record
Town/Parish
County/City
Day
Month
Year
Age
Description
Occupation
Master
Witness 1
Witness 2
Witness 3
Area of origin (Africa, Asia, Caribbean, North America)
Country of origin
Notes

These fields allowed the extraction of some data relating to the sex ratio of males to females; age (I decided to divide all the statistics relating to

Introduction

age into ten-year cohorts ending with an even number because of the implications of assigning the age of 21, legal majority, to individuals); the part of the world from which the person came (and sometimes the individual country or even place within it); and occupation. However, in the vast majority of cases only name and colour/ethnic origin were given in the records.

The second, considerably smaller, database is of children born to Black parents in this country, where their origin is mentioned in the records. There were other cases in records where the colour or ethnic origin of the parents were not given but could be discovered from other sources, such as the baptisms of the children of Ignatius and Anne Sancho. These children I noted on the index card for their parents, but in this database I only included those whose colour or ethnic origin were stated. I set this up because I was interested in how children and their parentage were recorded, as I soon observed that it was the parents' details that were given, rather than a racial classification of the child, so it was not easy to integrate them into the main database. The fields here are:

Surname
First name
Second name
Sex
Type of record
Town/Parish
County/City
Day
Month
Year
Age
Father's name
Mother's name
Description of child
Description of father
Description of mother
Birthplace of child (if different from the location of the record)
Notes

A third, smaller database was set up for the part of this book analysing crime and Black people. The individuals were also entered on the first database. The fields here are:

Surname
First name/names
Sex
Age
Occupation
Master
Crime
Date of the crime
Place where the crime occurred
County
Role (defendant, prosecutor, witness or mentioned in evidence but not called)
Sentence
Recommended for mercy or not
Outcome (reprieved or sentence carried out in full)
Residence of individual in Britain
Area of origin (Africa, Asia, Caribbean, N. America)
Country of origin
Notes

This enabled the extraction of statistics about the types of crime in which Black people were involved, the roles they played in court proceedings and whether the individuals accused of crimes (whether Black or white) were found guilty as charged or of a lesser crime. I also wanted to gain information about places of origin and places of residence in Britain (if not where the crime occurred) but this information was rarely given, so these fields proved less useful than I had hoped.

I decided to limit my thesis to England and Wales, partly because the differences in law in Scotland, Ireland and the various off-shore islands (the Channel Islands, the Isles of Scilly and the Isle of Man) make comparisons between the status of Black people in England and Wales and these places difficult to establish; but mainly because most records are held locally and those outside London are therefore time-consuming and expensive to investigate, although the extensive library of the Society of Genealogists made it possible to explore the registers of several hundred parishes around the country.

I chose the starting date of 1660 for two reasons. The first was that, although acquiring African slaves pre-dated 1660, it was not until 1663 that the Royal Adventurers into Africa specifically stated in its charter that one of the objectives was to supply the American colonies with 'Negro-servants'. The second reason for the choice of starting date was that it marks the Restoration of Charles II after the Commonwealth period. During the Commonwealth the responsibility for registering births and marriages was passed from the parish authorities to Justices of the Peace and most of these records have been lost. Although most parishes continued to perform (and usually record) baptisms and marriages, these records are incomplete, and so would be less valid statistically. The British slave trade was abolished in 1807 but it seemed more sensible to extend the period of the database to 1812, when the introduction of printed registers for baptisms and burials limited the amount of additional information that clerks had routinely recorded in parish registers because of there being no guidelines as to what should be entered.

As the database is constantly being updated, the numbers given in this book are already incomplete and I have preferred, where appropriate, to give percentages, which seem to remain constant each time recalculations are made.

Although the database I produced provides statistical information, I am primarily interested in exploring the lives of Black people in this country, not simply registering their presence, which is already well known. In order to reconstruct individual lives I have used the standard techniques of the genealogist. My own book *Tracing Your Family Tree in England, Ireland, Wales and Scotland* (2nd edn, 2008) details these. This is a time-consuming process: each person's life takes about a week (35 working hours) to investigate, so I have been unable to do more than a few. In some cases I have been able to track descendants for several generations or even to the present.

It became apparent that there were very few Black people in Wales during the long eighteenth century, outside ports and the major towns. More work will need to be done on the reasons for this and the lives of those few who have been found there, but Black people are also absent from records in large areas of England, so I have included Wales in the title of this book and mention some individuals in the text. Considerably more research on the lives of Black people in both England and Wales may be able to extract further demographic data, like average age at marriage, number of children, age at death and both social and geographic mobility, which can be compared to the indigenous population. This book is very much a preliminary exploration.

A note about Old Style dates

The first day of the new year in England and Wales was 25 March until 1752, when it was changed to 1 January. This means that before 1752 dates between 1 January and 24 March would be recorded as falling in what looks like the previous year. To prevent confusion, these dates are now given as, for example, 1 January 1750/1.

A note about money

Before decimalisation in 1971, Britain's currency consisted of 12 pennies (12d) to the shilling (1s) and 20s to the pound (£1), which might also be written as 1*l* (or *libra*, Latin for 'pound'). It is notoriously difficult to translate money into its present-day equivalent, partly because prices of everyday commodities were proportionately different from what they are today and partly because workers might receive part of their income in kind, rather than in cash. Very broadly speaking, during the period covered by this book 15s (75p) was a weekly wage: in the late seventeenth century this was what a skilled craftsman earned, and by the beginning of the nineteenth century, due to inflation and other economic changes, it was what an agricultural labourer received.

Acknowledgements

In the course of compiling the database and working on the thesis on which this book is based, I received a great deal of help from a number of people. My supervisor, Professor David Killingray, is the first I must thank. He saved me from many basic errors and any that remain are my responsibility. Family historians have responded generously to my requests for references. They are too many to name here but have been acknowledged where appropriate in the text. Individuals like Audrey Dewjee, Dr Joan Kemp, Mary Croft and Glenda Thornton sent multiple references. Members of the Hertfordshire Family History Society have also continued to send references over an extended period, usually anonymously. Dr Jill Barber, who initially worked at the City of Westminster Archives Centre and is now with Hertfordshire Record Office, has always had a particular interest in the history of Black people in England. I profited from lectures and courses on Black people in Westminster that she organised there. She has also contributed many references from both Westminster and Hertfordshire as well as discussing the subject with me. Sue Kirby, then of the London Borough of Newham's Heritage Service, was a great source of support and commissioned me to carry out several research projects on Black people in the borough during the eighteenth century. At Huntingdonshire Record Office, Matthew Hall was particularly helpful when I visited. R.G. Thomas of Suffolk Record Office sent a list of references he had found in the archives there. Other record offices, like Gloucestershire, Northamptonshire and Birmingham, have put findings related to Black people in their localities on their websites and I have used these. Norma Myers saved me a lot of work by listing the cases at the Old Bailey involving Black people that she had already researched for her thesis.

I have had useful conversations with members of BASA, the Black and Asian Studies Association, particularly Dr Caroline Bressey, Daniel Grey and Marika Sherwood. I have also discussed the subject with Professor Vincent Carretta and Professor Gretchen Gerzina. Arthur Torrington, founder of the Equiano Society, has taken great interest in my work and provided many opportunities to attend events he has organised and to meet people also interested in the subject. Professor James Walvin was a generous examiner of my thesis and has been immensely encouraging and supportive in getting this work published. Friends who listened with great patience as I talked at some length about my discoveries and theories include Marie Andrews, Michael Harper and Sandra Moscardini. The staff on the computer help desk at Goldsmiths College were really helpful, especially when I encountered difficulties with the database, and they also responded patiently to many basic queries from someone who began her working life when electric typewriters were the state of the art. My thanks go also to Judith Oppenheimer for her superb copy-editing of the typescript.

Lastly, I would like to dedicate this work to my late mother, Vera Chater, who first aroused my interest in history and genealogy, and to my father, Reginald Chater. It is through his line that I may, or may not, have Black ancestry.

Notes

1. An unnamed child of one of my ancestors was buried in the same common grave as an unidentified Black man, GL, Ms 9232/3, Registers of St Botolph Aldgate, August 1771.
2. Carr, E.H., *What is History?* (1961), p. 8.
3. Tosh, J., *The Pursuit of History: Aims, Methods and New Directions in the Study of Modern History* (1983, 2nd edn, 1991), p. 9.
4. George, M.D., *Life in Eighteenth Century London* (2nd edn, 1930), pp. 134–40. In 1937, in *Eighteenth Century London Life*, Rosemary Bayne-Powell mentioned the presence of Black people in London but gave no references: it was a popular rather than scholarly work and she probably used George as the source.

5. Hecht, J.J., *Continental and Colonial Servants in Eighteenth Century England*, Smith College Studies in History, Vol. XL (Northampton, MA, 1954).
6. In the 1970s trainee BBC journalists were taught to ask 'How angry are you?' The clichéd question became 'How did/do you feel?' in the 1980s. (Information from a personal conversation with the late Ivor Yorke, one-time Head of Journalists' Training at the BBC.)
7. Shyllon, F., *Black People in Britain* (Oxford, 1974), pp. x and 242.
8. *Ibid.*, pp. 84–5.
9. Linebaugh, P. *The London Hanged* (1991); Linebaugh, P. and Redeker, M. *The Many-Headed Hydra: the Hidden History of the Revolutionary Atlantic* (2000).
10. Craton, M., *Empire, Enslavement and Freedom in the Caribbean* (Oxford, 1997), p. xix.
11. It is regrettable that there is as yet no central registry of television programmes that can be viewed by everyone in the way that libraries contain books which can be borrowed, because the emotional legacy of slavery is something that is largely missing from written history. Very few people, Black or white, were as articulate in writing as the eighteenth-century grocer Ignatius Sancho (who was, it must be remembered, untypical of Black experience in England) and the written word does not, of course, convey either the tone of voice or the expression on the speaker's face. There have been many other programmes on the subject but, as they have no associated publication and are not easy to access, it is difficult to review their content. *Motherland*, made by Takeaway Media and broadcast by BBC2 on 14 February 2003, is another interesting example. It followed three individuals of Afro-Caribbean origin tracing their African (and white) ancestry through DNA. All three had their preconceptions and expectations overturned.
12. Tattersfield, N., *The Forgotten Trade* (1991); Schwarz, S. (ed.), *Slave Captain: the Career of James Irving in the Liverpool Slave Trade* (Clywd, 1995); Dresser, M., *Slavery Obscured: the Social History of the Slave Trade in an English Provincial Port* (2001); Harris, R., *The Diligent: a Voyage through the Worlds of the Slave Trade* (2002).
13. Coules, V., *The Trade: Bristol and the Transatlantic Slave Trade* (Edinburgh, 2007); Farrell, S., Unwin, M. & Walvin, J., *The British Slave Trade: Abolition, Parliament and People* (Edinburgh, 2007); Phillips, C. & Redeker, M., *The Slave Ship: a Human History* (2007); Walvin, J. *The Trader, the Owner, the Slave* (2007).
14. Fryer obtained many of the references from primary sources by contacting archivists in county and local record offices.
15. Shyllon, *Black People*, p. 128.
16. Gerzina, G., *Black England* (1995), pp. 86 and 92.
17. Hammon, B., *Narrative of the Uncommon Sufferings and Surprizing Deliverance of Briton Hammon, a Negro Man, – Servant to General Winslow of Marshfield,*

in New-England; Who returned to Boston, after having been absent almost Thirteen Years, etc. (Boston, MA, 1760).
18. Gronniosaw, U., *A Narrative of the Most Remarkable Particulars in the Life of James Albert Ukawsaw Gronniosaw, An African Prince, as related by Himself* (Bath, 1770?).
19. Sancho, I., *Letters of the Late Ignatius Sancho, an African* (1782), ed. Carretta, V. (1998). Strictly speaking, this is not an autobiography but a collection of letters, assembled posthumously by an admirer, to which a biography was appended.
20. Marrant, J., *A Narrative of the Lord's Wonderful Dealings with John Marrant, a Black* (1785).
21. Cugoano, O. *Thoughts and Sentiments on the Evil of Slavery: or the Nature of Servitude as admitted by the Law of God, etc.* (1787), ed. Carretta, V. (NY, 1999).
22. Equiano, O., *The Interesting Narrative and Other Writings* (1789), ed. Carretta, V. (2nd edn, 2003).
23. King, B., 'Memoirs of the Life of Boston King, a Black Preacher, Written by Himself, during his Residence at Kingswood School', *Methodist Magazine*, March 1798.
24. Jea, J., *The Life, History and Unparalleled Sufferings of John Jea, the African Preacher, Compiled and Written by Himself* (Portsea, c.1811).
25. King, R., Sandhu, S., Walvin, J. & Girdham, J., *Ignatius Sancho an African Man of Letters* (1996), pp. 48, 52–6 and 68.
26. A notable exception is Richard McGrady's *Music and Musicians in Early Nineteenth Century Cornwall: the World of Joseph Emidy – Slave, Violinist and Composer* (Exeter, 1991). The book began as a study of Cornwall's musical history but then the author discovered Joseph Emidy, who was born in Africa, enslaved and brought to Lisbon where he was given a musical education and played with an orchestra. An English sea-captain, in need of an on-board musician, kidnapped him. He spent several years at sea before being freed and spending the rest of his life in Cornwall, initially in Falmouth, then in Truro, using his considerable musical gifts to make a living. McGrady is a musician, not an expert in Black history, so his book is valuable because it uses a different area of expertise to show a Black person against the background of the society in which he lived.
27. Chater, K., 'Hidden from History: Black People in Parish Records', *Genealogists' Magazine* 26 (10) June 2000, pp. 381–4; and Chater, K., 'Where there's a Will', *History Today* 50 (4), April 2000, pp. 26–7.

Part I
Counting heads

Chapter 1

The Black population of England and Wales

Before the first national census in 1801, it is difficult to know how many people there were in Britain during the long eighteenth century. Although there are uncertain areas, what is generally accepted is that between 1701 and 1801 the population of the whole of England and Wales increased from approximately 5,836,000 to 8,700,000.[1] If the problems of calculating the total population of England and Wales are difficult, the task of estimating the proportion of Black people or those from any other ethnic minority is more daunting, even after the introduction of the census in 1801, because it was not until 1991 that ethnic origin was included in census returns. The main source of information about the population is Anglican parish registers, but many people are missing from them. Stillborn children and unbaptised people, as well as suicides and those who had been excommunicated, were interred either in unconsecrated ground or in a segregated part of the churchyard, usually the north side. A burial service would not be read over such people.[2] As burial registers are records of services rather than of deaths, they do not always include all those buried. It is therefore impossible to know how many unbaptised Black people were buried in churchyards without a service or in unconsecrated ground. Nor do Anglican registers often include Roman Catholics, Jews or the members of the myriad nonconformist sects that flourished from the late seventeenth century onwards. The legal disabilities suffered at various times by anyone who could not swear to the Thirty-Nine Articles of the Anglican faith meant that non-Anglicans were often reluctant to identify themselves to the authorities. In the nineteenth century it has been found that up to 40 per cent of a parish's inhabitants may be missing from the parish registers.[3] The first census in 1801 was simply a headcount and it was not until 1851 that an exact place of birth was required, but this is still not a reliable guide to ethnic origin or colour, as many white people were born overseas and came to Britain either to settle or on a temporary basis in order to conduct business or to be educated.

Defining a 'Black' person

Using parish registers raises the slippery question of how to define a Black person, which is still not satisfactorily answered. In parish registers a variety of terms was used and the clerk who described William Kirby, baptised in rural Kent in 1747, as a 'black Emore' is typical of the confusion that most clerks had about colour, race and nationality.[4] Table 1 shows the variety of terms in use. It was not until the nineteenth century that theories of race and classifications that have had such an effect on how Black people are perceived were formulated. I have not used twentieth- or twenty-first-century definitions of a 'black' person, not least because these are constantly being re-evaluated. It is a problem with which previous historians have also grappled. Folarin Shyllon chose not to use 'Negro' because it was 'a Western creation, invented to cut off Africans of the Diaspora from Africa and Africans, and is now discredited and untenable', but there is no evidence that this is what officials in the past intended to do: the African diaspora is a twentieth-century century concept.[5] Norma Myers decided to 'keep in touch with the language of the period'.[6] I too have chosen to record what was written rather than interpret it in the light of today's usages, which may well become tomorrow's 'discredited and untenable' terms. During the long eighteenth century sources such as newspaper advertisements used 'black' to describe native Britons with a dark skin. In general, the word was spelled with a small 'b' when describing skin colour and with a capital letter for a person, analogous to someone from another nation, but this was not invariable. As officials and other writers in the eighteenth century also capitalised French, Dutch, Spanish and the like, they may have regarded Black people as part of the populace of a nation. When writing of white people, even in cases where the two were being contrasted, 'white' was not capitalised. I have decided to follow this practice, using Black with a capital 'B' when referring to people and with a small letter when referring to skin colour.

The word 'Negro' was the most frequently used. This seems to be a fairly unambiguous description of race but it is simply the Portuguese/Spanish word for the colour black and may not refer to a specific racial category. Certainly it was used to describe a race from the mid nineteenth century, when racial classification was put on a scientific basis, but before then it is

Table 1 Descriptions used for Black people 1660–1812

Description	No. of occurrences	First occurrence[a]	Last occurrence[a]
African	23	1732	1812
Asiatic	1	1787	
Black	1,925	1665	1812
Blackamoor	392	1661	1808
Blackman	1	1783	
Black-woman	1	1702	
Brown	1	1799	
Chinaman[§]	1	1738	
Creole/Creolian	5	1758	1801
Dark	1	1796	
East Indian	11	1688	1794
Ethiopian	8	1671	1782
Gentoo (= Hindu)	4	1770	1787
Hottentot	1	1811	
Indian	111	1661	1812
Indian Black/Black Indian	5	1681	1730
Indian Mulatto	1	1762	
Lascar	17	1754	1811
Malay	1	1799	
Moor	20	1672	1767
Mulatto/Mulatta	62	1709	1812
Native of...	71	1711	1810
Negar (and variants)	24	1663	1756
Negress	5	1681	1804
Negro	2,001	1660	1812
Of colour[b]	28	1787	1812
Sambo	1	1784	
Tawny/Tawneymoor (and variants)	9	1662	1738
West Indian	3	1764	1795

Notes: [a] Occurrence in the database: the term may have been used both before and after the period 1660–1812.
[b] 'Of colour' was also used for people who were almost certainly of Chinese origin, to judge by the places from which they came, so it was not always possible to separate the Chinese out.

more difficult to be certain how individuals were using the word, whether it was used for race or nationality. It is also difficult to tell what distinctions were made between 'Negro' and 'Black', the second most frequent description. Both appear in entries written by the same clerk.[7] 'Black' was also used for people from the Indian subcontinent and for Europeans with a dark complexion, although this was usually with a small letter. Some of the 'Blacks' may have had some white ancestry: there is a great variety of skin colour among people from the Caribbean and America, resulting from miscegenation. 'Negro' was possibly used for those with very dark skin and more purely African features. There was often no distinction between those of African and East Indian origin. 'Black Indian' is occasionally found. A few on the database are described as 'Negroes' from the East Indies. This may indicate that 'Negro' was used indiscriminately for both race and colour. Alternatively, the people so described may have originally been brought from Africa to India by the Arab, Portuguese or Dutch slave trades or by British masters who had acquired a servant of African origin elsewhere and moved to the East Indies.[8] Sometimes the origin of a person described as 'Black' in a parish register can be found from other documents, but in the majority of cases this word suggests a non-European. Although some of the people described as Moors seem to have been of Arab origin, the terms Black and Moor seem to have been interchangeable in the late seventeenth and early eighteenth centuries: in the baptismal register of Holy Trinity Minories between 1710 and 1717 the word 'Black' is used, while in a copy of the register for that period the word 'Moor' appears for the same people.[9] 'Ethiopian' does not necessarily mean a person from the country, formerly called Abyssinia, in East Africa on the Red Sea. It seems to have been a synonym for African generally, but, as the map in William Dampier's account of his voyage to Australia in 1699 shows, Ethiopia was then used of the area of central sub-Saharan Africa now occupied by part of Congo, the northern part of the Democratic Republic of Congo (formerly Zaire) and the Central African Republic.[10] Some of those described as 'native of' may have been white people born abroad, as may have been the 'West Indians'. The word 'native' (from the Latin *natus*) was used in many registers to describe white people born in another parish. For many on the database there was no description: they are presumed to be Black because of a combination of factors, primarily age at baptism and place of birth.

In Britain during the long eighteenth century there were no official definitions for the ancestry of mixed-race individuals as there were at the time in America, both North and South, in the Caribbean and later in

The Black population of England and Wales

South Africa, where legal discrimination made classification necessary. Lacking any official guidelines in England, the clerks' perceptions decided how people's origins were recorded. Mulatto, or sometimes mulatta for a woman, as the description of a mixed-race person, was occasionally used.[11] There were not, however, the fine distinctions of ancestry found in America and the Caribbean. There is, as yet, no instance of the use of this term in a baptismal entry to describe the child of a Black and a white parent. On the database there is a single example of 'sambo' used as a description, but there are no quadroons, octaroons, quintaroons, mustees or musteefinos, all terms used in the American and Caribbean colonies to signify people with different proportions of white ancestry. The only man described as a 'sambo' came from North America, where this was the term used to describe a person who was one-quarter white. He may have assumed that the English clerk required his racial classification. Before oranges were regularly imported into Britain, 'tawney' described the colour now called orange after the fruit (which was a less vibrant shade than it is now), but there are references to 'a Tawney', which suggests that it was also believed to be a nationality or racial description. Some of these people seem to have been of Arab origin, or possibly pale-skinned people from the Indian subcontinent.[12] Others, like John Glover, who was involved in the Gordon Riots, were mixed race. At his trial at the Old Bailey, one witness said he saw several 'Blacks and Tawnies' in a crowd and another said Glover had a copper-coloured skin and was 'a different kind of Black'.[13] Ann Duck, the daughter of a Black man and a white woman, described an incident in which a man told her that he did not like her 'tawny' complexion.[14] 'Half-caste', later used for the offspring of white and Indian people, does not appear. In both the British Caribbean colonies and in the erstwhile French territories of the Americas, 'Creole' was originally used for someone, Black or white, born there.[15] Later, from the early nineteenth century, it came to be used for those of mixed race.

Size of the Black population in England and Wales

The only time before the twentieth century when any attempt was made to quantify the total number of Black people in the country was in the latter half of the eighteenth century, when the abolitionist movement was beginning. In 1764 the *Gentleman's Magazine* estimated that there were 'near twenty thousand Negroe servants' in the capital, and in the following year the *Morning Chronicle* said there were some thirty thousand in the whole country.[16] In the evidence Granville Sharp presented to the court in the 1772 case of James Somersett, which led to the landmark Mansfield Judgment, he gave a figure for the whole country of between fourteen and fifteen thousand, but did not say what evidence, if any, there was to confirm it. Edward Long originally thought the number was three thousand and only revised it upwards when he learned of these higher figures.[17] This wide disparity is an indication of how difficult it is to obtain a true figure. It is comprehensible that Sharp should have accepted what he saw in a published source, but Long was one of those who thought that Black people were a threat to British society. Why he should have produced such a low estimate when he believed that Britain was in danger of being swamped by aliens is puzzling. Nor did Lord Mansfield question Sharp's figure, which was probably derived from newspaper estimates.

Black people were highly visible at the level of society and in the places in which journalists and law makers lived. Lord Mansfield himself had a mixed-race great-niece in his own household. Wherever they went, upper- and middle-class people must have seen Blacks, because many were the servants of the upper classes, employed in highly visible positions. They opened doors to visitors, they served meals, they drove coaches in the streets. Sharp, as a known supporter of and campaigner for Black people, met them on a regular basis and therefore probably took particular notice of them. Both the aristocracy and the army used them in decorative or ceremonial roles, which also gave them high visibility. Fryer details the long tradition of employing Black musicians as Army bandsmen,[18] as contemporary prints also attest. In 1815, after the British slave trade had ended, Black musicians led the way as the Guards marched every morning from their barracks in Kensington to Hyde Park.[19] John Ellis noted that Black soldiers began to disappear from the British Army only in the mid nineteenth century.[20] In London legislators and opinion formers would have seen many others: sailors, beggars, poor people living on the margins of a prosperous capital city and port.

Beyond the highly publicised cases Sharp and other abolitionists brought, Black people also appeared in the lower courts where Mansfield occasionally sat as judge, where they were defendants, plaintiffs and witnesses. Members of society were therefore conditioned to accept high figures because it accorded with their own, limited experience. On the evidence of the database, I would conclude that Edward Long's original estimate was the most accurate figure: there were probably only a few thousand Black people in London in the early 1770s. In the thirty years (equivalent to one generation) between 1742 and 1772 there are only some 550 people on the database in the London area, where the concentration of Black people in the whole country was highest. This does not, of course, include every Black person in the metropolis, some of whom would have been transient, but it is impossible that so many thousands should be missing. Some three thousand (to use Long's estimate) could well not have come to the authorities' notice in some way, or may not have been recorded as Black for the various reasons discussed in Chapter 5. Almost fifteen years later, in 1786, the Committee for the Relief of the Black Poor estimated that there were between three and five thousand in the capital.[21] Although by this time people coming from the West Indies were apparently reluctant to bring Black slaves/servants to Britain, where they would be considered free and not obliged to return to the slave-owning colonies, any drop would have been compensated for by the arrival of Black people from North America following the War of Independence there. The Committee's figure is very similar to Long's, so should perhaps be regarded as more accurate than the newspaper estimates.

The Black population outside London

But the London area was (and still is) a special case. Wrigley and Schofield estimate there were some ten thousand parishes in England and Wales.[22] An exact number is impossible to give because, over the five hundred years covered in their work, the number was not fixed. Parishes were amalgamated when churches were destroyed (as in the Great Fire of London) or when populations fell. More frequently, they were created as communities grew. Much of the countryside, to judge by parish registers, never had any Black presence before the twentieth century. In the period covered by the British slave trade only one or two Black people appear in the registers of some rural parishes. They were usually a servant of a local aristocrat or member of the gentry. Provincial cities and towns had more, but here the numbers rarely reached double figures, unless in ports that had a historic involvement with the slave trade (Illustration 1). London, Bristol and Liverpool had, of course, a continuing Black population, but ports that had only dabbled in the slave trade, like Whitehaven in Cumberland or Weymouth in Dorset, had a small Black presence, which extended into the hinterland. Ports on the east coast, like Lowestoft in Suffolk, which did not have a slaving connection, had the occasional Black inhabitant, probably a seaman from a merchant ship who settled there, but the numbers were no larger than in an inland town, like Bury St Edmunds, also in Suffolk. The east side of the country, away from the

Number of slaves transported

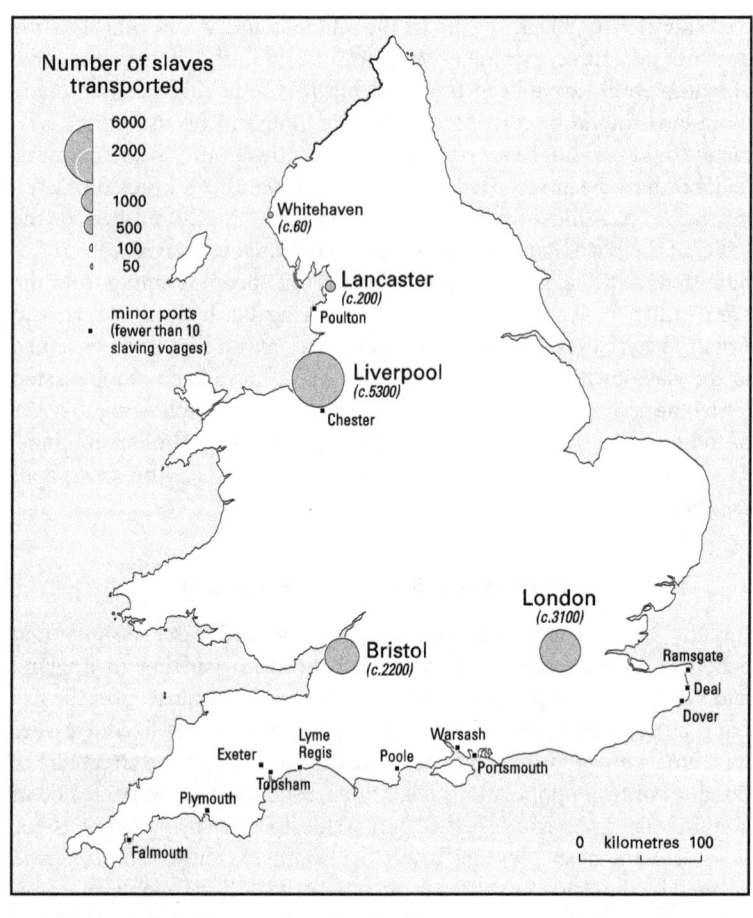

- 6000
- 2000
- 1000
- 500
- 100
- 50

· minor ports (fewer than 10 slaving voages)

Whitehaven *(c.60)*
Lancaster *(c.200)*
Poulton
Liverpool *(c.5300)*
Chester
London *(c.3100)*
Ramsgate
Deal
Dover
Bristol *(c.2200)*
Exeter
Lyme Regis
Poole
Warsash
Portsmouth
Topsham
Plymouth
Falmouth

0 kilometres 100

1. The slave trading ports of England, with approximate numbers of known slaving voyages. As well as originating voyages, ports on the south coast often dealt with slave-trading ships from London.

ports which traded with Africa and the Americas, seems to be the part with the smallest percentage of Black people, but more research needs to be done.[23] In Wales there also seem to have been comparatively few Black people during the long eighteenth century.[24] There are occasional entries in parish registers in ports like Cardiff[25] and Haverfordwest and the larger towns, like Denbigh and Newport. The central area, however, was (and still is) overwhelmingly rural and the lack of Black people in parts of the countryside without a resident wealthy estate owner, or one who had links with the colonies, is also the pattern in regions of England, like the Fens and the Lake District. The reasons why there seem to have been no Black people in these areas are themselves significant and need further exploration.

Shyllon concluded that the figures given in the journals previously quoted were greatly exaggerated and he estimated a figure of ten thousand Black people over the whole period of the British slave trade, but did not give his reasoning.[26] Norma Myers concurred with this figure, perhaps following Shyllon, and wrote 'on a national level Blacks were spatially distributed throughout [the country]'.[27] She examined only London and Liverpool in detail, but the distribution was uneven. In London it was easy to evade the authorities, so a number of Black people would not necessarily appear in parish records, but in the provinces the situation was different. In the countryside parish officials had much more control over inhabitants than they had in London because strangers were more immediately apparent and there were fewer places where people could evade attention. Major employers, who were mainly from the ruling class and generally belonged to the established church, could also insist on their employees attending church. Artisans and the lower middle classes were often nonconformists, but are apparently the least likely strata of society in which to find Black people. In villages and small towns there was a certain amount of social pressure to conform and attend a place of worship, preferably the Anglican church, but there was usually a grudging acceptance that nonconformists were Christian, although badly misguided.

The picture is complicated by the position of Black people vis-à-vis the settlement laws, but the pattern of distribution, even on the limited amount of work done so far, is clear, as every kind of locality, from isolated rural parishes in areas off the main roads and river routes, to cities, via market towns, has been sampled. It is virtually impossible that there are any hitherto undiscovered, substantial settlements of Black people, taking substantial as more than twenty Black individuals in one place at one time. Not only were Black people rare outside the major ports of London, Bristol and Liverpool, but the Anglican church was also a much stronger force in rural areas because it controlled local government. Adherents of the nonconformist churches, unless they formed over 10 per cent of the inhabitants, are considered a negligible proportion of the total population[28] and the percentage of first-generation Black members of such congregations must have been infinitesimal. The number of Black people in rural parishes is probably accurately reflected in the parish registers, so it is reasonable to use the lower figure of ten thousand Black people in England and Wales as the total number who spent a substantial amount of time here who would, in terms of the law, be regarded as 'settled'. This is, rather neatly but coincidentally, an average of one Black person per parish for the 150 or so years of the British slave trade. However, this takes no account of those, like mariners, who were in the country for a short period, or those servants who spent only a few years here with their masters, either from America, the Caribbean or a continental European country, like France or Spain, which had territories in the New World.

Sex ratio

European slave traders generally preferred male slaves, but the ratio of male to female and adults to children varied during the period of the slave trade, usually in response to decisions made by the various African sellers (who controlled this aspect of the trade) but sometimes due to factors in Europe and America. For example, when British legislation in 1788 and the early 1790s increased the space allowed each slave on board ships, the number of children fell.[29] Though the ratio of men to women sold into slavery and transported to the New World between the late seventeenth century and the first half of the nineteenth century is generally accepted as 64 per cent men and 36 per cent women,[30] the figures for those in England and Wales are very different. Over the whole period of the British slave trade, men make up 78.8 per cent and women 18.45 per cent, with 2.75 per cent unknown. Most doubtful cases come from names given to both men and women, especially Francis/Frances. The convention of using the first spelling for men and the second for women began around the mid seventeenth century,[31] but Francis was occasionally used for women in the eighteenth century. Other names, like virtues such as Charity or Christian, could be given to either men or women. Probably the majority of the 'unknowns' were men: masculinity was, and still is, regarded as the norm, so deviation from this would be specified. This means that approximately 80 per cent of the Black population in England and Wales was male and 20 per cent female. There are a number of possible reasons for this. The first is that in ports the number of male mariners heavily weights the numbers. In the early stages of compiling the database, before the riverside parishes in London were entered, the proportion was approximately 75 per cent male to 25 per cent female. This is the figure that another researcher, Audrey Dewjee, has also found.[32] Her work concentrates on

Yorkshire, on the east side of England, where there was no port trading regularly with the Americas, so substantial numbers of mariners would be absent. However, Black people brought as domestic servants from the colonies to Britain (who appear to have made up the majority of Black people in England) would also have been predominantly male. In the seventeenth and eighteenth centuries, male servants outnumbered female ones. The latter were mainly restricted to attending to the personal needs of the mistress and her children or doing laundry work.

Origins

No origin is given for 76 per cent of the people on the database. Of those for whom it is specified, most are from the Caribbean (10.73 per cent), followed by Africa (6.05 per cent), the East Indies (5.23 per cent) and then North America (4.3 per cent). A very small number, 0.13 per cent, are from elsewhere. Some places are difficult to identify. 'Caledonian Island' may be New Caledonia in the Pacific – one person came from there. The place of origin of one 'Negro' from HMS *Hindostan* was given as Bertria. Another came from Anjano in the East Indies, but I have not been able to identify these places more precisely. It is not known how many were originally from Africa but were then shipped to North America or the Caribbean and subsequently brought to England. In earlier records the phrasing is often 'from X', but in later records 'born in X' is more usual. Sometimes just the area of origin, not a particular country or island, is given but, where this is specified, most are from the Caribbean. By a small margin, the majority were from Barbados (138), followed by Jamaica (135), Antigua (41), St Kitts (39), Bermuda (14), St Domingo (12), Grenada (8), Santa Cruz (7), Martinique, Tortola and Dominica[33] (6 each), Demerara, Monserrat, and Nevis (4 each), Bahamas, Guadeloupe, St Thomas, St Vincent and Surinam (3 each) and one each from Cuba, Honduras, St Croix, St Eustacia, St Lucia, St Martins and Trinidad.

Although places of origin are given for many from Africa, these are mainly slave trading areas. As slaves were brought from many parts of Africa they are not a reliable guide to exact places of origin. In addition, most of Africa was not, in the eighteenth century, divided into countries. This European manner of dividing up territory was not introduced until the mid nineteenth century. West African peoples in particular were migratory, not tied in the way European farmers were to particular plots of land, so the centres of population gradually shifted over time.[34] It is therefore not useful to detail the apparent places of origin given in sources when these are on the slave-trading coast of West Africa. By far the commonest place of origin is simply given as Guinea. In addition there are individuals from Sierra Leone (11), Madagascar (8), St Helena (5), the Cape of Good Hope (4), Egypt and Mozambique (2 each) and one each from the Canary Islands and Cape Mount (now in Liberia).

The British involvement with the East Indies and China, conducted between 1600 and 1858 through the East India Company (EIC), must in a large part account for the proportion of people from Asia. The EIC was granted a monopoly of trade with the Indian subcontinent and the Far East in 1600. The situation here was very different from that of the African trade. Indian rulers did not object to people from the various European powers, initially Portuguese, then French and British, settling inland. Indeed, many Indian states used the armies of the various European powers to pursue internal disputes and power struggles. In Africa the tribal chiefs would only allow European traders to set up posts along the coast and strictly regulated their activities. They purchased European weapons but did not use foreign forces to fight their internal battles. This was similar to the position in China, where European traders were confined to Canton and Macao, and this is probably why only four people on the database were recorded as coming from China. This necessarily cursory overview may explain why the majority of people of Asian origin who came to Britain were recorded as from India (91). The Dutch were the major European power in the Far East, but links between Britain and the Netherlands probably brought a few people from their colonies to England: five were from Sumatra. In addition, there were one each from Malaya, Macassar, the Philippines and Timor. Six were simply recorded as being from the East Indies.

Until the War of Independence (1775–1783), North America was a British colony. The settlers' ties to the mother country meant some needed to visit Britain to conduct commercial or family business and others returned to settle, and they brought their Black servants with them. After the end of the war, Canada remained under British rule. Some British loyalists relocated there, some went to the Caribbean and others returned to Britain. The majority of Black people whose place of origin was within North America came from North or South Carolina (52), followed by New York (33), Virginia (23), Georgia (9), Maryland (8), Philadelphia (7), Florida (4) and one from Canada.

Wherever the Black people who came to England and Wales originated, the majority of them are to be found in the London area, either passing through or resident. Because of its importance as the seat of government and commerce, it deserves special consideration and analysis.

Notes

1. Flinn, M.W., *British Population Growth 1700–1850* (1970), pp. 16–18, summarises the problems in reaching a definitive figure.
2. A daughter of Ukawsaw Gronniosaw died unbaptised. The local Baptist minister refused her burial and it was only after Gronniosaw said he would bury her in his garden that the minister of the local Anglican parish agreed to do so, although he refused to read a service. Gronniosaw, *Narrative*, p. 46.
3. Wrigley, E.A. and Schofield, R.S., *The Population History of England 1541–1871* (1981), p. 3.
4. SoG, unpublished transcript, KE R/66–69, 'Registers of Bromley, Kent', 18 November 1747.
5. Shyllon, *Black People*, p. x.
6. Myers, N. *Reconstructing the Black Past: Blacks in Britain 1780–1830* (1996), p. ix.
7. William Weymouth 'a negro' and Maria Blackall 'w[idow] a Black woman' were married in St Gluvias, Cornwall on 28 June 1801. Taylor, T. & Phillimore, W.P., *Cornwall Marriage Registers: Marriages Vol. XIII* (1908).
8. Jayasuriya, S. de S. & Pankhurst, R., *The African Diaspora in the Indian Ocean* (Lawrenceville, NJ, 2001).
9. GL, Ms 9239 and Ms 9238.
10. Dampier, W., *A Voyage to New Holland* (1703 and 1709, republ. Gloucester, 1981) pp. 34–5.
11. This comes from the Spanish/Portuguese word meaning 'little mule', presumably a reference to hybridity.
12. The word was also used to describe Native Americans, although not in the few records relating to them that I found.
13. *Proceedings* 1779–80, VI, no. 398.
14. *Ordinary's Account*, 7 November 1744.
15. From the French *créole*, Spanish *criollo*, both deriving from the Latin *creare* = to create.
16. Walvin, J., *Black Presence*, p. 46.
17. Long, E., *Candid Reflections upon the judgement lately recorded by the Court of King's Bench, etc.* (1772), quoted in Shyllon, *Black People*, p. 101.
18. Fryer, P., *Staying Power: the History of Black People in Britain* (1984), pp. 79–88.
19. Symond, L. *Journal of a Tour and Residence in Great Britain during the Years 1810 and 1811, etc.*, republ. as *An American in Regency England*, ed. Hibbert, C. (1968), p. 30.
20. Ellis, J.D., 'Drummers for the Devil? The Black Soldiers of the 29th (Worcestershire) Regiment of Foot 1729–1843', *Journal of the Society for Army Historical Research* 80, 2002, p. 197.
21. Braidwood, S., *Black Poor and White Philanthropists: London's Blacks and the Foundation of the Sierra Leone Settlement 1786–1791* (Liverpool, 1994), p. 23.

22. Wrigley & Schofield, *The Population History of England*, p. 3.
23. Local historians, like Audrey Dewjee and Dr Joan Kemp, both working in Yorkshire, have discovered a number. Private correspondence. They were most likely servants of people who had connections with the colonies.
24. There is some genetic and other evidence of African origin dating from Roman times, or even earlier. Ahmed, A. & Ibrahim A., *The Black Celts: an Ancient African Civilization in Ireland and Britain* (Cardiff, 1992).
25. The earliest reference yet found to a Black person in Wales during the long eighteenth century is the baptism on 30 May 1687 of Joseph Potiphar, a Black servant, in St John's, Cardiff. Dabydeen, D., Gilmore, J. & Jones, C. (eds), *The Oxford Companion to Black British History* (Oxford, 2007), p. 508.
26. Shyllon, *Black People*, p. 102.
27. Myers, *Reconstructing the Black Past*, p. 35.
28. Eversley, D.E.C., 'Exploitation of Anglican Parish Registers by Aggregative Analysis', in Wrigley, E.A. (ed.), *An Introduction to English Historical Demography* (1966), p. 51.
29. Klein, H.S., *The Atlantic Slave Trade* (Cambridge, 1999), p. 162.
30. Lovejoy, P., 'The impact of the Atlantic Slave Trade on Africa', *Journal of African History* 30, 1989, pp. 378–9, quoted in Walvin, J., *Black Ivory* (1992), p. 319.
31. Withycombe, E.G., *The Oxford Dictionary of English Christian Names* (Oxford, 2nd edn, 1949), p. 114.
32. Private correspondence.
33. There was some confusion between St Domingo (now St Domingue) and the island of Dominica in the Lesser Antilles, so these figures should be regarded with caution. 'St Dominca', for example, is occasionally found and is probably St Domingo, but this is not certain.
34. Vansina, J. 'Population Movements and the Emergence of New Socio-political Forms in Africa', in *The UNESCO General History of Africa: Vol. V: Africa from the Sixteenth to the Eighteenth Century*, ed. Ogot, B.A. (abridged edn, Oxford, 1999), p. 25.

Chapter 2

The Black population of London

It is estimated that between 1700 and 1801 the population of London grew from around 500,000 to 958,863,[1] but demographers trying to estimate the population of London and the proportion of it that was Black before the nineteenth century face additional problems beyond those mentioned in the previous chapter. All that is known with certainty is that there was a minimum of 1,200 Black people in the metropolis in the mid 1780s, at the time of the American War of Independence.[2] This figure relates to the poor and unemployed people who came to London from America and does not include those already settled there, either the servants of the well-to-do or those who had left service and set up a business which could support them.

The best indication of changes in London's population comes from the Bills of Mortality. Although a number of cities compiled them, the longest and most complete run is for the Cities of London and Westminster and the surrounding parishes, which are divided into the City Without the Walls and the outparishes of Middlesex and Surrey (Illustration 2). These areas encompass what might be called Greater London in the mid-17th century and reflect the areas of densest population at that time, although the northern and southern parts of the outparishes of Middlesex and Surrey respectively were largely rural. Monthly accounts and a yearly summary from each of these parishes were published into the middle of the nineteenth century. Originally intended to give early warning of outbreaks of the plague, until 1667 they recorded only burials. After that date they also noted the number of baptisms, presumably to track the population's recovery after the Great Plague of 1665. The main problem with using them is that they were compiled only from Anglican parishes, but the capital had a significant number of people who were not attached to the Church of England, and there are indications that Black people were among these other religious communities.

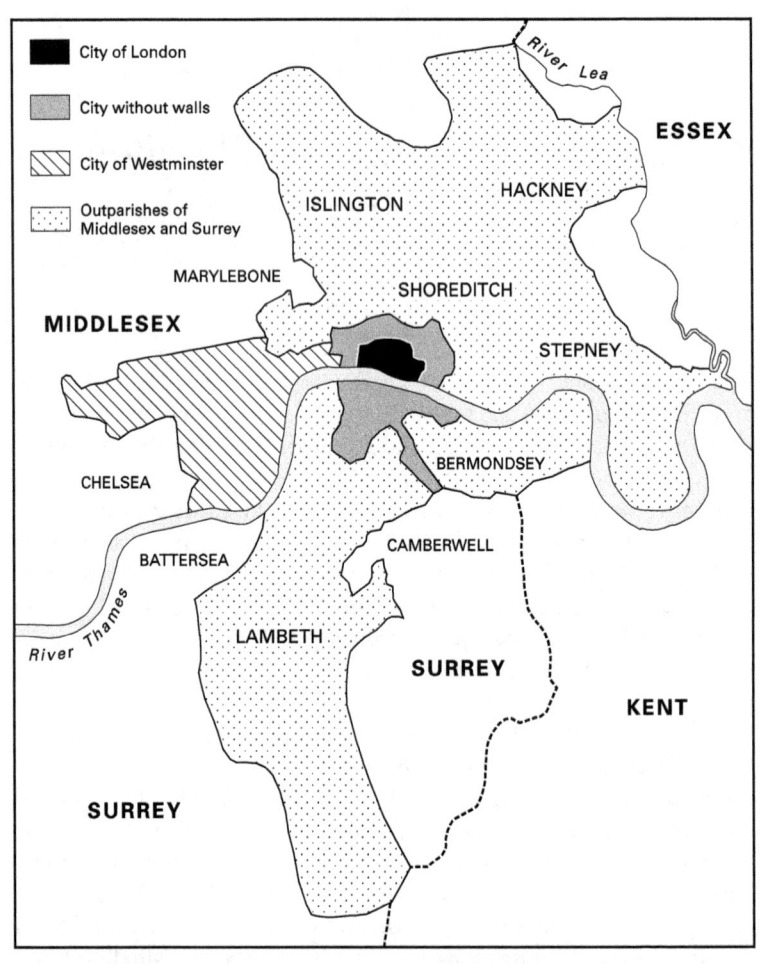

2. The areas of metropolitan London covered by the Bills of Mortality

Non-Anglicans

Outside the capital, the presence of nonconformists creates problems in estimating population figures, but in London this is compounded by the sheer number of denominations and sects which flourished there. Ukawsaw Gronniosaw, for example, became a Baptist. There were also numerous immigrant groups from overseas who had their own places of worship. Black people do not seem to have had any separate holy places, even those who were Muslim. Many of the records of the various non-Anglican and foreign churches, however, include Black people, as did the Dutch Chapel in St James, which largely served the Dutch community. The English names in the registers seem to belong to people who were married to Dutchmen and women, but there is at least one baptism of a Black person among the 251 entered there.[3]

One faith group that found England more congenial than its native land were the Huguenots, who came as refugees. In the years before and after the Revocation of the Edict of Nantes in 1685, up to a quarter of a million French and Walloon people fled their countries and thousands settled in the Cities of London and Westminster, joining the remnants of an earlier influx. In 1700 there were fourteen French churches in Westminster and at least two Huguenots had Black servants who were baptised in their *temples*.

By 1695 there were some 860 Jews, mainly Sephardim, with a smaller number of Ashkenazim, settled in London. The community had grown to around six thousand by the middle of the eighteenth century. Comparatively precise figures can be given because the Jews, unlike the persecuted faiths, kept good records.[4] Judaism is not a proselytising religion and before the twentieth century conversion was extremely rare. Jews occasionally registered the births of their children in the local parish registers, apparently to establish their settlement rights, and it seems that some may have done the same for their Black servants, like Francis Jo, the servant of Abraham Massiah, baptised in the City of London in 1755.[5] Alternatively, Jo may genuinely have been converted to Christianity.

Members of the British gentry who were Roman Catholics also had Black servants. One is mentioned in the Calvert divorce case which started in 1707. William Ashley, known as 'Black Billy', was the Calverts' groom.[6] Many large country houses, including those of Roman Catholic families, had private chapels. The divorcing couple would have been married and had their children, and possibly William their groom, baptised privately there. Ambassadors from Roman Catholic countries were attached to the Court of St James and allowed to have chapels for their worship, which were also used by indigenous co-religionists.[7] Following the French Revolution in 1789 there was a great influx of people who later attended the churches which in the last decade of the eighteenth century began to spring up as tolerance towards Roman Catholics extended to allowing them their own places of worship.[8] Catholics had, of course, been meeting surreptitiously since the Reformation, but kept few records for fear they could be used against them. The Black people baptised in legation chapels seem not to have been connected to the English aristocracy, nor to the foreign dignitaries at court. On 4 March 1746, for example, James Nicholas, 'an adult Ethiopian', was baptised in the Venetian Chapel in London. His sponsors were Samuel Grace and 'old Mary Reynolds of St Mary le Bone'.[9] Thomas Lambert 'negro' was baptised in the Chapel of the Imperial Legation of Austria in 1774. His godparents were George Codrington and Anastasia McCarthy.[10] This suggests that they were not attached to diplomats, but were part of the general Catholic population.

Although the numbers of these miscellaneous nonconformist, foreign, Jewish and Roman Catholic congregations were individually small, together they may add up to a significant number of adherents who will be missing from Anglican records. It is clear from surviving records that Black people were almost certainly a part of all these small religious communities, except the Jews and the Quakers. The apparent absence of Black people from the voluminous records kept by Quakers is an oddity, especially given their prominent role in the abolition movement, and needs more research.

Black 'communities' in London

Since the late 1980s the word 'community' has become much used and today it has a broad and imprecise meaning. Its primary definition is simply those who live in the same locality, but it has been widened to include those who have something in common: religious (the Roman Catholic community, the Jewish community, the Muslim community, etc.), sexual orientation (the gay community), occupational (the financial community) or some other factor, like the deaf community. Exploring the problems of what constituted a community of Black people in America during the period of slavery, Peter Kolchin observed:

> The slave community has become one of the central – albeit least well defined – concerns of recent historians of slavery. Eager to rebut images of slave passivity and docility, many of these historians have elevated the slave community into an all-embracing agency that gave order to the slaves' lives, expressed their deepest aspirations, and prevented their complete victimization.[11]

Some historians refer to a 'Black community' in eighteenth-century London and their meanings are equally ill defined. Black people in Britain were more likely to have mutual interests than their American counterparts. Whereas in the Americas there was a sharp legal distinction between those who were free and those who were slaves, in Britain before 1772 they all had the same ambiguous, ill-defined legal status. In the colonies Black people followed a variety of occupations, but in England and Wales the overwhelming majority were domestic servants, at least for part of their lives. Black British seamen were often officers' servants, as was Equiano, and it is not always clear whether those in the military were regular soldiers or servants of officers. Black people in Britain, therefore, were much more likely to have similar occupations, but these were shared with the white people with whom they worked on equal or near-equal, terms. There were, as far as can be ascertained, no jobs in England and Wales confined to Black people alone, like the field hands on plantations in the Americas.

The Sons of Africa is sometimes cited as a Black political society. One of its members, Olaudah Equiano, is often represented as a leader of the Black community. It is odd, if there were an eighteenth-century Black community in London, that he never seems to have met Ignatius Sancho, the most famous Black person in London at that time. When Equiano returned to London from the Americas in 1777, politicised by his experiences in the slave-owning colonies, he was in his late twenties or early thirties. Ignatius Sancho had been running his grocer's shop in Westminster for some years. Sancho died three years later, in 1780. Surely Equiano must have heard about this shopkeeper and his illustrious customers and would have visited him for reasons of solidarity if there were some Black community, united by colour and ethnic origin. Sancho makes no mention of him in his letters, but this is not surprising, since Equiano did not yet have the eminence he later gained. By the time Equiano came to write his *Narrative* (first published in 1789), however, Sancho's letters had been collected and published and his views on the iniquities of slavery were known. Had Equiano met him, he would surely have mentioned this in his autobiography, although it must be added that he makes no mention of any of the other 'sons of Africa' either. The only Black person he mentions seeing in London is a 'white negro woman', probably Amelia Lewsham, who had albinism and was exhibited or exhibited herself for money.[12]

Both Equiano and Sancho identified themselves as 'Africans', but were otherwise very different. Equiano, the former mariner, was a man of action who travelled widely, both overseas and in the British Isles. He published his own work, was assiduous in promoting and selling it, took an energetic role in the Sierra Leone project and was involved with other political campaigners. A couple of weeks after his marriage Equiano actually left his wife to go on a speaking tour. Sancho was apparently less active, partly no doubt because of his age and ill-health, but his letters present a picture of a man living quietly with his wife and children, enjoying domestic pleasures and dealing with ideas through correspondence, not action. Although he ran a business, his main interests were plainly in literature and music. He urged others, like the novelist Lawrence Sterne, to express his views to the public, rather than address them directly himself.

These men had little in common beyond their colour and origin. The whole point of a community is that the differences between its members are subsumed in a concern which overrides other interests and which is incorporated into their everyday lives. There is no evidence of such an overwhelming focus among the Black people, famous or obscure, in seventeenth- or eighteenth-century London. At times, such as the delivery of the Mansfield Judgment in 1772, Black people were undoubtedly reminded of what they had in common and were drawn together, like those who celebrated the verdict. In their day-to-day lives, however, they seem to have associated mainly with those with whom they had most in common: fellow servants, mariners or those they dealt with in business or socially. The *Proceedings* of the Old Bailey contain many instances of a Black person as part of a group of white people, or Black criminals working with white ones, and no one questions why or comments on this as remarkable.

St Giles's Black-birds

Some historians, however, have claimed that three Black communities existed in eighteenth-century London. The first is in St Giles. This rests on a single reference, first quoted by M. Dorothy George, who noted that after the end of the American War of Independence in 1783, those Black people who came to England 'quickly fell into distress. Negroes became conspicuous among London beggars and were known as St Giles black birds'. Although she does not give a reference for this, it is clear from a footnote that she is referring to Carl Wadström's *Essay on Colonisation* (1794).[13] George described the poor Irish community in St Giles in some detail but specifically denied that there was a free Black community in the parish of St Giles or anywhere else, saying 'They did not live in colonies with their countrymen'. More recent historians, however, fastened on this single phrase from Wadström's work because the idea that Black people had established their own society away from the control of white people appealed to the politicised ideology created by the development of Black studies in America in the mid twentieth century. When historians turned their attention to Black people in Britain they were primed to look for a similar Black culture. Because the legal and social conditions of Black people in Britain and America were entirely different, it was difficult to prove that those here had managed to retain a separate identity and culture. The discovery of an apparent Black community in London, the heart and seat of the British Empire, built on the trade and exploitation of Black people, was obviously of major importance.

It is worth quoting the whole passage from Wadström's *Essay on Colonisation* that led up to the phrase that created a myth:

> The Blacks living in London are generally profligate because uninstructed and vitiated by slavery: for many of them were once slaves of the most worthless description, namely the idle and superfluous domestic, and the gamblers and thieves who infest the towns in the West Indies. There are several laws against carrying, or enticing slaves from the Ilands [sic], without the knowledge of their owners. Yet some of these fellows contrive to conceal themselves, or are concealed by others on board ships on the point of sailing; a better sort come to attend children and sick persons on board, and others are brought by their masters, in the way of parade. Many of them, naturally enough, but perhaps without sufficient reflection, prefer a 'crust of bread and liberty' in Old England, to ease, plenty and slavery in the West Indies. For, excepting the too frequent excesses of capricious, tyrannical, or drunken owners; the treatment of *such* slaves is as good as that of the truly useful field-negroes is bad. In London, being friendless and despised, on account of their complexion, and too many of them being really incapable of any useful occupation, they sink into abject poverty and soon become St Giles's black-birds. (Italics in the original)[14]

Wadström seems to be suggesting that the Black people here were ex-slaves from the West Indies, although it was those who came from America following the War of Independence that the authorities were most concerned about at the time he was writing, establishing the Sierra Leone project to resettle them in Africa in response to their plight.

Originally the parish of St Giles in the Fields stood in open ground just north of the boundary with the City of Westminster. To the east, the parish of St Andrews Holborn and the Liberty of the Rolls stood between it and the City of London but, as the metropolis grew, it became built up, especially following the Restoration. By the latter part of the seventeenth century the inhabitants were those who gained their livelihood by fulfilling the needs of the rich and aristocratic members of the nearby Court in Westminster, like artisans who made the luxury goods they bought, writers and actors who diverted them intellectually and the prostitutes who entertained them physically. Westminster's prosperity also attracted beggars who depended on largesse. The poor had a long history in the area, since a hospital for lepers was founded there in 1141 and the chapel built for them became the parish church of St Giles in the Fields in the thirteenth century. The hospital remained until the reign of Henry VIII.[15] St Giles was originally a large parish but the northern part was divided off and became the parish of St George Bloomsbury in 1731 and the southern part is often now subsumed into the area loosely known as Covent Garden.[16] Within the parish in the seventeenth and eighteenth centuries, however, there were several different areas. Around Dyot Street, off St Giles High Street, was a large, poor Irish community which made St Giles a byword for violence and lawlessness, but many respectable and well-to-do people lived in the parish, especially in and around Great Queen Street. A Freemasons' Hall was built there in 1775–76 where public dinners were attended by the great and the good. Members of what might be called smart Bohemia lived in this street, although by the end of the eighteenth century most had moved westwards as the area fell out of fashion. Notable residents included the dramatist Richard Sheridan; James Hoole, a writer famous in his day as a translator and dramatist; and the artists Opie and Hudson, who taught Joshua Reynolds. A number of famous actors and actresses also lived here and around Drury Lane.

Dictionaries of historical slang and colloquial phrases provide no clues to the origin of the phrase 'St Giles's black-birds'. Francis Grose's *The Vulgar Tongue* (1785)[17] was the first English dictionary of slang and did not include 'black-birds'. Grose said 'Giles's' or 'St Giles's Breed' meant 'fat, ragged and saucy'. He noted that Newton Street and Dyot Street in the parish were 'the headquarters of most of the thieves and pickpockets about London', but made no mention of any Black community there.[18] These streets were in the area later known as the Rookery. Another contemporary compiler of slang terms was Sir John Fielding, a magistrate who lived in Bow Street, Covent Garden, who served from 1754 to 1780. He recorded the slang and colloquial expressions used by the underworld, what came to be called 'thieves' cant'.[19] The list contains no mention of 'black-birds'. Although Fielding said that Black people were seduced from service, he did not refer to any distinct Black community and, as a magistrate in the area, he must have been in the best possible position to know of one. His half-brother Henry's (also a magistrate) *An Enquiry into the Causes of the Late Increase of Robbers* was largely concerned with abstract

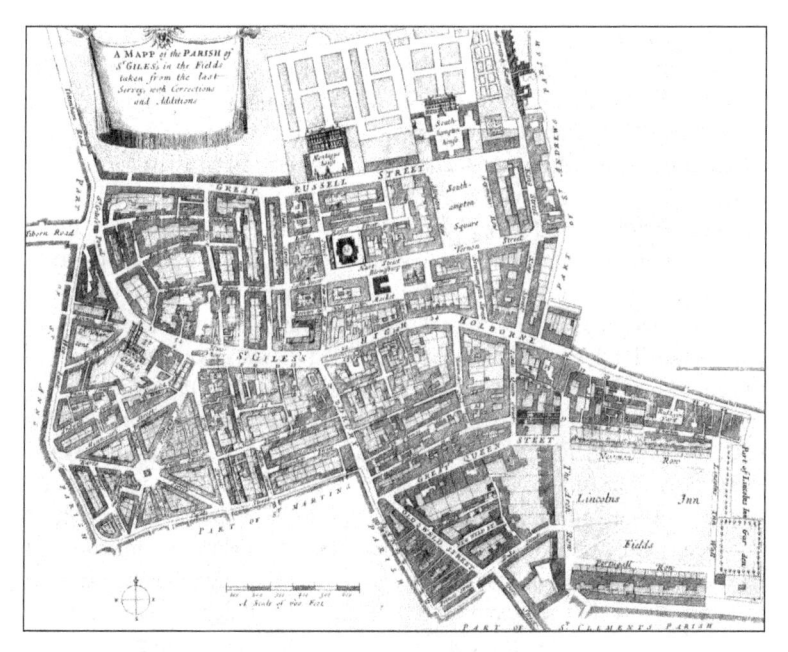

3. The parish of St Giles in the Fields. Based on John Strype's 1755 edition of John Stowe's Survey of London.

legal issues but did include a description, given to him by the High Constable of Holborn, of the squalid and overcrowded conditions in St Giles. Henry Fielding added that most of the inhabitants of the town's outskirts were Irish, but it is not clear whether he was specifically referring to St Giles or was writing more generally. Either way, he does not mention any separate Black community anywhere in London.[20] Brewer's *Dictionary of Phrase and Fable* (1870, revised 1952) makes no mention of 'black-bird'. Eric Partridge's *A Dictionary of Historical Slang* does include it, but gives its meaning as 'An African captive on board a slaver: nautical' and says it was rare. More generally, Partridge says, it meant 'a Polynesian indentured labourer, virtually a slave'.[21] Used as a verb, to black bird meant 'To capture Negroes and esp. Polynesians' and black-birders were those who engaged in this practice. The dates of these usages are all mid nineteenth century, long after the British slave trade had ceased. Partridge's *Dictionary of the Underworld* has two definitions for 'black-bird'. The first was a blackmailer or swindler and the second 'a white man trading in negroes male and female', which came from American slang c.1929. Although slang has usually been employed in everyday speech long before it is written down, these dates are far too long after 1794 to suggest that the phrase was then current. Even if Wadström were the first to use it in print, others must surely have done so in the half century or, in the case of the American reference, one hundred and thirty-odd years before Partridge found it.[22]

A substantial concentration of Black people in a particular location would have been worthy of comment by a visitor, either from the provinces or overseas, or by a journalist, but no one seems to have done so. Pierre Jean Grosley, a French lawyer, recorded his impressions in *A Tour to England* (1765). He mentioned passing through Seven Dials when a mob ran amok, disappointed because a man condemned to stand in the pillory had his sentence deferred. If there had indeed been a community in St Giles, there surely must have been a significant number of Black people among the Seven Dials mob, but Grosley made no mention of this.[23] Somewhere between visitors' and journalists' lies the work of Jack Harris, who produced *Harris's Lists* of ladies of easy virtue that were still being published around the time Wadström was writing. There are a few Black women in them, although no rent boys, probably because sodomy was a hanging offence. There was, however, no concentration of Black prostitutes in St Giles, as might be expected if there were a community there.[24] Plate 3 in Hogarth's series *The Rake's Progess* shows a Black woman among a group of prostitutes in Drury Lane, which formed the boundary between St Giles and St Pauls Covent Garden to the west and St Clement Danes to the east. Other research on St Giles has also failed to find any references to a community.[25]

A Victorian writer, Thomas Beames, devoted two chapters to St Giles in the Fields during the past, observing that:

> It appears this famous Rookery on the SE side of Tottenham Court Road that had recently [in 1850] been demolished was from a comparatively early period, the resort of the Irish and the place they first colonised. It has long been remarkable for poverty and vice.[26]

Beames quoted another writer (presumably John Bayley), who said that the Seven Dials area was 'noted for the assemblages of idle and dissolute persons'. Beames was, however, aware of ethnic minorities in the area. He quoted from *The British Traveller*'s description of a club in Seven Dials which 'consisted wholly of foreigners, chiefly of Frenchmen'.[27] What Beames' research in contemporary and near-contemporary writings failed to uncover was a Black community in the late eighteenth century, either in the area which became known as the Rookery, which had a substantial Irish presence, or in Seven Dials, an area within the parish. Nor did the Victorian writer Edward Walford find any Black community in St Giles in the sources he used, although he did quote a reference from John Smith's *Ancient Topography of London* (1810) to a Black woman in neighbouring St Clements who shaved men 'with ease and dexterity'.[28] Walford, too, wrote about the notorious Irish community in the parish.

The phrase 'St Giles's Black-birds' does not appear in any of the major works of fiction. Throughout the first half of the eighteenth century there was a fashion for realistic novels and plays about low life. Daniel Defoe, himself born in St Giles, wrote *Moll Flanders* (1722) and *Roxana* (1724) in which there are many references to parts of London, although not specifically to St Giles, without any mention of the city's Black inhabitants. Tobias Smollett was the next major novelist of this period whose works contained realistic descriptions of London life, including its various ethnic minorities. In *Roderick Random* (1749) the eponymous hero takes lodgings with a Scotsman in St Martin's Lane, the northernmost part of which (now forming part of Monmouth Street) was in St Giles in the Fields. Smollett also mentions both Jews and Huguenots in this area. Roderick Random recruits two men for protection. These tatterdemalions, named Fitzclabber and Gahagan, are plainly Irish, not Black. Random also visits Moll King's coffee house, which was a real place with a Black barmaid called Tawney Betty, who is not mentioned.[29] Smollett did not, however, ignore Black people in England. Black trumpeters appear fleetingly in *Humphry Clinker* (1771) among the episodes set in Bath.[30] Henry Fielding, the half-brother of the magistrate Sir John Fielding, and who himself became a magistrate, would have been in a good position to know of any Black semi-criminal community in St Giles but there are no Black characters in his novels, although some, like *The Life and Death of Jonathan Wild the Great* (1743), dealt with the law. Others, like *The History of Tom Jones* (1749), had incidents set in London but Black characters appear in none of his works.

It might be argued that, like Charles Dickens in the nineteenth century, these authors saw Black people regularly but did not include them in their works. Not all poets, novelists and dramatists, however, ignored the Black presence. There is, for example, a little-known song, 'The Black's Lamentation', which purports to be the story of a man confined in New Bedlam because he was spurned by a white girl.[31] In 1790 an anonymous novel, *Memoirs and Opinions of Mr Blenfield*, included Shirna Cambo, a character based on Ignatius Sancho. The adaptation of

Aphra Behn's *Oroonoko or the Royal Slave* (novel published in 1688, play produced in 1695), dealt with African nobility. James Townley's *High Life Below Stairs* (1759), set in a country house, included a Black servant among the characters, but there was no suggestion he was involved with crime or with any Black community: his life was bound up with his fellow (white) servants. An operatic afterpiece *The Padlock* (1768), written by Isaac Bickerstaff (music) and Charles Dibdin (words), included the character Mungo, a Black servant.[32] Isaac Jackson's *The Divorce* (1780) also had a Black servant in the cast. The most famous play in which criminals appear is John Gay's *Beggar's Opera* (1728), set in London. Although there are no explicitly Black characters, in the 1770s the role of Polly was taken by a young Black actress.[33]

The fashion for low-life subjects was, however, much earlier in the century than Wadström was writing. The publication in 1765 of Horace Walpole's *Castle of Otranto* introduced a new genre, the Gothic romance. There was also a sudden flowering of women writers concerned with genteel domestic life. These two forms, the Gothic and what might be called the 'woman's novel' displaced the low-life genre from the height of literary fashion. Gothic novels were largely concerned with villainous aristocrats and were often set in exotic places, so would hardly mention St Giles. The domestic works created by well-bred women would not include it either, since they were unlikely to venture there. One popular writer, however, remained faithful to the low-life genre. Pierce Egan's adventures of Tom and Jerry, published as *Life in London* in 1822, twenty-seven years after Wadström's *Essay*, described the supposed peregrinations of three men around the various entertainments on offer in the capital. George Cruikshank produced a series of engravings of scenes from the work. One depicts Egan's characters meeting Massa Piebald, a Black man with white hair, who was elected chairman of the revels, and played the fiddle to entertain his mainly white audience in the Holy Land in St Giles, so called because of its concentration of Irish inhabitants (Illustration 4). Other illustrations in the series included Black people but always with white companions. What Egan and Cruikshank made plain was that Black people were integrated into the local peoples' lives in both East and West London. Egan described poor people, both Black and white, enjoying themselves together. It was a sentimentalised picture of poverty but it showed a single community, rather than two separate communities divided on racial lines as they would have been in the Americas. There was no suggestion, as Wadström claimed, that Black people were friendless and despised because of their colour. Egan, like Sir John Fielding, was interested in the language

4. Tom and Jerry in the Holy Land, from Pierce Egan's *Life in London*

used by the lower classes and enjoyed recording it. He would surely have used such a colourful word as 'black-birds' had he come across it.

Edward Burford's studies of low life in Covent Garden mentioned St Giles in the Fields and his detailed study, based substantially on contemporary memoirs, unearthed a few Black denizens of Covent Garden, like Tawney Betty, the barmaid at Moll King's coffee house. Tawney Betty is even depicted on a mourning card for her employer, suggesting she was famous in her own right.[34] Were she an everyday sight, she would not have been worthy of special distinction. Burford also quoted a German visitor in 1710 who noted Moors of both sexes 'hawking their bottoms about the Strand and Covent Garden'.[35] James Walvin was the first historian to say that there were Black communities in St Giles and Wapping[36] and he was followed by Gretchen Gerzina.[37] Gerzina did not, however, claim that Black people had a separate community anywhere in London but said they gravitated to white slums.[38] Neither they nor any other historian working on the subject have found it remarkable that the well-known supporters of the slave trade, notably Edward Long and Philip Thicknesse, who were quoted extensively, did not mention this supposed community of poor Black people in the slums of St Giles. The anti-abolitionists would surely have used such a community as an example of how, as Wadström said, they were better off as slaves in the West Indies than as beggars in London.

While researching his thesis on the Black poor, Stephen Braidwood did not find any significant baptisms in the parish registers of St Giles in the Fields between 1783 and 1787. He wrote:

> It is conceivable that significant numbers of Black people, living in conditions of poverty, may not have been mentioned in the local parish registers: yet this seems unlikely in view of the number of poor Blacks we have noted in East End parishes. Alternatively contemporaries may have identified poor Blacks with St Giles in the Fields chiefly because the parish was associated with beggars. In 1789 a newspaper article alleged that many of the Black Poor in London had been corrupted by the example of their associates in the purlieus of St Giles and Wapping.[39]

Braidwood also checked the registers of St Giles Cripplegate, in the City of London, where he found three baptisms, and St Giles Camberwell, then a rural suburb in Surrey, where he found no baptisms of Black people.[40] He concluded: 'For the present it seems that the origin and validity of the term 'St Giles Blackbirds' must remain in doubt.'[41] I would concur, because although there are a number of baptisms of Black people in the registers of St Giles in the Fields between 1660 and 1812 they are no more numerous than in most of the other parishes in the metropolitan area, like St Anne Soho, which adjoins it. There seem to be considerably fewer (as a percentage of the total) than in the nearby Westminster parishes of St James, St George Hanover Square, St John Smith Square and St Clement Danes in Westminster, where wealthy people lived.[42] In addition there seems to be a single reference (Wadström's) to 'St Giles's black-birds', rather than the 'contemporaries' he cited. All modern academics who have used the phrase 'St Giles' black-birds' seem to have derived it from the same source – Wadström's original, either directly or from another work in which it was quoted.

Between 1722 and 1812, a few of the Black people who came before the court at the Old Bailey, as defendant, plaintiff or witness, seem to have been connected to the parish. There are, however, difficulties in identifying where people actually lived: it was the place where the crime was committed that was cited in the indictment or referred to in witnesses' evidence. In one case, John Vernon, a Black servant who had previously worked for a titled man but was 'out of place', was lodging in St Giles when he was robbed there.[43] John Downs (a Black) was lodging in Fleet Street but was robbed while having a drink in St Giles.[44] There are also many cases where the crime occurred in Westminster, on the other side of the parish boundary, so the perpetrator might have lived in St Giles but gone to a more prosperous area to steal.[45] The parish did come up in many other cases as a place where crimes (mainly assault) were committed and all the parties involved lived there, but the majority of people in these cases either were stated to be Irish or appear to be so from their names. It is impossible to prove anything from negative evidence but it does seem significant that all the works cited above, both factual and fictional, have failed to uncover or describe a Black community in St Giles. So how was it that only Carl Bernard Wadström saw what must have been a very distinctive sight in the London area? The short answer is that he was not describing a community.

Wadström was a Swede who travelled widely in Europe. In the eighteenth century, as well as being the language of diplomacy, French was the language that anyone in Britain with pretensions to gentility spoke.[46] Wadström must also have been fluent in the language, especially as Sweden had long-standing diplomatic links with France. He later wrote an *Adresse aux corps legislatif et au directoire executif de la republique française* [Address to the legislature and executive government of the French Republic], published in Paris in 1795. Although it is difficult to know whether Wadström wrote both the *Essay* and the *Adresse* himself or used translators, 'black-birds' was a literal translation of the French word, rather than of its colloquial meaning. Wadström did not say these poor Black people *joined* St Giles's black-birds, that there was a place they could go to, a community: he said they *became* St Giles's black-birds, which sounds more like an occupation. The French for blackbird is *merle* and, as well as its ornithological sense, the word has the idiomatic meaning of a rascal, not quite a wrongdoer or criminal, but someone who sails close to the wind. In his play *Eaux de Bourbon*, Florent Carton Dancourt (1661–1725) wrote 'c'est un dénicher des merles, se dit un homme habite à rechercher ce qu'il peut lui etre agréable ou utile, et adroit à en profiter' [he is a robber of blackbirds' nests, that means a man accustomed to searching out what can be pleasant or useful to him, and skilful in profiting from it]. Jean Josephe Vadé (1719–57), in his play *Niçaise*, uses the phrases 'un vilaine merle, un homme desagréable' [an ugly or villainous blackbird, a disagreeable or ugly man].[47] The *Grand Larousse Encyclopedique* (1957 edition) quotes both these definitions and adds *fin merle* [fine blackbird] which means '*personne très rusée*' [very cunning person]. Thomas Beames, whose book on the rookeries of London is mentioned above, wrote of Thurot, a French adventurer who lived in St Giles, as 'an apt specimen of the half smuggling, half gambling, living-by-their-wits population who made St Giles's their rendezvous at this time [1779]'.⁴⁸ This description is a good translation of the idiomatic use of *merle*.

Wadström probably heard English people in the highly educated circles in which he moved speak of '*merles*', meaning rogues. He (or any translator he might have used) probably assumed that both French and English had the same secondary meaning of *merle*/blackbird. Wadström did not say there was a Black community in London: he simply used a French colloquialism to characterise unscrupulous people living by their wits in St Giles. Dorothy George was the first to pick the phrase from the whole passage and to take it literally. Those who followed without doing any further research created a myth.

Other Black 'communities' in London

The other 'communities' in London that historians believe existed are in Wapping and Mile End, both in the East End of London. The Wapping location, a riverside settlement on the north bank of the Thames, is the most frequently cited. The existence of a community, or even a substantial number of Black people, here also seems to rest on a major misapprehension caused by the disproportionate number of Black people entered in the baptismal register of St George Wapping.⁴⁹ This parish was created from St Dunstan Stepney, a large parish stretching from Hackney (then a suburb) south to the river. The church of St George was consecrated in 1729. Its first rector, the Reverend Herbert Mayo, contributed to the appeal for money to fund the Sierra Leone project and was also a member of the Committee for the Abolition of Slavery.⁵⁰ Mayo was particularly assiduous in converting and baptising Black people. As his obituary said, 'I suppose no clergyman in England ever baptised so many Black men and Mulattoes [*sic*]'.⁵¹ He was also conscientious about making the entries in the baptismal register. He did not, as some ministers did, delegate this task to the parish clerk. This means that it is possible to compare the phrasing of entries made at different times: any variations will be significant, rather than caused by different practices by two or more people. When the registers and the day books are examined it is immediately obvious that the entries relating to most of the Black people contain different information from those of the other parishioners, and I would argue that these differences demonstrate that the majority of those baptised did not live in the parish. From the establishment of the parish in 1729, Mayo carefully included the occupations and addresses of the adults and the parents of the children he baptised, which were also entered in the day books. Until

The Black population of London 51

Table 2 Baptisms of Black people in Wapping 1730–1812

Period	Address in Wapping and/or occupation given	Colour and birthplace only given
1730–39	0	0
1740–49	4	0
1750–59	4	0
1760–69	4[a]	1
1770–79	3	12[b]
1780–89	6	69[c]
1790–99	2	30
1800–12	0[d]	20

Notes:
[a] Plus the baptism of the son of an Indian servant.
[b] Plus the baptism of a man born at St Christopher's (St Kitts) whose colour/race was not given.
[c] Plus four baptisms of people born in America whose colour/race was not given.
[d] Plus the baptism of a Black man born in Africa and living in Rosemary Lane, East Smithfield, Whitechapel, which had a high concentration of lodging houses for seamen; and one of a 'man of colour' born in Macao, China, who was probably Chinese.

the 1770s there were only a few Black people baptised every decade. Most were servants with an address in the parish, or were annotated 'Ma[rine]r', referring to someone temporarily in Wapping before joining another ship. But then the number sharply increased and no occupation or address was recorded for almost all the Black catechumens, candidates for baptism, in either the register or the day books (see Table 2).[52] Mayo did, however, carefully enter where the Black people came from. This would link to the need to determine the person's place of settlement, should this later become of importance (see Chapter 5). There were exceptions, which suggests that some Black people did live in the parish, and this figure is approximately the same as the number recorded with addresses in the previous decades, i.e. accepted to be residents of the parish.

The parish burial registers reveal a different picture. Between 1729 and 1812, only twelve people explicitly stated to be Black, and two whose names suggest they may have been, were buried.[53] There may be others (one of the registers is badly damaged and the ink has faded totally from several pages of the last one, covering 1777–1812), but any additional numbers cannot be great. Five of the twelve Black people buried were unknown, either 'found in the street' or 'from the Workhouse' (where sick and dying people without a home would be taken). Parish authorities did make efforts to ascertain the names of unknown people found within their jurisdiction. That these people could not be identified suggests they were not resident and were not among the number baptised by Mayo. They are most likely to have been itinerant beggars or destitute sailors, of whom there were also many men, presumably white, buried in the parish. Of the other seven buried in the parish, the addresses of four were given. They were probably the servants of better-off residents of Wapping.

Finding out what happened to all these Black people baptised in Wapping would be a long and in most cases an ultimately fruitless task. Most have names indistinguishable from those of the general population and they seem to have moved on, as none apparently appears in the burial registers. There is, however, a document which gives one person's background and a little of her history before and after her baptism. Ann Clawson was baptised by Herbert Mayo on 25 August 1782. In the register she is described as 'from Se1negal in Africa suppos'd to be 24 Years old'.[54] Nine years later, on 10 November 1791, she was brought before a magistrate in St Martin in the Fields in Westminster to undergo a settlement examination. Her name there is recorded as Ann Closson. She stated that she had been brought to England from Africa by a Captain Moore. For about six years she lived as his servant in Kent Street in the borough of Southwark. Although she was given food, clothing and accommodation she had no wages. She 'quitted his service when baptised' and in 1790 hired herself as a yearly servant with wages of seven and a half guineas to Mr Neale, a surgeon living in St Martin in the Fields. After three months she left the surgeon's service to live with John Closson, a Black man living in Bethnal Green. A month later the two fell out and Ann went back to Mr Neale, negotiated a pay rise of half a guinea a year and returned to his service. Ten months later, in October 1791, she gave birth to an illegitimate child, fathered by a fellow servant, and Mr Neale dismissed her.[55] The information in this statement shows that, although baptised in Wapping, Ann Clawson or Closson, or Barker (this latter was given as an alternative name in her statement) never had any connection with this parish. She seems to have believed that baptism would free her, so had gone to Herbert Mayo to get this done. It seems likely that after she was baptised and had left Captain Moore she moved in with John Closson, as there is a gap of eight years between her baptism and going to work for Mr Neale and she was using Closson's name when she was baptised. He, or another Black person, probably told her about the clergyman and the supposed benefits that being christened by him would bring.

What seems the most likely explanation is that for a short period there were a number of Black people who came to the parish of Wapping, drawn there, like Ann Closson, by Mayo's willingness to baptise them. The belief that this conferred freedom would have made his parish a magnet for newly arrived Black people. As no addresses are given for the majority of Black people baptised in the period following the well-publicised Mansfield Judgment and the end of the American War of Independence, most of the others in the Wapping registers probably had similar motives and as little connection with the parish as Ann Closson. Mayo's obituary noted that 'Several of them never came into the port of London, without waiting upon him . . .'.[56] It does not say that the Black people he baptised lived in his parish, just that they visited him there.

Undoubtedly a small number of Black people were resident in Wapping. As a riverside settlement, it would have had the usual contingent of Black mariners passing through and a small number who worked out of Wapping because they had partners and children there, like the mariner Anthony Stewart 'a Black', whose son Charles, by Lucy, was baptised in 1788. His address is given as Denmark Street.[57] However, there is no evidence of a substantial community of Blacks, nor that the numbers living here were any higher than they were in any of the other riverside settlements. The resident Black population was small and remained about the same size over the years.

Mile End

A third place that has been suggested as the location of a possible Black community is Mile End, a settlement, as Wapping originally was, in the large parish of Stepney. The White Raven public house was one of the places where money was distributed to poor Blacks when the Sierra Leone project was being planned. It was actually in the parish of Whitechapel, at the beginning of Mile End Road, on the border with the parish of Stepney. By the eighteenth century there were two areas of settlement within it. Mile End New Town grew up in the last quarter of the seventeenth century, along the road out of the City in the western part of the parish, on the border with Whitechapel. The other settlement, to the east, and surrounded by open ground, became known as Mile End Old Town.

Although other historians had noted the distribution of relief at Mile End, Braidwood seems to have been the first to call it 'a locality which we have already noted as a centre of the Black population'. He observed that most of the Black people baptised in Stepney came from Mile End Old Town.[58] At this time, Mile End Old Town was an area of middle-class sea captains and senior members of the marine industry, like William Snelgrave, the slave trader, and his son, also William, who was involved in marine insurance. There were also a number of residents connected with the East India Company and the Hudson's Bay Trading Company.[59] It is their servants who account for the number of Black people Braidwood found. This rather undermines his argument that by 1780 'the majority of Blacks were living, not as slaves or servants in wealthy households but as freemen and independent householders or tenants, often in poverty'.[60] He gave no evidence for this assertion. In his study of Mile End Old Town between 1740 and 1780 Derek Morris found only a few inhabitants stated to be Black or from the East Indies.[61] No independent householders or tenants are specifically described as Black. This does not mean that there were not some Black householders, simply that there is no evidence of this. Certainly Stepney's proximity to the river would mean that a number of Black seamen would be found in the parish, but most seemed to have lived closer to the river, in the hamlets of Wapping, Shadwell, Limehouse and Ratcliff, to judge from the parish registers. There were more: the Snelgraves mentioned above had a Black servant, John Scipio, who was buried in the parish churchyard without any reference to his colour.[62]

There is a possible explanation for the choice of the White Raven as a distribution centre. In 1765 Captain Henry Kent opened a hall for hiring out servants. This stood in the parish of Stepney, next to the Trinity alms-houses on the other side of Mile End Green from the public house.[63] Kent died in 1780 but the business probably continued there, because it was a prime site for people coming into town to enquire for temporary servants during their stay. It was not so much that a disproportionately large number of Black people lived in Mile End (although some undoubtedly did), but that the place was known for its employment agency. It was therefore a sensible place to locate a relief centre: those who did not get hired could at least be fed and the authorities could keep an eye on them.

It is likely that a similar consideration led to the choice of the Yorkshire Stingo, a public house in Paddington, as another relief centre for Black people. No one has suggested that Paddington had a concentration of Black inhabitants, so why else would it be regarded as a good site for a relief centre? There were a number of Black people in neighbouring Marylebone, but these were not destitute: they were the servants of the richer inhabitants. Both public houses were in locations where people entered the City of London from the east (in the case of Whitechapel, where the White Raven was located) or came to Westminster from the west (in the case of Paddington, the site of the Yorkshire Stingo). Those travelling into the metropolis leaving their usual servants behind would have needed temporary servants while they were in town, so employment agencies at these points would have done good business and attracted unemployed people seeking work.

Concentrations of Black inhabitants elsewhere

There are a few other parish registers in London containing a disproportionately large number of entries relating to Black people but they should not be used as a kind of ethnic minority census. It is very important to look at the nature of the parish rather than count the entries without question. St Marylebone, for example, has many baptisms of Black people in its records, but this is probably because a number of merchants from the West Indies lived there and they must have brought servants with them. There is, however, a far higher proportion of Black people in the register of Holy Trinity Minories, just outside the walls of the City of London. This was a poor area so it might be assumed that it was where Black people collected together. However, it was also one of the churches whose minister conducted what were called irregular marriages.[64] Normally people who did not wish to have banns called for three weeks in their local parish church had to obtain a licence from the bishop of the diocese in which they lived, or from the Archbishop of Canterbury if they wanted to be married outside their diocese. For historic reasons some parishes, like Holy Trinity Minories, did not fall under the control of a bishop and so were able to issue their own licences. Ceremonies conducted on these terms are known as irregular marriages. Many of the Black population believed that baptism conferred freedom. It seems likely that the ministers who conducted clandestine and irregular marriages were also willing to baptise Black non-parishioners. St George's Chapel in Mayfair was another church outside the Bishop of London's authority where irregular marriages were conducted and its registers show an even greater disproportion between Black and white baptisms than do those of Holy Trinity.[65] St Katherine by the Tower also performed irregular marriages. Although this legal loophole had been closed by 1780, it is possible that Holy Trinity and St Katherine by the Tower retained a reputation among Black people. Another reason which might distort the number of Black baptisms in St Katherine by the Tower is the presence of a hospital there. Sick Black people who did not have a support network of friends and family (and there must have been many) would go to hospitals where those in danger of death would have been baptised by the authorities concerned about their souls.

The Black population of Westminster

There seem to be no modern studies of the population of Westminster. One of the problems is that the number living there fluctuated: the winter season brought hundreds of the well-to-do and their servants flocking in from the countryside. Although historians usually mention only the East End being involved in the shipping trade, it extended along the river, so Millbank also had a transient population of mariners. Until the Great Fire of London in 1666 the population of Westminster was comparatively small, but merchants whose houses were destroyed camped out in the fields around the royal palace at St James. The Restoration of Charles II in 1660 brought an influx of people to serve his court, including craftsmen who made the goods his luxury-loving regime craved. The growth of population after the Restoration can be seen in the increase in the number of parishes. There were two ancient parishes, St Clement Danes and Westminster. By 1660 Westminster had already been subdivided into St Martin in the Fields (1550), St Mary le Strand (1558) and St Paul Covent Garden (1653) but, as the population grew, more parishes were created: St Anne Soho (1685), St James Piccadilly (1685), St George Hanover Square (1725) and St John Smith Square (1728). Within individual parishes there were also chapels, which kept separate registers, like St George's Chapel in Mayfair. The Queen's Chapel of the Savoy, dedicated to St John the Baptist, was part of a medieval royal palace within St Clement Danes but came under the jurisdiction of the Duchy of Lancaster; between 1680 and 1756 it acted as a parish church.[66] Royal Peculiars in Westminster were Westminster Abbey and the Chapels Royal in St James's Palace, Whitehall and Marlborough House. The latter was known as the German Chapel Royal. In addition, there was a private chapel in Buckingham Palace. Black servants who were part of the Royal household are likely to have been christened in one of these.

Between 1660 and 1812 at least a thousand Black people are recorded as living in or passing through Westminster. Although it is possible that some are included twice (the Jeffrey Moras baptised in 1730 is almost certainly the Jeffrey Morat/Murat tried at the Old Bailey in 1736 for attempted murder[67]) there are likely to have been many more, but the burial registers of the Westminster parishes were, unfortunately, among the least informative in the metropolitan area. They rarely gave any information beyond the name, and, from about 1800, the age of the person buried. In the City of London and most other parts of the country relationships and other information were often given. St Clement Danes was exceptional in recording occupations from a very early date but, like the others in Westminster, rarely gave colour, ethnic origin or family relationships. Black people are also infrequently identified as such in marriage registers. The only marriages in Westminster where colour is mentioned took place at the Savoy Chapel during the two years that the minister there was conducting illegal marriages after the passing of the 1753 Marriage Act. In this period all the marriage entries contain much more information about the parties than was required by law, presumably because the minister wanted to protect his position. One involving a Black person was by licence (so the bride and groom might have come from anywhere).[68] The other two were by banns, which meant that one or both parties were living in the parish.[69] One other marriage in the Savoy Chapel may be of a Black person.[70]

Baptisms of Black people, probably a good guide to the relative size of their presence over the long eighteenth century, peaked in the decade 1770–1779, when they constituted 0.35 per cent of total baptisms. After 1790 there was a sharp drop, although the population of Westminster was steadily increasing. Comparison of the number of baptisms of Black people with the total number in Westminster shows that increases and decreases in the two were not linked. Indeed, during the twenty years from 1750 to 1769, although the total number of baptisms in Westminster fell, the number of Black people christened increased. A number of hypotheses can be suggested. The first is that the employment of Black servants (Westminster was the seat of government and the Court) among the aristocracy and the powerful increased during the latter half of the eighteenth century. The second is that the activities of the abolitionists caused an increase in the number of Black people who believed that baptism would confer freedom. Only 11.44 per cent of the baptismal entries of Black people give the name of a master or mistress, either explicitly or by implication. The third is that the Mansfield Judgment in 1772 was widely believed to give Black people freedom, although Mansfield reiterated a previous ruling that baptism did not confer freedom, so masters who had previously withheld consent to baptism no longer did so. The fourth is that this judgment may also have increased the number of Black people coming to this country, where they believed they would gain their freedom. It is noticeable that the origin of those baptised is much more frequently given after this date (although, as discussed elsewhere, this might be because of the implications of the judgment for the operation of the poor laws). The last is that the ending of the American War of Independence brought Black people who had supported the Loyalist side to England and a significant number of them came to Westminster.

The sharp decrease from 1790 may also have a number of causes. The first is that all those who had wanted but, for one reason or another, were not able to be baptised had the ceremony carried out in the 1770s or 1780s, following the Mansfield Judgment. The second is that the number of Black people coming from America or the Caribbean because they believed they would be free in England stabilised after an initial surge. The third is that the rich no longer brought Black servants about whose loyalty they had reservations from the Caribbean because they feared they would lose them or have to pay them to remain. There may, of course, not be one single reason for these imbalances, but a combination of the factors listed above, and more research is needed.

Sex and age

Seventy-five per cent of those baptised in Westminster were male, 22 per cent female, and for 2 per cent sex was not given and the names were ambiguous. This ratio is comparable to that for the whole country. Many ages, if not most, were estimated, but the majority of those baptised in Westminster were adolescents, between the ages of 11–20, followed by the 21–30 cohort, then 1–10, 41–50, 31–40, and lastly, 51–60. In addition, twenty-eight were simply described as 'adult'; one was 'at maturity'; five were annotated 'boy', one 'girl' and one 'young man'. It must be remembered that these were ages at baptism. Whether the age profile reflected that of Black servants generally cannot be known, because it is difficult to tell how long they had been either in the country or, in the case of servants, in their masters' service before baptism. Nor is it known in the earlier period whether they were born in Africa or in one of the colonies. From 1745, the names of parents were sometimes included. These were generally European names, suggesting that they were the children of slaves.

Origins

The place of birth or previous country of residence of most of the Black people in Westminster (74 per cent) was not stated. The largest group came to England from the Caribbean (37.5 per cent), followed by Africa (26.5 per cent), Asia (20.5 per cent) and North America (16.5 per cent). Whether those from the Caribbean and North America were born there or in Africa is not known. As might be expected, Jamaica (23) and Barbados (20) are numerically the largest groups, followed by Antigua (11), St Kitts (6), Tortola (3), St Domingo and Tobago (2 each) and one each from Bermuda, Demerara, Dominica and St Vincent. The slave-trading areas of Africa are the most frequently given places of origin in this continent, so cannot be considered a reliable guide to the actual place of birth, but four were recorded as from St Helena and one from the Cape of Good Hope. In addition, there was one 'Ethiopian', but where he came from is a moot point. All those from Asia who were baptised in Westminster came from India. Carolina (15) was the most frequently mentioned place of origin in North America, followed by New York (6), Boston (2) and Florida (2). There is also one described as a 'Spanish Indian'[71] and one who had come from France.[72]

Previous historians have said that the majority of Black people in the London area were to be found in the East End, particularly in the riverside parishes. They assumed that Black people were poor, so they looked for them only in poor areas. The population in Westminster, however, was much larger and also seems to have been more settled: many of the Black people in the docks were mariners, and thus transient. Of the Black people in Westminster, only seven are unnamed. Two were servants in trials at the Old Bailey,[73] another a baptism[74] and the rest were burials. There are fewer unknown Black people here than anywhere else in the London area, suggesting that few here were destitute beggars or transients: they were known and had links to the inhabitants.

The Black population of the City of London

As the mercantile centre of Britain, and later the British Empire, the City of London was at the hub of commerce. It is therefore unsurprising to find a Black presence there from very early days. The Square Mile of the City of London covers the area within the old Roman walls. Until the Great Fire of 1666 the City was where the majority of people in the London area lived: the City of Westminster was a comparatively small settlement of people attached to the Court. Before the Great Fire, there were 110 parishes in the City. Some only covered a few streets,[75] but those that were partly in the City and partly outside the walls, like the various churches on the landward gates, were larger. Many of the eighty-seven churches destroyed by the Great Fire were not rebuilt but the parishes were amalgamated, a process which continued as people moved out of the increasingly crowded city. The City remained the financial centre of London but those connected to politics and the court gravitated to Westminster, so the kinds of people in the two cities became very different. There were relatively few members of the nobility in the City parish records, which largely consist of merchants, tradesmen and artisans but there were some mariners, mainly in riverside parishes. The Black population might therefore be expected to be different from that in Westminster.

The City Without the Walls

The Bills of Mortality in the London area distinguish between the ninety-seven parishes within the city walls and what was called the City Without the Walls, or the City Without. These included the ones at the ancient gates and the parishes whose boundaries encompassed areas both within and without the City.[76] The borough of Southwark, on the south bank of the Thames, was also included in the City Without.[77] The parishes of St Katherine in the Tower, though next to the City walls, and St Peter ad Vincula within the Tower came within the Liberty of Tower Hamlets, and for the purposes of the Bills of Mortality were included in the outparishes of Middlesex and Surrey.[78] For convenience and consistency in analysing figures, I have kept to the division of parishes between those within the City walls and those without. There is much more variation in the information included in register entries in the City parishes than in those of Westminster. Some, like most of the Westminster burial registers, record only names. Others give relationships, occupations and origins. The records of a few of the smaller parishes and chapels in the City are not extant. The outparishes of Surrey and Middlesex were omitted from the following analyses because they covered both areas of high population like Lambeth in Surrey and St Katherine by the Tower in Middlesex, and rural places like Clapham and Islington.

The fluctuations in the Black population in the City of London did not follow the general trends for the City itself or, it appears, the country as a whole. There seem to have been fewer baptisms of Black people in the City of London than in the City of Westminster, and the numbers peaked in the 1720s. This could be for two reasons: the first is the nature of the inhabitants. Most of those in the City were businessmen. They may have been less conscious of fashion than those at the Court, and so less likely to have Black servants as a status symbol. The second is that, as the City's inhabitants grew more prosperous, they moved out. The peak of baptisms of all people, Black and white, in the City was in the 1680s and thereafter they reduced gradually until the 1740s, when there was another noticeable reduction. This probably reflects the move of the wealthier citizens, those who were more likely to have Black servants, to the suburbs. Black servants of the merchants who lived outside the City would be baptised in the parish where the family lived, rather than where their masters worked. Joseph Sedgwick, for example, was a merchant, born and married in the City of London, where his first two children were also born. Around 1734-35 he moved from the City to Stratford Bow on the Middlesex-Essex border, where another child was born and his family lived while the children were young. His two Black servants were baptised in Stratford Bow in 1740, but probably moved with the family to the City when they relocated there around 1744, as neither appears in the Stratford Bow burial register.[79] There were smaller spikes in baptisms in the 1700s and covering the years 1760-89. The reasons for these cannot yet be conjectured. Certainly they do not follow the general trends in the City, although the second spike is comparable to the trends in Westminster and the rest of the country.

Until the 1690s, the number of burials of Black people apparently equalled or exceeded the number of baptisms. It is unwise to draw conclusions from this seeming anomaly but it is worth noting that the City had a very high mortality rate generally: its population increased through migration. The peak of burials of Black people in the City apparently came in the 1680s, when the peak of burials in the general population of the City also occurred. Oddly, there is no record in any of the extant City parish registers of the burial of a Black person during the Great Plague of 1665. The authorities did find it difficult to administer the City during this period, but most churches maintained registers. There were plague pits in which bodies were interred because there was no room in the churchyards, but the names of those who died seem to have been recorded. Very few entries, however, gave anything more than a list of names and the cause of death.[80] Presumably such a traumatic event made all distinctions of class, relationship, colour or race irrelevant. Alternatively, most Black people then in the City would have been working for families that had the means to flee into the countryside.

Approximately 3.9 per cent of the Black people mentioned in City records had ambiguous names, or their sex was not given, and some 22.5 per cent of the Black people here were female. This latter is slightly less than the countrywide figure. Ages, or an indication of age, at baptism were recorded in the majority of City parishes. The age profile is more or less the same as for Westminster: the majority were aged 11–20, followed by 21–30, 0–10, 41–50 and 51–60. In addition, there were thirty-six described as 'adult' and one 'woman', who were probably over 21; twenty 'boys'; one 'girl'; three 'youths' and two called 'young'. These were probably under the age of majority.

Origins

The origins of 85 per cent were not given. The majority of those where a place of birth or origin was given came from the Caribbean (37.87 per cent), although it is not known whether these people were born there or in Africa, closely followed by the East Indies (33.33 per cent). Next was Africa (24.24 per cent), and then North America (4.54 per cent). In addition, one is described as a Creolian, which might suggest someone Black or of mixed race born in the Caribbean, although the term was also used of white people at the time; one, a 'lascar', was most probably from the Indian subcontinent but may have been from anywhere in Asia, and two were described as from 'Madera'. Where this was is not certain, although it is most likely the island of Madeira, under Portuguese rule. There were two 'Tawney Moors', who could have been either of Arab origin or of mixed race, and four 'mulattos', with no further indication of their ethnic origins or from where they came.

Those from the Caribbean included Jamaica (11), Barbados (3), Antigua and Dominica (2 each) and one each from Bermuda, Demerara, Nevis, St Vincent and Tobago. From Africa, apart from Guinea, there were one each from Sierra Leone, Madagascar and Mozambique. As the British slave trade did not extend to the east coast of Africa, the presence of the two Black people from the latter islands is not easily explicable. They may have come to London with ships which called there, either joining the crew as free sailors or having been purchased privately by the captain of a ship trading there. The Madagascan is described as the servant of the parish minister but there is no further information on the Mozambiquan.[81] One from North America was from South Carolina, the second from Maryland and the third from Florida.

The predominance of people from the East Indies, a greater proportion than in Westminster and the country as a whole, must reflect the importance of the City's trade with the Indian subcontinent and the Far East. The headquarters of the East India Company, which had a monopoly of the trade in this part of the world until 1833, were in the City. The comparatively small numbers from Africa and North America may reflect the lesser importance of trade with these areas in the City.

The Black population of the City Without the Walls

It is in the City Without the Walls that the fewest number of baptisms and burials of Black people are recorded in the metropolitan area, although the population was much higher than that of the City Within the Walls. This is probably because the people who lived here, especially in the streets immediately outside the City walls, were craftsmen.[82] Relatively few Black people learned a craft, for reasons which are discussed in Chapter 8, and from 1730 the city authorities had banned Black people from entering apprenticeships. Nor did the City authorities permit anyone who had not completed an expensive City apprenticeship, and thus gained the freedom, from working inside the Square Mile. Living next to the walls was therefore the best way for skilled craftsmen whose parents had not been able to afford the high premiums commanded by the City to gain a living while remaining within the law.

The majority of baptisms of Black people here came in the 1780s: roughly the same as in the rest of the country, but this was the decade after the peak in Westminster and much later than in the City Within. There was a smaller peak in the 1680s (when the baptisms of Black people in the City Within peaked), which may indicate that for some reason there was an influx of Black people at this time as well which is as yet unexplained. Baptisms among the general population of the City Without peaked in the 1720s and started to rise again in the 1800s. There were comparatively few baptisms of people stated to be Black in the City Without and there were even fewer burials. Most years apparently saw none: the largest number was five in the 1780s, when the Black population seems to have peaked.

The average age at baptism of the Black population of the City Without seems to have been marginally higher than in the City and in Westminster. Although the largest cohort in all three areas was 11–20, in the City Without a larger proportion of baptisms was of people aged 21–30 and a smaller proportion under the age of 11. In addition, there were eighteen simply described as 'adult' and one 'man', which suggests they were over 21; and two 'girls', one 'boy' and one 'youth'. The sex ratio of males to females (83 per cent to 18 per cent) was much higher than anywhere else in the country. These factors, combined with the few (eight) who are noted to be 'servants' may suggest that more of the Black population here were workers contributing directly to their employers' profits, rather than domestic servants.

No place of origin was given for 76 per cent (Figure 1). Where origin was given, the majority of Black people (53 per cent) came from the Caribbean, followed by 34 per cent from Africa, 20 per cent from the

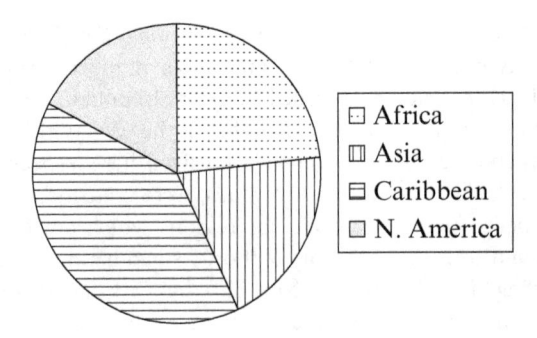

Note: The unknown proportion (76 per cent) is omitted.

Figure 1 Area of origin of Black people in England 1660–1812

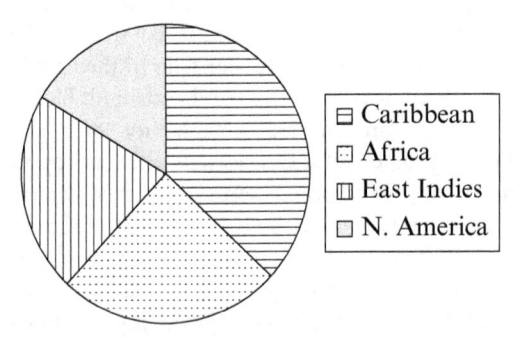

Note: The unknown proportion (74 per cent) is omitted.

Figure 2 Area of origin of Black people in Westminster 1660–1812

East Indies, 16 per cent from North America and a single person (2 per cent) from Canada (after 1783). Within the Caribbean they followed a standard pattern: Jamaica (15), Barbados (7), Bermuda and St Kitts (3 each), Antigua (2) and one each from Martinique, Nevis and St Domingo. The origins of those from North America were given as four from North or South Carolina, one from New York and one from Canada. Those stated to have been born in the East Indies were usually simply described as 'Indian' or from the East Indies, but they included six from places in India and one each from the Philippines and China. This profile is more similar to Westminster and the rest of the country than to the City Within.

☐ East Indies
☐ Caribbean
☐ Africa
☐ N. America
■ Other

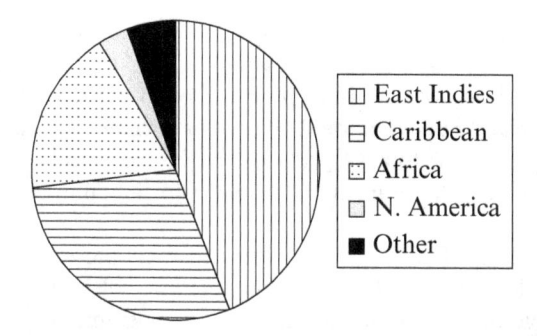

Note: The unknown proportion (85 per cent) is omitted.

Figure 3 Area of origin of Black people in the City of London 1660–1812

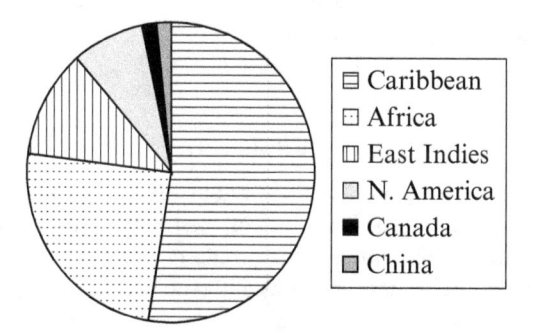

☐ Caribbean
☐ Africa
☐ East Indies
☐ N. America
■ Canada
☐ China

Note: The unknown proportion (76 per cent) is omitted.

Figure 4 Origins of the Black population of the City Without 1660–1812

The origins of Black people show the greatest difference between the three areas of metropolitan London. In both Westminster and the City Without, most Black people came from the Caribbean, followed by Africa, and a substantial number came from North America (Figures 2 and 4). In the City, most came from the East Indies, followed by the Caribbean, and the number from North America is considerably smaller (Figure 3). This is probably because of the City's mercantile basis and reflects the amount of trade with Asia done there. It is also in the City that the greatest number of references does not reveal the individual's place of origin.

The fluctuations in the numbers of Black people baptised in the three areas are also interesting. The numbers in Westminster, which were higher than in the City or the City Without, rose significantly from the 1750s, peaked in the 1770s and declined sharply in the 1790s. The City Without saw a similar profile, though the total number was much lower, and peaked in the 1780s, with a smaller spike in the 1680s. In the City itself, the total began to rise in the 1680s and peaked in the 1720s. Here the total numbers were approximately the same as in the City Without.

There is some fragmentary evidence in extra-parochial records of Black people being employed in non-domestic roles in the City and these people may not have had their colour or ethnic origin recorded in registers. In Westminster Black servants and their masters were routinely noted, but once they had left service their jobs seem to have been included in registers only occasionally. To find an occupation recorded for a Black person is rarer in both the City and the City Without than in Westminster. This may suggest that the Black people in City areas were doing a variety of non-domestic jobs, especially casual labour, on the riverside.

Conclusions

The metropolitan area of London, covered by the Bills of Mortality, contained three separate areas: the Cities of Westminster and London and the City Without. The demographic profile of people, both Black and white, in the three areas described was different, but drawing any conclusions as to the reasons for these differences would be premature before considerably more research has been done. It does, however, seem to add weight to the argument that there was no one Black 'community': people described as 'Black' came from a wide range of backgrounds and had different jobs. All that can be done here is to suggest further avenues to be explored. The first point to emphasise is that, for the vast majority of Black people in the records, nothing is given beyond their colour/ethnic origin. Although some entries give additional information which allows profiling of age and continent, even place, of origin, the results need to be treated with caution. Second, relatively little work has been done on the demographics of the London area in general, primarily because of the lack of necessary information. Bills of Mortality are not congruent with population figures, and other sources, like the church court depositions used by Peter Earle,[83] may be too small a sample to be completely representative, as well as seeming to omit those at either end of the social spectrum. A third problem is the sheer number of parishes in the City.

There was an element of planning in the construction of Westminster after the Great Fire that was absent from the City of London, which had grown up haphazardly from pre-Roman times. The Westminster parishes were larger and the population there was more homogeneous. Last, a great deal of information is simply missing, most notably from the burial registers of Westminster.

In all three metropolitan areas covered above, the peak age for baptism was adolescence (11–20) and this age profile is comparable to the rest of the country, but the difference in the sex ratio of Black people between Westminster and the City Without seems significant. Westminster's profile, with 75 per cent men, is similar to the country at large, while the City Without, 83 per cent men, is comparable to ports generally and must reflect the number of mariners in this area. Unfortunately, the comparatively large proportion of those of unknown sex in the City makes it difficult to determine whether the ratio there was closer to Westminster or to the City Without.

It is clear that considerably more research needs to be done on the Black population of the London area in order to explore the differences between the parts of the densely populated metropolitan area: the suburbs, where many of the more prosperous City merchants and probably their Black servants lived, and the outer, more rural parishes of Middlesex, Surrey, Kent and Essex. Further work on what was happening both in the City and in the colonies during these periods is necessary before any hypotheses can be formulated as to why there should be such variations. Such detailed research should also produce information which would help to answer some of the other questions raised by this statistical overview, particularly the occupations and roles played by Black people in the life and commerce of London.

Notes

1. Findlay, R., *Population and Metropolis* (Cambridge, 1981), p. 51. The 1801 census figure is probably a slight underestimate: it seems that only the inhabitants of houses were enumerated, so people on board ship, those sleeping rough and others were omitted.
2. Norton, M.B., 'The Fate of some Black Loyalists of the American Revolution', *Journal of Negro History* 58 (9) 1978, pp. 402–26, quoted in Myers, *Reconstructing the Black Past*, pp. 22–4.
3. Kretschmar, F.G.L.O., *De registers van de 'Dutch Chapel Royal' 1694–1775* (Amsterdam, 1964), 17 March 1716/7. Although there had always been Dutch people in the city, after the accession of William III in 1668 a sizeable Dutch

presence is found, mainly based in Westminster. There were also groups in Hammersmith, Richmond and Rotherhithe but no records that they may have kept have survived.
4. Katz, D., 'Philo-Semitism and the Readmission of Jews to England 1603–1655' (Oxford, 1982) quoted in Samuel, E. 'London's Portuguese Jewish Community', in Vigne, R. & Littleton, C. (eds), *From Strangers to Citizens: The Integration of Immigrant Communities in Britain, Ireland and Colonial America, 1550–1750* (2001), p. 240.
5. GL, Ms 5088, Registers of All Hallows London Wall, 17 September 1755. Abraham Massiah or Massieas appears in the records of Bevis Marks synagogue. *Bevis Marks Records(Part II): Abstracts of the Ketubot or Marriage-Contracts of the Congregation from the Earliest Times until 1837* (1949), pp. 84 and 94; *Bevis Marks Records (Part VI): the Burial Registers (1733–1918) of the Novo (New) Cemetery of the Spanish and Portuguese Jews' Congregation, London* (1997), p. 376.
6. Lambeth Palace Court of Arches, D. 556, quoted in Stone, L., *Broken Lives: Separation and Divorce in England 1660–1857* (Oxford, 1993), p. 58.
7. Only the later registers of these chapels survive: the Venetians' date from 1744, the Bavarians' from 1748. The records of the Portuguese chapel in Warwick Street seem to have been taken to Lisbon when the Bavarian embassy took it over in 1788, so the extent to which it was used by British Catholics and Black people converted to Catholicism is unknown.
8. The first buildings of the churches of St James Spanish Place and St Patrick Soho Square were erected in 1791 and 1792. The latter was intended for the large Irish community in neighbouring St Giles in the Fields. St Mary Moorfields was rebuilt in 1820 with money received as compensation for the destruction in the Gordon Riots of 1780 of a house which Catholics had been using for worship.
9. Catholic Family History Society, *The Registers of the Venetian Chapel in London* (1996). Richard James 'born in East India at Madras' was also bap. here on 28 May 1787, p. 39.
10. CWA, photocopy of the registers of the Imperial Legation of Austria on open shelves, 10 September 1774. The original is in the Westminster Diocesan Archives. Codrington may have been a member of the family of that name who had extensive estates in Barbados.
11. Kolchin, P., *American Slavery 1619–1877* (Canada, 1993), p. 149.
12. Equiano, ed. Carretta, *Interesting Narrative*, p. 220.
13. George, *London Life*, p. 134.
14. Wadström, C.B., *An Essay on Colonisation* (1794, facsimile edn, Newton Abbott, 1968), p. 228.
15. There was a connection between both the London churches dedicated to St Giles and poor people. John Stow records that Henry V endowed a hospital for the poor at St Giles Cripplegate, which was later suppressed by Henry

VIII. Stow, J., *The Survey of London* (1603), ed. Wheatley H.B. (rev. edn, 1956), pp. 269-70. The hospital at St Giles in the Fields was founded in the reign of Edward III, then sold to a City merchant in the reign of Henry VII. Stowe, *ibid.*, p. 392. This hospital was also suppressed by Henry VIII, Weinreb, B. & Hibbert, C. (eds), *The London Encyclopaedia* (1983), pp. 710-11.

16. The parish of St Paul Covent Garden was created within St Martin in the Fields in 1653.
17. Reprinted Chichester, 2004.
18. Grose, *ibid.*, p. 134.
19. Fielding, J., 'A Dictionary of Cant Words and Terms', *The Newgate Magazine or Malefactors' Monthly Chronicle*, Vol. II (1766), pp. 834-44.
20. Fielding, H., *An Enquiry into the Causes of the Late Increase of Robbers and Other Writings* (1751), ed. Zirker, M.R. (Oxford, 1988), pp. 143-4.
21. Partridge, E., *A Dictionary of Historical Slang* (1937, abridged edn, 1972), pp. 76-7.
22. Partridge, E., *Dictionary of the Underworld* (1968), pp. 76-7.
23. Grosley, P.J., *A Tour to England* (1765), quoted in Sambrook, G.A. (ed.), *English Life in the Eighteenth Century* (1960), pp. 59-63. Grosley's work also provides negative evidence that Black people were not, as Wadström said, 'friendless and despised, on account of their complexion', because he records no account of Black people being so treated.
24. *Harris's Lists* contains details of names, addresses, appearance, special talents and other miscellaneous information about prostitutes mainly, though not exclusively, in Covent Garden. They were published from the 1740s by John Harris and continued to be produced under the same title after his death in 1765, until at least 1793. It is fair to add, however, that the *Lists* were aimed at gentlemen: the cheapest prostitute in them charged a crown (5s) so they were obviously not in the same class as poor streetwalkers.
25. Gage, J., 'The Rise and Fall of the St Giles Rookery', *Camden History Review* 12 (1984), pp. 17-23.
26. Beames, T., *The Rookeries of London, Past, Present and Perspective* (1850), p. 32. The Irish community was long standing and often mentioned by contemporaries.
27. The parish registers of St Giles in this period had many entries of people with French names: there was also a substantial French population in neighbouring St Anne Soho.
28. Walford, E., *London Recollected: Its History, Lore and Legend*, Vol. 3 (1872-78), pp. 206ff.
29. Smollett, T. *Roderick Random* (1749, Everyman edn 1927), pp. 291 and 276.
30. Smollett, T. *Humphry Clinker* (1771, Penguin Books edn 1967) p. 60.
31. Wardroper, J., *Lovers, Rakes and Rogues: a New Garner of Love-songs and Merry Verses, 1580-1830* (1995), p. 107, originally published c.1810 in a street

ballad collection now in the BL, 1875.d.16. Wardroper noted that this was 'an uncommon theme'.
32. Roger Fiske, editor of Michael Kelly's *Reminiscences* (1826, Oxford edn 1975), p. 75n, mentions two white actors competing for the part.
33. Jackson, J., *History of the Scottish Theatre* (Edinburgh, 1793), quoted in Edwards, P., 'Black Personalities in Georgian Britain', *History Today* 31 (9), September 1981, pp. 39–43. The unnamed Black actress had also, according to Jackson, played Juliet in Shakespeare's *Romeo and Juliet*.
34. Reproduced in Burford, E.J., *Wits, Wenchers and Wantons* (1986), p. 63.
35. *Ibid.*, p. 36. This is presumably Baron Zachariah Conrad von Uffenbach, who wrote *London in 1710*, transl. W. Quarrell & M. Moore (1934), since his work is included in the bibliography. I have not, however, been able to find this quotation there. Von Uffenbach did note Black people, saying that he had never seen 'such a quantity of Moors of both sexes in England . . . Males and females frequently go out begging' (p. 88). This is similar to Burford's reference – possibly he did not check the original or was embroidering on it.
36. Walvin, *Black Presence*, p. 14.
37. Gerzina, *Black England*, p. 24.
38. Writers about Black people in Britain, however, have looked for them in slums. They found them there but it was where most people, of whatever colour, in eighteenth-century London lived. There seem to have been no attempts to find them in prosperous areas but, on the basis of baptisms, the parishes in the City of Westminster, where the rich and noble lived, seem to contain the greatest concentration of Black people.
39. Braidwood, *Black Poor*, p. 58, referencing *The Diary or Woodfall's Register*, 29 October 1789. What may be significant here, although Braidwood did not say so, is that the article did not explicitly say that these associates were Black.
40. The only other churches dedicated to St Giles near London are in Ickenham and in South Mimms, both in north Middlesex. They were, and still are, villages. There are no baptisms or burials of Black people in either.
41. Braidwood, *Black Poor*, pp. 58–9.
42. Settlement examinations and removal orders are a useful source of information about people coming into a parish, but unfortunately those of St Giles for this period have not survived. There is only one Black person from St Giles in the settlement examinations of neighbouring St Martin in the Fields. CWA, 'Rough examination book of St Martin in the Fields', 23 May 1817, p. 111, in CWA, *Sources for Black and Asian History at the City of Westmister Archives Centre* (2005), p. 64.
43. *Proceedings* 1773–4, II, no. 146.
44. *Proceedings* 1780–1, II, no. 230 and III, no. 321. The case of Elizabeth Gammer and Mary Rhodes, indicted for assaulting Thomas Edwards, the Black servant of Reginald Bray, Esq. in a drinking house in Drury Lane (part of which is

in St Giles), may be another, but Edwards' place of residence is not given. *Proceedings* 1731-2, I, no. 38.

45. Another problem is that street names are not often given and, if this is a common name, like Church Street, it is impossible to specify where exactly was meant. Some addresses also seem to have been either given or transcribed erroneously. James Fitzgerald, who was Black, was indicted for theft in Parker Street. There seems to have been no Parker Street in London but there was a Parker Lane off Drury Lane in Covent Garden and the owner of the house mentions visiting Lichfield Street, which is close to St Giles. *Proceedings* 1771-2, VII, no. 641.

46. The Lennox sisters, daughters of the 2nd Duke of Richmond, read French as easily as English and the letters between them are full of French phrases. Tillyard, S., *Aristocrats: Caroline, Emily, Louisa and Sarah Lennox 1740-1832* (1994). The upper-middle-class Wynne sisters, daughters of an Admiral, and their husbands also used phrases from this language. Freemantle, A. (ed.), *The Wynne Diaries 1789-1820* (Oxford, 1952). Even prosperous artisans had their daughters taught French. *Proceedings* 1766-7, II, no. 28.

47. Littré, E., *Dictionnaire de la Langue Francaise* (Paris, 1957); Herail, R.J. & Lovatt, E.A., *Dictionary of Modern Colloquial French* (1984). I also spoke to someone who had, after taking a degree in French in 1996, worked in Paris for a couple of years but had not heard the expression.

48. Beames, *Rookeries of London*, p. 38.

49. Stephen Braidwood carried out research that found 3 per cent of baptisms in selected parish registers in the East End of London between 1783 and 1787 were of Black people. One hundred and sixty-eight were mentioned in the registers of nine London parishes. Six in the East End, 'one of the poorest sections of the city accounted for 144 of the Blacks with 71 in one parish St George in the East'. Braidwood, S.J., 'Initiatives and Organisation of the Black Poor 1786-1787', *Slavery & Abolition* 3 (1989), p. 211-27.

50. Braidwood, *Black Poor*, pp. 26-7.

51. *The Orthodox Churchman's Magazine*, 11 January 1802, p. 30.

52. Braidwood seems not to have cross-referenced the day books: these sometimes give more information than appears in the register entries, although in the case of this particular parish the two are very similar. Notes in the burial register show that it was compiled from the day book, so the same was probably true of the baptismal register. This practice seems to have been common in other parishes.

53. LMA, Registers of St George in the East: James-Lock Blackman, bur. 24 November 1738 from Cab[le] Street; Blackmoor-How Wardal, bur. 11 March 1739 from R[atcliff] H[igh] W[ay]. His occupation is given as 'distiller'. There was a family surnamed Blackmore in the parish and his first name suggests he may have been related to them.

54. LMA, Registers of St George Wapping.

55. CWA, F5074, p. 65. This examination also sheds light on how Black people seem to have had a considerable sense of autonomy. Ann Closson's actions show a degree of freedom that suggests neither she nor her employers regarded her as enslaved.
56. *The Orthodox Churchman's Magazine*,11 January 1802, p. 30.
57. LMA, Registers of St George Wapping, 18 July 1788.
58. Braidwood, *Black Poor*, pp. 69 and 26–7.
59. Morris, D., 'Stepney and Trinity House', *East London Record* 13 (1990), pp. 33–8.
60. Braidwood, *Black Poor*, p. 212.
61. Morris, D., *Mile End Old Town 1740–1780: a Social History of an Early Modern London Suburb* (2002), p. 20. His research used a wide range of documents and has also been published on CD-ROM in the form of a database detailing every inhabitant appearing in records relating to land tax, property leases and deeds.
62. LMA, Registers of St Dunstan Stepney, 16 May 1760.
63. Morris, *Mile End Old Town 1740–1780*, p. 20.
64. Benton, T., *Irregular Marriage in London before 1754* (1993) contains more information about individual parishes.
65. HS 15, *The Register of Baptisms and Marriages at St George's Chapel, Mayfair 1735 to 1754*.
66. As a memorandum in the registers notes before entries for January 1722, between 1714 and 1722 the baptisms, marriages and burials were entered by mistake in the registers of St Mary le Strand. First register of the Savoy Chapel, in the care of the incumbent.
67. CWA, Registers of St James Piccadilly, 14 April 1730; *Proceedings* 1735–6, III, no. 22.
68. Registers of the Savoy Chapel in the care of the incumbent, '(a Black) 27 years of Age B[achelo]r & Ann Menpauss 25 D[itt]o Sp[inste]r', 14 October 1755.
69. Registers of the Savoy Chapel in the care of the incumbent: John Turner 'a Black, & Mary Roberts [by Banns]', 8 April 1755; William Timewell '(a Black) & Martha Craken [by Banns]', 9 September 1755.
70. Registers of the Savoy Chapel in the care of the incumbent. The groom's name was John Blackamoor but this might be a white person: Blackmore, and its variants, is a British surname.
71. CWA, Registers of St Margaret Westminster, unknown man, bur. 18 February 1799.
72. *Proceedings*, 1766–7, II, no. 128.
73. *Proceedings*, 1744–5, IV, no. 189 and *Proceedings* 1782–3, V, 1 June 1783 (case no. not given).
74. CWA, Register of St George Hanover Square, 6 April 1781.
75. The rebuilt Cathedral of St Paul's covered the area occupied by the parish church of St Faith, which still retained some kind of parochial jurisdiction because it continued to keep separate registers.

76. The parishes were: St Andrew Holborn; St Bartholomew the Great; St Bartholomew the Less; St Bride; Bridewell Precinct; St Botolph Aldersgate; St Botolph Aldgate; St Botolph Bishopsgate; St Dunstan in the West; St Giles Cripplegate; St Sepulchre and Holy Trinity Minories. In addition, events in the Pesthouse were recorded, although no records seem to have survived.
77. In the eighteenth century it contained the parishes of St George Southwark; St Olave Southwark; St Saviour Southwark and St Thomas Southwark.
78. The outparishes of Middlesex and Surrey also comprised St Giles in the Fields, Clerkenwell, Lambeth, Shoreditch, Bermondsey, Newington, Islington, Whitechapel, Rotherhithe and Stepney.
79. *Registers of St Olave Hart Street* (HS 46), 25 May 1697; GL, Ms 4783, Registers of St Clement Eastcheap, 12 May 1728; GL, Ms 5716, Registers of St Benet Paul's Wharf, 21 September 1729; GL, Ms 9225/3, Registers of St Botolph Aldersgate, 17 September 1730 and 25 July 1734; LMA, Registers of Stratford Bow, 25 February 1739/40 and 13 October 1740; Tower Hamlets Local Studies Library, Land Tax Records for Stratford Bow 1743.
80. St Giles Cripplegate was exceptional in giving relationships, including servants. GL, Ms 6418/6-18.
81. GL, Ms 5746/2, Registers of St Alphage London Wall, 30 May 1704; GL, Ms 4348, Registers of St Margaret Lothbury, 30 June 1787.
82. The parish of St Giles Cripplegate, for example, distinguished between those who lived inside the walls (marked F for Freedom) and those outside (marked L for Lordship) and also included occupations in baptism and burial entries. GL, Ms 6418/6-18. The few Black people baptised and buried here had no occupation recorded, nor did French Protestants, of whom there were a number.
83. Earle, P., *A City Full of People: Men and Women of London 1650-1750* (1994).

Part II
Black people and the law

Chapter 3

Free or enslaved?

Discussion of the subject of Black people and the law in England during the long eighteenth century has been given considerable attention and has focused largely on their status as slave or free, concentrating on the handful of cases in which the question of the legality of slavery in England and Wales was brought to court. From 1542, Wales came under the same laws and legal system as England. It is not technically a separate country, but a principality,[1] so subsequent references to England also apply to Wales. Because slavery has been the subject of so much analysis I do not propose to examine the theoretical discussions in detail: there is little I can add. The main objective of this book is to examine the experiences of the average Black person in England and Wales during the period of the slave trade, and the question of slavery apparently impinged very little on the lives of the overwhelming majority. By examining so obsessively only the few legal cases and the handful of references in other documents related to slavery, historians have perhaps produced a distorted picture of its importance in England. The following is therefore intended to raise alternative considerations that may not have been written about in the same depth that has been given to the issue of slavery.

It is common to look at slavery in the past using present-day definitions and making assumptions based on how it is currently defined and regarded, but this is not how it would have been perceived in the long eighteenth century. During this period slavery existed legally in most of the world and was not generally regarded as morally unacceptable. The present-day Anti-Slavery International is the world's oldest international human rights organisation. It had its origins in a meeting in London on 22 May 1787 'for the purpose of taking the slave trade into consideration', becoming the Committee for Effecting the Abolition of the Slave Trade. Before 1787 there were individuals who saw slavery as wrong and the British Quakers had set up an informal committee to consider the question in 1783, but this was the first concerted attempt to abolish the British slave trade. Anti-Slavery International's first four factors defining a slave would have been recognised in the past.[2] A slave is:

1. forced to work through mental or physical threat;
2. owned or controlled by an 'employer', usually through mental or physical abuse or threatened abuse;
3. dehumanised, treated as a commodity or bought and sold as 'property';
4. physically constrained or has restrictions placed on his/her freedom of movement.

Although 'slave' is a useful shorthand term, today's popular association of the word with a very narrow section of the historically enslaved, those taken from West Africa to the Americas, is misleading. A form of slavery had, in fact, been introduced in England by an Act of Parliament in 1547, aimed at forcing vagabonds into work. It was not successful and was repealed.[3] In the eighteenth century the idea was revived by three celebrated Enlightenment figures.[4] There was no suggestion that the forms of slavery they advocated would be confined to people of a particular colour or race: it was poverty that would be the defining factor. Nor did the proposals include the treatment of these indigent people as chattels to be sold or separated from their families, or that their children would inherit their status, like slaves in the colonies or in Scotland, where a poor law passed in 1597 did allow vagrants and their children to be enslaved.[5] These proposals, however, also came to nothing.

In the colonies to which condemned criminals were sentenced for periods of transportation, their situation was often compared to that of the Black slaves there. White transportees were sold at public auctions, where they were physically examined to determine their fitness for labour, and at least some of them were ill clothed and ill fed, subject to whippings and, if they attempted to run away, fitted with heavy iron collars to prevent further escapes. They differed from Black slaves only in that their status was not inherited by any offspring they might have. However, the limited period of their enslavement made them less valuable and so they were, they considered, less well treated. As Elizabeth Spriggs wrote from Maryland in 1756:

> What we unfortunate English people suffer here is beyond the probability of you in England to conceive. Let it suffice that I, one of the unhappy number, am toiling almost day and night, and very often in the horses' drudgery with only this comfort that: 'You bitch, you do not half enough:' and then tied up and whipped to that degree that you'd not serve an animal;

scarce anything but Indian corn and salt to eat, and that even begrudged. Nay, many negroes are better used . . .[6]

Over the period of the main British slave trade, the popular concept of a slave changed. Between the late seventeenth century and the middle of the eighteenth century, as Linda Colley has pointed out, most people in Britain would think of a European in the Ottoman Empire.[7] Europeans were not the only people engaged in a slave trade: the Arab slave trade was much longer established and many Europeans, including British people, were enslaved as well as Africans. Most were seafarers in and around the Mediterranean, but in the late seventeenth century there were raids on isolated coastal villages in England, Wales and Ireland. Because Arabs did not keep records in the same way that Europeans did, it is more difficult to estimate the numbers of white slaves involved but they may be as high as one million (and many millions more Black slaves).[8] There were regular appeals for money to ransom them, collected through parishes (Illustration 5), and the records also note payments made to men travelling home after being ransomed.[9] Some Europeans published accounts of their experiences, so in the seventeenth century and into the eighteenth English people would have associated slavery with people like themselves, largely in the Muslim world, although there are accounts of Englishmen enslaved elsewhere.[10] Until the second part of the eighteenth century the majority of the British population would probably never have seen a Black person and the comparatively few who did would not equate the occasional gorgeously attired and apparently pampered servant of the aristocracy, or even an itinerant entertainer or beggar, with slavery. It was not until a series of treaties with the Ottoman Empire in 1757 that the trade in white slaves largely ceased, but even in the latter part of the eighteenth century there were occasional reports of enslaved English people in and around the Mediterranean countries.[11]

After the treaties with the Ottoman Empire, the focus of public consciousness switched to the abolition of Black slavery in the Americas, although Granville Sharp had begun his personal campaign to define the legal status of Black people in England through the courts in 1765. Adam Hochschild dates the beginning of a formal, concerted campaign to 1785, when Thomas Clarkson published his prize-winning essay on slavery.[12] He was joined by other like-minded men, but before this time the average British person would have been largely unaware of conditions for slaves in the colonies. These were not seen in Britain, which had a big enough agricultural workforce to make plantation slavery unnecessary. In the Americas, slavery became synonymous with blackness, but in England the definitions remained less

5. Record in the vestry minutes of the parish of West Ham of 20*l* 1d collected for the redemption of white slaves in Algeria (1670/1)

The Minister and Churchwardens did present unto the vestry an Accompt [= account] of the Monies they had from house to house Collected upon the Briefe for ye Redemption of the poore Christians now in Turkish Slavery, And the names of the severall persons Contributing was read & a Duplicate thereof signed to bee Returned to the Bishop according to the Direction of the Briefe together with the money, w[hi]ch did amount unto the summe of Twenty Pounds and one penny And it appearing by the said Accompt, that the above named Mr. Edward Bisse had not given anything towards the s[ai]d Briefe, & that hee refuseth to [give – deleted] Contribute to any Occasion whatsoever, but only to what by law hee may be forced unto It was ordered that the 5*l* 19d should not be advanced to him as above said.

[Edward Bisse had claimed the amount of 5*l* 19d for expenses in connection with work he had carried out for the parish authorities]

clear cut. There were many popular songs, most obviously 'Rule, Britannia' (1740) by James Thomson, which contrasted British freedom with slavery elsewhere, as in the line 'Britons never will be slaves'. Another, 'Hearts of Oak' (1759) also had a naval theme, encapsulated in the first verse:

So cheer up my lads, 'tis to glory we steer,
To add something more to this wonderful year.
To honour we call you, as free men not slaves,
For who are so free as the sons of the waves?[13]

Despite this pride in British freedom, the word 'slave' was not confined to Black people and was occasionally used to refer to white members of the indigenous population. In a trial at the Old Bailey in 1742, for example, one of the witnesses was a boy who, another witness remarked, 'goes of Errands: he is, what some call, a Slave' but gave no further explanation, and none was requested.[14] Women also equated their position in society with slavery, especially after the campaign to abolish slavery gained momentum and they began to draw parallels with their own experiences and lack of power. But long before that, in 1682, Aphra Behn, the author of *Oroonoko or the Royal Slave*, had written of women's relationships to men as 'The slave, the hackney of his lawless lust!'[15] In 1703 Lady Mary Chudleigh had written bitterly,

Wife and servant are the same
But only differ in the name.
...
Fierce as an Eastern Prince he grows
And all his innate rigour shows.[16]

The French Revolution (1789) also led women to question their position, which had effects in Britain. In 1793 Madame Blandin-Desmoulins of Dijon asked for despotism against women to be renounced because 'no virtue could be expected of slaves'.[17]

Undoubtedly Black people in Britain were coerced into working and were physically abused, but so were their white counterparts. Physical punishment of family members and servants by the male head of the house was accepted as normal. The only Black person known to have died at the hands of a master or mistress during the period covered by the British slave trade was an unnamed boy, beaten to death by a sea captain in December 1772.[18] This abuse, however, was not because of his colour or race: white apprentices, servants and sailors died from similar treatment. The best-known cases are those of the white parish apprentices killed by Sarah Metyard and her daughter in 1762 and by Elizabeth Brownrigg in 1767. The Metyards and Brownrigg, whose family had cruelly abused at least two other girls, were hanged, as was Captain John Sutherland, who murdered a white cabin boy on his ship in 1809 (Illustration 6).[19]

6. The murder by John Sutherland of his cabin boy, nineteenth-century artist's impression produced by the Navarre Society. Captain Sutherland was executed for his crime in 1809.

Fryer and Dabydeen both noted advertisements for runaways which describe them as having scars, which they assumed were the result of physical punishments.[20] This leaves out other possible causes. Dabydeen quoted two advertisements which mentioned scars on the neck. These, however, are unlikely to have been caused by the usual methods of chastisement, a stick or a whip, which are used on the head or body, but most likely resulted from the wooden or metal halter used to shackle African slaves being taken to the coast in a train of slaves fastened together to be sold. Those captured in raids or battles in Africa, for example, may well have acquired wounds there or, less dramatically, may simply have had accidents. Without further evidence, it is impossible to know exactly how such scars were acquired, but other possibilities than ill treatment by masters must be considered. Scars were a useful way of identifying both white and Black people before the advent of photography and often appear in descriptions of criminals or runaways of any colour. In 1779, for example, a newspaper carried a report of an attack at Newnham in Herefordshire by footpads, one of whom was described as 'much pitted with the smallpox and has a scar under one of his jaws.'[21]

Manumissions

All slave-owning societies seem to have provision for manumission, so such a procedure is one piece of evidence for the legal existence of slaves. Seymour Drescher has explored how Black people became free in England and says there were essentially four methods: indentures as a servant; a letter of reference from an employer; assumed prior manumission by self-assertion; and sacral manumission.[22] The first two, which also applied to white people, seem to be stretching the definition of slavery beyond the point at which it has any meaning. Drescher's assertion that Black slaves were brought into North-West Europe, where property laws over people did not exist,[23] ignores the fact that men did have property rights over their wives and their wives' property and possessions until the latter part of the nineteenth century, and also over their children. These, however, were not absolute and had limits. This misapprehension means he that misses an important point. Slaves brought to England could have been kept in permanent subjugation by classifying them, whether or not they were adult, as children or legal minors, but there was never an attempt to introduce such legislation. Nor were the owners/masters of Black people singled out for taxation purposes. There were taxes on a range of goods, targeted at the wealthy and fashionable, like land, windows, hair powder, silver plate, carriages, dogs, etc. A tax on male servants was levied between 1777 and 1830 and on female servants between 1785 and 1792. These taxes, however, applied to all servants, although to place a very high tax on Black ones would have made them even more symbolic of conspicuous wealth. That there were never separate regulations covering Black servants indicates that they were in the same legal position as their white counterparts. Drescher also says that Black people were absent from wills and estate inventories. However, in his will, proved on 4 November 1680 in the Prerogative Court of Canterbury, John Gregory of East Ham, Essex bequeathed his wife Dorothy 'all my Plate, the Coach and horses, all the hay and Corn and the Black ...'.[24] William Snelgrave, the slave trader, who was resident in England, granted Scipio 'a Black man whom I bought at Jacquin on the coast of Guinea' his freedom in his will.[25] These cases are not the only ones of their kind. The conclusion must be that not enough wills have been examined.

There was no official ceremony or procedure to mark manumission for Black servants/slaves in England and Wales. But there do seem to have been formal manumissions. Welch describes a number of manumissions of slaves in the records of the Lord Mayor of London in the early nineteenth century, relating to women from Barbados. Welch writes that 'freedmen and women were forced to turn to the Lord Mayors' Offices in the various cities of Britain'.[26] There is no suggestion that these slaves came to England; rather, it seems that they remained in Barbados to enjoy their freedom. It is possible that there are other manumissions in the records of English law courts which have not yet been found. Drescher also accepted as fact that manumission was 'an interaction between the courts on the one hand and the massive flights of the servants on the other: The Black servants ultimately voted with their feet, "withering away" the institution in a self-emancipation of flight'.[27] As will be argued, the numbers of runaway Black servants were not 'massive' and in percentage terms were probably comparable to the numbers of runaway white servants and apprentices, of whom there were more white than Black. Later in his article, however, Drescher noted 'dozens' of Black servants putting 'places wanted' advertisements in the newspapers during the eighteenth century. If the institution had withered away, why were so many servants actively looking for new positions as domestics? Drescher concluded, but struggled to prove, that manumission in eighteenth-century England was 'sacral', that is achieved by sale to a deity, i.e. baptism. It was certainly believed by some Black people themselves but many judges, not least Lord Mansfield, denied this. Nor has any direct evidence been found that masters believed it, although there are a number of examples of them not disputing a Black servant's decision to leave service after being baptised, like Ann Closson, previously mentioned. Drescher's argument was based on negative evidence: if slaves were not freed by a social or legal ceremony then this must have been done by religious means, i.e. baptism. This conclusion results from a false premise: that there must have been slaves in England because Black people were there. Drescher came close to arguing that slavery did not exist in England but never actually said this explicitly, although he did quote in a footnote Orlando Patterson's observation that there was no known slave-holding society where the whip was not considered as an indispensable instrument. Drescher saw it as significant that the whip was not the punishment of choice in England.[28] This, with all the other sources he cited, surely means that he should have concluded England was not a slave-holding society and so the concept of manumission would have been absent. Because he believed that Black people were absent from wills and inventories, he missed references to the freeing of Black servants in probate documents which showed that their masters thought they could be manumitted.

Like other historians, Drescher admitted that 'we lack some of the most significant tools for the analysis of American slavery'. I think there is a misprint here. From the context, he meant either English slavery or that it is impossible to compare English and American slavery. This error is perhaps indicative that he was exploring slavery in England using an American context. He called slavery in England a 'latent social problem'. For this definition he assumed that American practice was a norm, and so where other nations' practices differed, these were regarded as problematic. It is, however, especially important in this area to look at the British background, particularly as America was a colony during the largest part of the British slave trade. British practice should perhaps be regarded as the norm and what happened in the colonies as an aberration.

Wages

There were no regulations relating to domestic servants. Under the Statute of Artificers (1563) wages for thirty occupations were strictly regulated; the last remnants of the Act were not finally repealed until 1824, by which time the law was mainly a dead letter. 'Servants' were included in this Act, but this word referred to agricultural labourers, not domestic servants. Apprentices were not paid during the period of their apprenticeship – typically seven years – but their indentures constituted a contract of employment, so their lack of wages might be considered to be outside this argument. One of the indicators of a slave is non-payment for work but, crucially, it is performed under threat of retribution because the master has complete control of the slave. Though Shyllon said 'Black slaves in Britain, as chattels anywhere, were not entitled to and did not receive wages', research shows the position to have been much less clear cut. He gives no evidence for his assertion and adds that Isaac Jackman was 'merely exercising a dramatist's free hand' when, in *The Divorce* (1780), the playwright has one of his characters, a Black servant, claiming to receive a wage of 10 guineas a year.[29] No contemporary, however, seems to have found this unlikely. Wills made by Black servants, like John Scipio[30] and Ruth Thomas,[31] show that they had money and possessions to bequeath, and some of this must have come through payment from their employers. By the time of his death in January 1771 Jack Beef, the Black servant of John Baker, a magistrate in St Kitts who had brought him to England, had accumulated enough savings to be able to plan his return to St Kitts.[32] Wills made by sailors show that they received wages and prize money. Sometimes this was a substantial amount. In 1764 George Harford, a Black sailor on the *Stag* man-of-war, received some £40.[33]

The question of when Black servants in Britain began to be paid wages as a matter of routine is not yet settled. Some historians think there was a transitional period during the eighteenth century when some were paid and some were not.[34] However, as late as 1815, Louis Simond observed that white servants in inns did not receive wages.[35] There were other white servants, especially children, like page boys, who were not paid and who received only their board, lodging and clothing. In 1818 the *Huntingdon, Bedford, Cambridge and Peterborough Gazette* reported a dispute between two parishes about the settlement status of a man named White who had initially been employed for victuals, being paid wages only after he reached the age of 20.[36] This shows that such issues were not confined to Black people: white people also worked for no pay. It is impossible to calculate the ratio of paid to unpaid Black servants because there is little information in official documents. The only source where such details were regularly given is in settlement examinations, because whether a servant was paid or not and how long he/she had worked for an employer were crucial facts the authorities needed to discover. Comparatively few of these documents have survived and very few Black people appear in them. To a lesser extent bastardy examinations also give some insight into life histories, though not often the paid/unpaid distinction. There are other, indirect ways of deducing status. Most of the Black people admitted to parish workhouses would have been accepted as having a claim on the parish (and therefore have been in paid employment for more than the statutory year). I would also suggest that the way baptism and burial entries in parish registers are worded might also give some indication of paid/unpaid status (see Chapter 5).

Perhaps the most convincing argument that some people regarded Blacks as chattels comes from 'For Sale' advertisements in newspapers. Myers found twenty-four advertisements for sales (not auctions) between 1709 and 1792.[37] This gives an average of approximately one every three years. A total of twenty-eight advertisements and newspaper reports of sales was quoted by Fryer, Scobie, Walvin, Gerzina and Shyllon combined.[38] I have found another in a regional newspaper.[39] It is likely that others took place privately. Some sales were prompted by death or bankruptcy. There were, however, no regular public auctions. Most were individual sales and the largest number of people sold at the same time that has so far been found was eleven in Liverpool in 1766.[40] In addition, the registers of Thorley in Hertfordshire contain a reference to the baptism in 1773 of 'A Black aged about 19 or 20 belonging to Mr George Horsley and was named at Auction – Thomas'. Where this auction took place is not stated.[41] The register of Poole, Dorset, records the baptism in 1755 of an unnamed 'Negro woman. Purchased by Mr Thomas Olive', but neither is there any indication of where this sale happened.[42]

Neither the advertisements nor the wills previously mentioned use the word 'slave'. Nor did visitors seem to regard the Black people they encountered as slaves. Carl Moritz, for example, came to England from Germany in 1782. He observed the presence of several but regarded them simply as interesting members of society.[43] Another visitor, an American, Benjamin Silliman, was outraged at seeing a well-dressed Black man in the company of a white woman in London's Oxford Street. He complained that British people had not yet 'learned' that Black people were inferior, but did not describe the man as a slave.[44] It is rare to find a Black person living in England described as a slave in any English records. On the database there are only thirteen references using the term.[45] The word almost invariably used, where there is any description, is 'servant'. This is, I would argue, partly to do with status under the poor laws, as there were special circumstances applicable to servants, discussed in Chapter 5.

Beyond the catch-all word 'servant' there are other ambiguities in how Black people are described, especially in parish registers. Some are unequivocally described as 'belonging to' someone. Others are described as the servant of a named person but others are recorded as 'at Mr X's', or 'living with . . .', like an unnamed Black child 'from Mr Riches' buried in the City of London in 1686/7.[46] It would be easy to assume that this kind of phrase meant the person concerned was a slave/servant, but this would not always have been the case. In 1665, an unnamed 'Blackman from Bedwells house' who had died of the plague was buried in the parish of West Ham, then in Essex. From other records, it appears that the Bedwells had a house with only two hearths in the settlement of Stratford and Mrs Bedwell was paid by the parish to nurse sick people.[47] At this period, this couple were unlikely to have a Black servant, let alone a slave. Given that the deceased died of the plague, the most likely explanation is that he was the servant of a family fleeing from London who fell ill on the journey and was left with an experienced nurse in Stratford, then a coaching stop on the road to Colchester. Similar phrasing is used in the will of Sir William Batten, who died in 1667. He left a legacy to 'my servant' Mingo, 'a negro but now dwelleth with me'.[48] Some Black people themselves said they were 'living at Mr X's' or 'living with' someone, which suggests they did not see themselves as permanently tied to a master. At the Old Bailey in 1774 a Black man, John Vernon, said he 'lived in the service of Sir Robert [blank] but I was out of place at the time the fact happened.'[49] At a trial in 1783, William Henry, also Black, said, 'I lodge at Pelham-street, Brick-lane. I am a servant out of place. I lived last with one Mr Meadows.'[50] It is possible therefore that some of those in parish registers for whom an address, but no relationship, is given were lodgers; perhaps conducting business for their masters; being loaned to a member of the family or friend of their master's; between hirings; or there for some other reason, like an unnamed 'negro manservant of Mr John Newtons from Mr Raworthe' buried in 1665 in the City of London.[51]

The legality of slavery

Slave owners who brought their slaves from overseas colonies to England either assumed that they were also enslaved here or did not inform their slaves otherwise, who were in no position to question this. Some people in the colonies, long before the Mansfield Judgment, did recognise that there was no slavery in England. In 1730 in Bermuda an Act was passed in which it was stated 'the Priviledges of England are So universally Extensive as not to admit of the Least thing called Slavery'.[52] Slavery was an established institution in Africa, so the slaves themselves might also assume that it was universal, because they had no experience of living anywhere that it was not the norm, especially in the period preceding the abolition movement. Later, however, the masters of some Black servants seem to have become aware that their position in England was different. Charles Comba is recorded as a 'covenanted servant' at his baptism in 1761 in Harmondsworth, Middlesex.[53] In the early days of the Caribbean colonies white people became covenanted servants, pledging themselves to serve a given number of years. They were later replaced by slaves but the practice continued in the American colonies until much later.[54] Comba's master, Thomas Bullock, may have come from the West Indies or North America and thought the same system applied in England. Alternatively, he may have been aware that the situation was different and aimed to prevent his Black servant from leaving his service while in England. The Reverend Mr John Pilgrim had two Black servants, Henry and Sarah Windsor, who were baptised in the parish of Old Windsor, Berkshire, in 1761. Pilgrim's will, proved on 24 April 1778, did not include Henry in the list of property and chattels he bequeathed to his wife. Instead, he left Henry an annuity on condition that he remained in his wife's service until her death. Neither Henry's colour nor his ethnic origin is mentioned in the will.[55] Pilgrim seems to have accepted that Henry had a choice about where he worked. In 1771 Joseph Thomas Newman was baptised 'after an Affadavit being made previously before Justice Girdler that he was no Persons Property but to all Intents and Purposes sine juris'.[56] Such an affidavit is so far unique. It is unlikely to have been obtained at the insistence of the parish: this was in the City of London, where numerous Black people were baptised without any reference to their status or masters. Presumably Newman wanted this entered in an official record for reasons of his own: he was perhaps recently arrived from a colony where slavery existed and it was routine practice to carry proof of free status.

A few people called 'slaves' in documents are women, like the unnamed 'mulatto slave', the mother of Ann Thomas, baptised in Teddington, Middlesex, in 1752.[57] In these cases, their masters were perhaps the child's father but unwilling to admit this. The parish authorities were supposed to discover the fathers of illegitimate children in order to enforce payment for the child's upkeep and prevent this falling on the ratepayers, but few would have been prepared to carry out the potentially humiliating legal procedure on someone of high social standing in their community. The clerks may have written 'slave' in order to fix the responsibility for the child's upkeep on the woman's master. When the putative father of an illegitimate child is a Black man, he seems never to have been described as a slave, although his master's or mistress's name is usually given, as in the case of Thomas Caesar, 'son of Mary Crocker a base child by Mrs Elizabeth Footes Black call'd Caesar', who was baptised in Calstock, Cornwall in 1748.[58] The distinction between unpaid Black people in England and Wales and the indigenous white population was therefore not clear cut. Some of both sections of the population worked for no wages. Some were ill treated. Neither inherited slave status. One case, however, was to prove definitive in determining the conditions of service of Black people.

The Somerset case

Slave owners from overseas colonies frequently brought slaves to Britain and a handful of cases involving such people came before the courts, including Dinah Black (1687), Katherine Auker (1690), an unnamed man who died during the course of the hearing (1757), Jonathan Strong (1767), John and Mary Hylas (1768) and Thomas Lewis (1771). Abolitionists hoped to gain a definitive ruling against slavery but these cases were resolved by reference to individual circumstances, or, in the case of the unnamed man, by his death and therefore had no wider implications. It was the case of James Somerset, or Sommersett, in 1772 which resulted in the momentous ruling known as the Mansfield Judgment. Somerset was purchased in Virginia by Charles Steuart, or Stewart, a customs officer, who brought him from Boston, Massachusetts to England in November 1769. Somerset left him, and was probably christened on 12 February

1771 in St Andrew Holborn, London, perhaps in the hope that this would liberate him.[59] Later that year, on 26 November, Stewart had Somerset captured and put on board the *Ann and Mary*, a ship bound for Jamaica. Three sympathetic witnesses, Thomas Walklin, Elizabeth Cade and John Marlow, obtained from Lord Mansfield, the Lord Chief Justice, a writ of *habeas corpus*, a legal test of the right to imprison someone.[60] This required the ship's captain, John Knowles, to produce Somerset in court and on 7 February 1772 the case came before the Court of King's Bench, the highest court of common law in England and Wales.[61]

Granville Sharp, the abolitionist, became involved in the case. There were five counsel on Somerset's side. William Davy and John Glynn argued that slavery was a product of local laws and did not exist in England and Wales. James Mansfield (not related to the judge) and Francis Hargreave argued that the law only permitted a man to contract to serve a master for life, not to enslave himself, and even that might be unenforceable. Alleyne argued that the cruelties suffered by slaves in America could be introduced here if slavery were found lawful. On Stewart's side, his two counsel, William Wallace and John Dunning, relied on the legality of slavery and the slave trade in Africa, Virginia and Jamaica as well as the inconvenience to slave owners and the wider financial implications of releasing a slave from his owner's service.

Aware of the economic and social implications of any judgment he made, Mansfield ordered several recesses, in which he unsuccessfully attempted to persuade Stewart to release Somerset, or one of Somerset's supporters to purchase him. Historians have seen these delays as an attempt by Mansfield to avoid making a decision. Though this must have been a factor, Mansfield also needed to research what English law had to say on the subject of slavery. There was at the time no handy guide to laws as was later produced by, for example, *Halsbury's Laws of England*.[62] What Mansfield presumably used was Danby Pickering's *The Statutes at Large*, a collection of the full text of every Act of Parliament passed since Magna Charta (the spelling Pickering used) in 1215, which began publication in 1761. By 1771, it had reached twenty-nine substantial volumes. Mansfield must have needed much of the time occupied by recesses to work his way through them, to cross-refer the Acts, to consider their implications and to research any precedents established in hearings. Finally, on 22 June 1772, Lord Mansfield delivered his judgment: Somerset could not be sent overseas without his consent: 'Whatever inconveniences, therefore, may follow from the decision, I cannot say this case is allowed or approved by the law of England; and therefore the Black must be discharged.'[63]

The primary reason Mansfield gave for his decision was the impossibility of making a ruling in one country based on another's laws, even if that country were a colony of Britain and therefore technically subordinate. Mansfield was particularly aware of the limitations of English law in the colonies. In 1764 he had written to George Greville, then Chancellor of the Exchequer, about a Royal Proclamation imposing British law on newly acquired territory in Canada:

> Is it possible that we have abolished their laws, and customs, and forms of judicature all at once? – a thing never to be attempted or wished. The history of the world don't furnish an instance of so rash and unjust an act by any conqueror whatsoever: much less by the Crown of England, which has always left to the conquered their own laws and usages, with a change only so far as the sovereignty was concerned . . . The fundamental maxims are, that a country conquered keeps her own laws 'till the conqueror expressly gives new. A colony which goes from hence to settle in a waste country . . . carries with them such part of the laws of England as is adapted to, and proper for their situation.[64]

Following the settlement of the 'waste country' of North America and the Caribbean islands, colonists from Britain had passed their own laws, including Acts defining slavery and how it was to be managed. Although the institution of slavery had existed before the Norman Conquest in England, there was no provision for it in common law, established in the years following the accession of William I,[65] and still the basis of English law. Mansfield referred to other judges' pronouncements on the subject of slaves in Britain. The most important was the opinion given in 1729 by the Attorney General (Sir Philip Yorke) and the Solicitor General (Charles Talbot), who said that slaves coming from the West Indies with or without their masters did not become free, baptism did not confer freedom and their masters could compel them to return to the plantations. In 1749 Philip Yorke, by then the Lord Chancellor, reiterated that baptism did not confer freedom. Mansfield found these were simply legal opinions and had not been delivered in circumstances that gave them the weight of law, but he confirmed that baptism did not emancipate slaves. Mansfield's review of the various laws covering service found nothing about slavery because this was something the mother country had never formulated, although he never explicitly said this. Instead, he stated that only 'positive' law, specific Acts of Parliament defining it, could support it. The logical conclusion must be that, if there were no laws defining slavery, it did not exist. Mansfield said 'it was impossible [Somerset] could be a slave in England'. His careful phrasing 'a slave in England' suggests

Somerset could legally be a slave elsewhere, as was the case.[66] Mansfield concluded that, while in this country, Somerset was free and could not be compelled to go abroad. Although some historians have severely criticised him for such a cautious and limited judgment, it is difficult to see how, as the law then stood, and indeed stands today, he could have come to any other conclusion.[67] The culmination of the case, the release of Somerset, was greeted with joy by Black people and with dismay by slave owners. Both groups believed that it meant the emancipation of slaves in England and Wales, but they were mistaken. There was no need to emancipate them: they were already free in this country, whatever their status in the colonies.

The abolitionists took note of Mansfield's opinion that it was not the place of the courts to decide on such a momentous issue in the absence of any laws defining a slave and under what terms he or she could become or remain enslaved.[68] No more cases were brought to court and eventually the fight was switched to Parliament, although the kidnapping and shipping of Black servants back to the Caribbean colonies continued. It was even possible for a slave ship captain, Thomas Ralph, to advertise for the return of his slave, also called his apprentice, in 1780.[69] A few, however, may have returned voluntarily to the colonies. In 1773 two 'Black girls, slaves, aged 25, servants to Mrs White' sailed with Elizabeth White from Liverpool to Jamaica.[70]

Mansfield's review of English law concluded that slavery had not existed and did not exist in England and Wales. There were slaves and masters from the colonies who did not understand the law and some modern historians fall into the same error. David Dabydeen, for example, says 'Blacks were legally slaves at this time [1728/9], not paid servants'.[71] The absence of wages is not equal to slavery and at this time only agricultural servants, not domestic ones, were covered by legislation. Although this is long before the Mansfield Judgment, the date is irrelevant because, as Mansfield found, there had never been slavery in England since the establishment of common law. What masters and their servants believed affected their behaviour, but not their legal position.

Runaways

Some historians contend that it was the slaves themselves who caused the institution of slavery in England to become a dead letter by running away. As Shyllon wrote in 1974, '*some* of them [Blacks] sought their freedom. The newspapers of the eighteenth century carried *various* advertisements concerning the descriptions of runaway Africans' (my italics). Three years later, this had become 'scores'.[72] Certainly, between the writing of the two books Shyllon had unearthed a few more advertisements, but certainly no more than a single score. By the time Fryer's *Staying Power* was published in 1984 more advertisements had been found. He concluded that 'a great number of Black people resisted servitude in the only way open to them: by running away'. He also claimed advertisements were 'often inserted into Bristol's local newspapers' and said, 'In those last two months of 1761, the pages of the *Public Ledger* fairly bristled with hue-and-cry advertisements'.[73] In fact there were six, one advertising for two absconders. 'Many' of the Asians, too, ran away, yet Fryer found only two advertisements to quote.

Historians generally call them 'Hue and Cry' advertisements, although the newspapers themselves started the notice with 'Run Away'. To call them Hue and Cry advertisements may not be technically correct. A hue and cry was an obligation on every person to pursue a criminal and apparently needed to be approved by a magistrate. Since, at the time the majority of these advertisements were appearing, the legal status of unpaid Black servants/slaves was not fully established, those who ran away were not really breaking the law unless they had signed indentures to serve for a certain number of years. Those who absconded with some of their master's property (and this might include their clothes, which are usually described), were thieves.[74] As long as the theft had been reported to a magistrate, this type of advertisement alone should be referred to as a hue and cry. Calling all advertisements for runaways 'Hue and Cry' suggests a parallel with the situation in the New World, where escaped slaves were tracked with dogs.[75]

No one has attempted to compare the number and nature of these advertisements with those for members of the indigenous population. As even a cursory look through contemporary newspapers shows, the eighteenth-century press was full of notices for runaway servants, apprentices, members of the armed forces, women leaving their husbands and fathers deserting their families, and many advertised rewards for information or the return of the runaway. Fryer noted that advertisements 'rarely speak of runaways over 20'.[76] Although he did not make the observation, the overwhelming majority were male. Norma Myers found thirty-five advertisements for runaways in eleven newspapers during the twenty-five years that she sampled between 1665 and 1795. All in her study were male and she thought this proved a preference for male servants. This is a factor, but the other possibility is that young men were then most likely group to abscond. Myers' research suggested a crude average of 1.4 advertisements for Black runaways per year. Whether this is a high or low figure is impossible to know without a comparative study of the general population and an accurate figure for the Black population. I have discovered an advertisement in a regional newspaper for a Black runaway not found by previous researchers, and there are probably a few others, but this is still not an enormous number.[77] Simon Schama said that in London, 'The pursuit of these runaways was the work of slave catchers who prowled the coffee houses and inns, eager to collect the many rewards posted in London and American newspapers.'[78] Anyone relying on slave catching as a permanent occupation would, on these figures, be in for a very thin time. Not much work has been done on runaways in general but, in his study of crime in Essex, Peter King examined two local newspapers, the *Ipswich Journal* 1760–64 and the *Chelmsford Chronicle* 1765–91. There were very few Black people in this area at the time. His research revealed just over one runaway advertised for per fortnight over thirty years. The majority were aged between 18 and 20, followed by those aged 15–17.[79] Paul Mansfield, a local historian, found that in the period 1773–78 the *Sherborne and Yeovil Mercury* carried an average of two advertisements a week for runaway apprentices.[80]

Although Black servants in the long eighteenth century are often all regarded as 'enslaved', it seems that the attitudes of their masters were different, depending on whether they came from a colony where slavery legally existed or whether they spent their lives, or most of their lives, in England or Wales. Until 1772, those who came from the colonies bringing a domestic slave with them seem to have assumed that they remained slaves in England and Wales: that ownership was as for any other chattel, such as a horse or a piece of jewellery, which they could bring from the colonies to the mother country and still own. The laws regarding such possessions, however, were the same in the mother country: it was only people, as the Mansfield Judgment clarified, who were not covered by laws on ownership in England and Wales. Masters who had not lived in the colonies, or who spent a comparatively brief time there, seem to have regarded their Black servants in the same light as their English or Welsh ones, as John Pilgrim's will, quoted above, suggests. It is more difficult, or even impossible, to determine what the Black servants themselves thought.

To those who had been born in the colonies, where slavery was the norm, or who had been slaves in Africa, the difference in attitude to servants in England and Wales must have come as a surprise. It might be suggested that they remained psychologically enslaved, but the magistrate John Fielding noted that it seemed to have taken Black people relatively little time to adjust to the idea of freedom. '[They] no sooner arrive here than they put themselves on a Footing with other Servants.'[81] It is always easier to get used to a situation in which one has greater autonomy than to adjust to restrictions. Once he had experienced the relative equality of shipboard life, Olaudah Equiano seems to have chafed under the ownership of the various masters who regarded him as a slave, even though he had spent at least some (if not all) of his formative years in America. Other Black biographers also seem to have found it easy to become autonomous: Gronniosaw rejected the bride his friends proposed for him. Converts, like John Jea, might be said to have been born again into the freedom that they believed Christianity gave them. Some, of course, like white servants who remained in service, may have preferred the protection a good master gave and were not desperate for their freedom, which could simply have meant freedom to starve. Their clothing, food and accommodation were provided and many were also given medical care and pensions at the end of their working lives. More has been written about those who were unhappy in service, partly because there is always more evidence about those who want change and partly because of the intellectual fashions of the twentieth and twenty-first centuries, which have concentrated on the struggles of oppressed underclass. Those people, both Black and white, who lived quiet, unremarkable lives have not attracted much interest, even though they were the majority.

There is no suggestion that masters considered that the children of their Black servants/slaves were also enslaved, as they were in the colonies. No such case seems to have come before the courts in England, nor has any been found in any document, though a number of Black men and women are known to have had families here. I would conclude that slavery did not exist as an institution in England and Wales, though there were individuals who were regarded by their masters as slaves. It is a fine, but crucial distinction.

Notes

1. This is why today it has an assembly rather than a parliament, as Scotland does.
2. There are also modern factors, such as bonded labour, forced marriage of women and girls, and forms of child labour that are injurious to their health. Some of these existed in eighteenth-century Britain.

3. Slack, P., *The English Poor Law 1531–1782* (Cambridge, 1990), p. 10.
4. Rozbicki, M.J., 'To Save Them from Themselves: Proposals to Enslave the British Poor, 1698–1755', *Slavery & Abolition* 22 (2001), pp. 29–50.
5. The last remnants of this were not done away with until 1799, although the Court of Session's verdict in the case of *Knight* v. *Wedderburn* in 1778 had concluded that slavery in Scotland was illegal. Knight was Black.
6. TNA, HCA 30/258, quoted in Coldham, P.W. *Emigrants in Chains: a Social History of Forced Emigration to the Americas of Felons, Destitute Children, Political and Religious Nonconformists, Vagabonds, and Other Undesirables 1607–1776* (Baltimore, MD, 1992), p. 131. Other similar experiences are detailed on pp. 115–34.
7. Colley, L., *Captives: Britain, Empire and the World 1660–1850* (2002), pp. 63–4.
8. Davis, R.C., *Christian Slaves, Muslim Master: White Slavery in the Mediterranean, the Barbary Coast and Italy, 1550–1800* (2003), quoted in Milton, G., *White Gold: the Extraordinary Story of Thomas Pellow and North Africa's One Million European Slaves* (2004), p. 304.
9. Barns, S.J., *Walthamstow History and Vestry Minutes* (1925) contains a transcript of a parish account book containing payments in 1724 'to five Naked Turkey Gally Slaves in their way home 2s 6d' and 'to passing of 9 poor Naked Gally Slaves 2s 9d', and in 1734 'to several poor slaves 2s 0d'. These would have been white, not Black, people. Walthamstow was the location of the country home of Sir William Batten, Samuel Pepys' superior in the Navy Office. Batten, who died in 1667, had a Black servant, who was a family favourite, and the local people who remembered him or had heard tales of him would not have seen Mingo in the same light as these Englishmen.
10. Pearson, M.P. & Godden, K., *In Search of the Red Slave* (Stroud, 2002) is based on *Madagascar: or Robert Drury's Journal through Fifteen Years Captivity on that Island* (1729). Colley, *Captives* has sections on Britons held in captivity in North America and India, as well as in the Muslim world.
11. The *Leeds Intelligencer*, 17 January 1786, p. 3, reported that one of a group of English people captured from a Portuguese vessel and taken to Algiers chose to stay there, even though he had been released, in place of his brother, who had been a slave there for ten years. Only in 1816 did this particular part of the Arab slave trade end, with the destruction of Algiers by the British Navy and the freeing of the 1,642 white slaves held there.
12. Hochschild, A., *Bury the Chains* (NY, 2005), p. 89.
13. Lyric by David Garrick, music by William Boyce. 'Hearts of Oak' is the official march of the Royal Navy today.
14. *Proceedings* 1741–2, I, no. 26.
15. *The City Heiress*, quoted in Todd, J. (ed.), *Oroonoko, The Rover and Other Works*, p. 13.

16. 'To the Ladies'. At this time slavery was seen as being located along the Barbary Coast and in the Middle East.
17. Letter in *Révolution de Paris*, January 1793, quoted in Tomalin, C., *The Life and Death of Mary Wollstonecraft* (1974), p. 157.
18. Quoted in Anim-Adoo, J., *The Longest Journey: a History of Black Lewisham* (1995), p. 42. She gives no reference for this newspaper report. The jury at the inquest in 1828 on an Indian named Fanny Fetah brought in a verdict of manslaughter. Evidence was given that the girl had been beaten, but those who heard or witnessed this saw nothing excessive in her treatment: the family cook and another servant said they had 'corrected' Fanny themselves. *The News*, 27 January 1828, p. 30, reproduced in Barber, J., *Celebrating the Black Presence in Westminster 1500–2000: Hidden Lives* (2000).
19. Crook, G.T. (comp.), *The Complete Newgate Calendar* (1926), Vol. IV, pp. 46–7 and 59–60, Vol. V, pp. 42–5. The chief witness against Sutherland was a Black sailor, John Thompson. Unlike the situation in the colonies, Black people could and did testify against white people in the English courts.
20. Fryer, *Staying Power*, p. 23; Dabydeen, D., *Hogarth's Blacks: Images of Blacks in Eighteenth Century English Art* (Kingston-upon-Thames, 1985), p. 36.
21. *Hereford Journal*, 21 January 1779, p. 3.
22. Drescher, S., 'Manumissions in a Society without Slave Law: Eighteenth Century England', *Slavery & Abolition* 10 (1989), pp. 85–101. It is significant that Drescher observed that England lacked any law that dealt specifically with slavery.
23. *Ibid.*, p. 87.
24. TNA, PROB 11/364. Around 1678 John Gregory went to Barbados. However, he may, never have returned to England: the Prerogative Court of Canterbury had jurisdiction over English colonies as well as in England and Wales. Although the will requested burial in neighbouring West Ham there is no record of this in the burial register. Essex RO, D/P 256/1/2, Registers of West Ham. The registers for East Ham for this period are not extant. Gregory appeared at the manorial court of Burnells in 1678 (Stratford Local History Archives). He then appears in a list of landowners in the parish of St Michael in Barbados. Hotten, J.C. (ed.), *Persons of Quality: People Who Went from Great Britain to the American Plantations 1600–1700* (1873), p. 454. There are burials for two Black people in West Ham churchyard some years later: Abraham on 14 July 1717 and Maria on 13 July 1721, but they may not have been John Gregory's servants: a Cecily Gregory 'of Barbadoes' was buried there on 4 February 1696. She is likely to have been a relative of John Gregory and these two people may have been her servants.
25. TNA, PROB 11/732.
26. Welch, P.L.V., 'Madams and Mariners: Expressions of Self-confidence among Free Coloured Women in Barbados 1750–1834', paper submitted to the 29th Annual Conference of the Association of Caribbean Historians, 7–12 April

1997. This raises interesting legal questions: although England, as the mother country, contained courts of appeal for the colonies, this should have been either the Court of Kings Bench or the House of Lords. The choice of the City of London's Lord Mayor's Office is an odd one.

27. Drescher, 'Manumissions in a Society without Slave Law', p. 91.
28. Patterson O., *Social Death*, p. 4, quoted in Drescher, *ibid.*, p. 98, fn 21.
29. Shyllon, F.O., *Black Slaves in Britain* (Oxford, 1974), p. 242.
30. Chater, K., 'Where There's a Will', *History Today* 50 (4), April 2000, pp. 26–7.
31. GLC Ethnic Minorities Unit, *A History of the Black Presence in London* (1986), pp. 14 and 16. Ruth Thomas appears to have loaned money to her master's wife.
32. Baker, J., *The Diary of John Baker*, ed. Yorke, P. (1931), p. 15. Some of this probably came from wages, and the rest from the tips or vails that servants customarily received from visitors to a house.
33. *Gloucester Journal*, 14 June 1764. For this information I am grateful to Roger Jaques, a descendant of a collateral branch of the family of the man who murdered George Harford for this money.
34. Lorimer, D., 'Black Slaves and English Liberty: a Re-examination of Racial Slavery in England', in Lorimer, D., *Colour, Class and the Victorians* (Leicester, 1978), pp. 121–50, and Fryer, *Staying Power*, p. 203.
35. Simond, L., *Journal of a Tour and Residence in Great Britain* (first published 1815, repr. as *An American in Regency England*, ed. Hibbert, C. (1968), p. 19.
36. *Huntingdon, Bedford, Cambridge and Peterborough Gazette*, 17 January 1818, p. 11.
37. Myers, *Reconstructing the Black Past*, p. 58.
38. *Tatler*, 1709; *London Gazette*, 13–17 January 1712; *London Gazette*, 2–5 July 1715; *Felix Farley's Bristol Journal*, 31 August 1728; *Daily Journal*, 28 September 1728; *Daily Advertiser*, 11 December 1744; *Bristol Journal*, 23 June 1750; *Bristol Intelligencer*, 12 January 1754; *Public Advertiser*, 9 June 1756; *Williamson's Liverpool Advertiser*, 20 August 1756; *London Advertiser*, 1756; *Williamson's Liverpool Advertiser*, 24 June 1757; unidentified Liverpool newspaper, 1757; *Felix Farley's Bristol Journal*, 2 August 1760; *Felix Farley's Bristol Journal*, 2 August 1760; *Public Ledger*, 31 December 1761; *Public Advertiser*, 11 February 1762; *Gentleman's Magazine*, 1763; *Williamson's Liverpool Advertiser*, 1765; *Williamson's Liverpool Advertiser*, 12 September 1766; *Bristol Journal*, 20 June 1767; *Bristol Journal*, 9 January 1768; *Liverpool Chronicle*, 15 December 1768; *Public Advertiser*, 8 April 1769; *The Gazetter and New Daily Advertiser*, 18 April 1769; *Public Advertiser*, 28 November 1769; unidentified notice in Lichfield, 1771 (Shyllon, *Black People*, p. 13); *Stamford Mercury*, 1771.
39. *Avis's Gazette*, published in Birmingham, 11 November 1771, carried an advertisement for the sale of a negro boy at Lichfield. This is probably the one to which Shyllon referred without attribution.

40. *Williamson's Liverpool Advertiser*, 12 September 1766.
41. Hertfordshire RO, Registers of Thorley, 9 April 1773. I am grateful to Dr Jill Barber of Hertfordshire RO for this reference. She noted that the rector of the parish was a Mr Horsley.
42. SoG, Mfm 3460-4, Registers of Poole, Dorset, 27 April 1755. Three days later, June and Susannah, 'daus of Thos. Olive & a negro woman', were baptised.
43. Moritz, C., *Travels in England in 1782*, quoted in Sambrook, G.A. (ed.), *British Life in the Eighteenth Century* (1960), pp. 7-8.
44. Silliman, B., *A Journal of Travels in England, Holland and Scotland. . . 1805 and 1806* (New Haven, CT, 1820), Vol. 1, p. 272.
45. Even in the earliest days of the Black presence the word 'slave' is rarely used. In the Return of Strangers made in the City of London in 1593, three maids, 'blakamores' [sic], were recorded as lodging in the house of Paul Baning, Alderman for the Ward of Farringdon Without. Mary de Tropane, herself a stranger, was living in St Helens Bishopsgate Ward and was noted as having no servant but employing 'one Blackamore'. Scouladi, I., *Returns of Strangers in the Metropolis 1593, 1627,1635, 1639*, Huguenot Society of London Quarto Series, Vol. LVII (1985), pp. 149 and 170.
46. HS 46, *The Registers of St Olave, Hart Street, London, 1563 to 1700*, 8 January 1686/7.
47. Essex RO, D/P 256/1, Registers of West Ham, 3 October 1665; Q/RTh5 'Hearth Tax for 1671'; DP 256/5 'West Ham Churchwarden's Accounts', 1665-66.
48. TNA, PROB 11/325.
49. *Proceedings* 1773-4, III, no.146. Both Black and white people said either that they were the servant of someone or living with a person.
50. *Proceedings* 1782-3, VII, no. 640.
51. HS 46, *The Registers of St Olave, Hart St, London 1563-1700*, 29 July 1665.
52. Act for the Security of the Subject to prevent the forfeiture of Life and Estate upon Killing a Negroe or other Slave, reproduced in Craton, M., Walvin, J. & Wright, D., *Slavery, Abolition and Emancipation* (1976), p. 175.
53. West Middlesex FHS, *Registers of Harmondsworth, Middlesex* (1991), 7 July 1761.
54. Coldham, P.W., *Emigrants from England to the American Colonies 1773-1776* (Baltimore, MD, 1988) lists people in TNA T47/9-12, returns of people leaving British ports, which the government collected for these three years. Many were indentured servants.
55. SoG, unpublished transcript BK/R 74; Brooks, J.W., The Registers of Old Windsor (1986), 5 November 1761; TNA, PROB 11/1041. Two other wills in TNA, PROB 11/551 (proved 1716) and PROB 11/703 (proved 1740), relate to John Pilgrim and Thomas Pilgrim, both of Barbados, which suggests the Rev. Mr Pilgrim had family connections in the Caribbean.

56. HS 38, *Register of St Bene't and St Peter, Paul's Wharf, London*, 19 February 1771.
57. SoG, unpublished transcript, MX/R 344, Registers of Teddington, 8 December 1752.
58. Cornwall RO, Registers of Calstock, 19 March 1748, in BASA *Newsletter* 35, January 2002, p. 27, sent by Renee Jackaman.
59. GL, Ms 6667/12.
60. Shyllon, *Black Slaves*, p. 125, states that they were Somerset's godparents. This is a plausible suggestion, but he gives no reference to substantiate his claim. No sponsors are included in the baptismal entry.
61. Scotland had, and still has, a separate legal system and the situation in relation to Black slaves there was finally resolved in the case of *Knight* v. *Wedderburn* in 1778. This uncompromisingly ruled that Knight was free. Such a definitive ruling was possible in Scotland because a system of slavery existed there and, despite this case, it continued until 1799. Millar, J. 'White Slaves with Black Faces: Scottish coalminers in the 17th and 18th centuries', *Family Tree Magazine*, 18 April 2002, pp. 66-7. Millar noted that one of these 'perpetual servants' wore a brass collar engraved '1701 Alexander Stewart property of Sir John Stewart'. Another had been acquired in exchange for a pony.
62. *Halsbury's Laws of England* has been published annually since 1907. It summarises the current state of legislation by topic.
63. An account of the events appears in many publications. The most recent is Wise, S.E., *Though the Heavens May Fall: the Landmark Trial that Led to the End of Human Slavery* (Cambridge, MA, 2005).
64. Madden, A.F. and Fieldhouse, D. (eds), *Classical Period of the First British Empire* (1985), pp. 16-17, reproduced in Samson, J. (ed.), *The British Empire* (Oxford, 2001), pp. 84-8.
65. This replaced the system of local courts administering local laws, which varied across the country. The law became uniform across the whole kingdom, hence 'common' law. Modifications and changes were, and still are, effected by statute law, Acts passed by Parliament, and precedents, decisions made by judges hearing cases. A summary of this appears in James, P.S., *Introduction to English Law* (12th edn, 1989), pp. 21-6, and no doubt in many other works on the history of the law.
66. Lord Mansfield's confirmation, not manumission, of his mixed-race great-niece's freedom in his will is an oddity. If he had already pronounced that slavery did not exist under English law, why would he need to make the point that Dido Elizabeth was free? Mansfield was probably being ultra cautious, aware that such a contentious issue might lead to further proceedings which could overturn his judgment. Perhaps he also feared that the Acts of Parliament he said were the only way to introduce slavery into England would be passed, as had been proposed by various eminent thinkers.

Free or enslaved? 101

67. Today people brought to England from countries like the Sudan or Mali, where there is, despite the Convention on Human Rights, de facto slavery, are free in this country but, should they return home, they may again become slaves.
68. There was no shorthand writer in court to take down the judgment and various versions of what Mansfield said were in circulation. Wise, *Though the Heavens May Fall*, pp. 185–91. What is now accepted as the full judgment can be found in *Howell's State Trials*, Vol. 20, cols 1–6, 79–82 (1816) and on <www.nationalarchives.gov.uk/pathways/Blackhistory/rights/docs/state_trials.htm>.
69. *Williamson's Liverpool Advertiser*, 4 May 1780. The law on British ships at sea, however, was also an ambiguous area. I am grateful to Professor David Killingray for this reference.
70. TNA, T 47/9–12 in Coldham, *Emigrants from England*, p. 23.
71. Dabydeen, *Hogarth's Blacks*, p. 127.
72. Shyllon, *Black Slaves*, p. 7; *Black People*, p. 11.
73. Fryer, *Staying Power*, p. 64.
74. James Woodforde's diary contains an entry which makes clear that he regarded the livery and greatcoat he bought for a footman as his property. Woodforde, J., *The Diary of a Country Parson 1758–1802*, selected and ed. Beresford, J. (Oxford, 1978), II, p. 212.
75. Most people have vague memories of Eliza, with her child in her arms, pursued by bloodhounds across the ice floes of the Ohio River in the novel Stowe, H.B. *Uncle Tom's Cabin* (1852, repr. Edinburgh, n.d. on my copy), pp. 57–72. When I checked this reference, having not re-read the book in forty years, I found it was considerably less dramatic than I remembered. There were no hounds, although I have a distinct mental picture of a dramatic illustration of slavering dogs only inches from fleeing Eliza. I presume that other people will have the same visceral reaction to the phrase, based on childhood books.
76. Fryer, *Staying Power*, p. 22.
77. *Kentish Gazette*, 18 August 1764, p. 1, advertised for Little Sam who ran away from Faversham.
78. Schama, S., *Rough Crossings* (2005), p. 40. He offers no evidence for the existence of professional slave-catchers. He adds, 'Once caught such Blacks were imprisoned, sold off (for there were regular sales and auctions in London) and bundled off to waiting ships at Gravesend, destined for Jamaica, Havana, Santa Cruz or Charleston.' No regular sales, let alone auctions, have been found in London or, indeed, any other British town.
79. King, P., *Crime, Justice, and Discretion in England 1740–1820* (Oxford, 2000), p. 186.
80. Mansfield, P., 'Indexing Old Newspapers', *Family Tree* 15, July 1999, p. 65.
81. Fielding, H., *Extracts from Such of the Laws as Particularly Relate to the Peace and Good Order of this Metropolis* (1768), p. 143, which has been quoted by many historians.

Chapter 4

Black people and the criminal justice system

Overwhelmingly, historians of Black British history have concentrated on the Mansfield Judgment and the cases that led up to it, but these are few compared to the number of court proceedings that involved Black people incidentally, rather than hinging on their status as enslaved or free. It was often difficult to determine whether Black people fell within the provision of the poor laws (discussed Chapter 5), although the evidence suggests that parish authorities applied the same rules to them as they did to other aliens and to white people. There was no doubt with regard to criminal law. Black people appeared in trials and other legal proceedings all over the country as defendants, prosecutors and witnesses.

By the eighteenth century a number of courts hearing civil and criminal cases had developed from the medieval Curia Regis. Alongside the lay courts were ecclesiastical courts, which had jurisdiction over probate, family matters like marriage, divorce and illegitimacy, and moral issues like fornication, abusive language and non-attendance at church. The ecclesiastical courts also governed the clergy and church rights, such as tithes and fees. In addition there were manorial courts, which mainly had jurisdiction over land tenure. The powers of both the ecclesiastical and manorial courts dwindled during the eighteenth and nineteenth centuries. Coroners' courts held inquests to determine the causes of death where there were suspicious circumstances and were supposed to hold an inquest on every person who died in prison, although this did not always happen. Most newspapers gave minimal coverage to routine inquests, publishing only the name of the deceased and the cause of death, but went into greater detail on those involving more noteworthy events, especially murder or suicide. Only the most sensational cases in the ecclesiastical or manorial courts were covered.

During the long eighteenth century, there was not such a clear distinction as there is today between civil cases, those where one person sues another over some disadvantage or injury to his/her interests, and criminal cases, where the state is deemed to have suffered and brings the prosecution. Although after the establishment of police forces in the 1830s the authorities began to take over the prosecution of criminals for assault, theft and other crimes which are today seen as the state's responsibility to prosecute; the first Director of Public Prosecutions was not appointed until 1880. Until then, it was primarily up to the injured party to take the person who had wronged him or her to court, although in the long eighteenth century plaintiffs were often given financial assistance to pursue a case, either by parish authorities or by tradesmen's associations formed to combat crime against their members.

Crimes were divided into misdemeanours and felonies. Misdemeanours were punished by fines, periods in the pillory, whippings and imprisonment, while felonies were punished by execution, transportation or maiming, such as branding, and forfeiture of possessions. Petty larceny (under one shilling) was counted as a misdemeanour. Murder, manslaughter, rape, burglary and larceny were defined as felonies. Within this apparently rigid and punitive system there were various ways that a defendant might be spared the full rigour of the law. Cases might be 'compromised' before coming to court by the parties coming to an agreement. If matters got as far as a trial, juries might exercise 'discretion' and reduce the crime by, for example, valuing stolen goods at less than the prosecutor claimed, in order to convert the crime from a felony to a misdemeanour. Some crimes carried a lesser penalty if the criminals could claim benefit of clergy because they could read, although this privilege ended in 1706. After sentencing, a royal pardon might be granted and/or the sentence commuted to transportation on petition from the jury or relatives and friends of the criminal.

Criminal cases went through three stages: Petty Sessions, Quarter Sessions and Assizes. Local Justices of the Peace (JPs) held Petty Sessions, which dealt with misdemeanours and minor offences, and also heard settlement and bastardy examinations, sometimes in their own homes and sometimes in church vestries. JPs referred more serious cases to the Quarter Sessions, held four times a year. These could be either County Sessions or Borough or City Sessions held by a town or city with a privileged jurisdiction. Quarter Sessions also dealt with a wide range of other legal matters, such as licences for a number of occupations, settlement disputes and removal orders, taxes, sacrament certificates, recusants and nonconformists, etc. Any of these matters might involve Black people and, in addition to crimes, there are occasional settlement examinations and disputes involving them. JPs could also refer cases directly to the Assizes, generally held twice a year. Judges (usually in pairs) went round the counties 'on circuit' within a specified area. Cheshire, Durham and Lancaster had Palatinate Courts (which were, confusingly, sometimes called Assizes). The Palatinate courts, the City of London and Middlesex (which included the City and Liberty of Westminster and the Liberty of Tower Hamlets) were outside the Assize circuits for legal and historic reasons. There were, as in the rest of the country, lower courts, but the equivalent of Assizes in Middlesex and the City were the Sessions of Oyer and Terminer and Gaol Delivery held at the Old Bailey until 1834, when the Central Criminal Court was established. Cases from the Instance Court of the High Court of the Admiralty, dealing with murder and piracy on the high seas, were also held at the Old Bailey. These latter sometimes involved Black people, like the trial of Captain John Sutherland, mentioned Chapter 3. In another case, in 1767 a seaman, John Wynne, was convicted at the Old Bailey of murdering a 'free negro' off the coast of Africa and was hanged at Execution Dock.[1]

Court papers related to the preliminary sessions consisted of statements, called informations, made by the victims of crime, and recognisances to appear in court, made before a JP. The records at Quarter Sessions and Assizes include indictments (usually annotated with the plea, verdict and sentence); calendars of prisoners to be tried; jury panels; minute books and court registers. The papers rarely include the witnesses' evidence. Sometimes witness depositions with coroners' papers may contain supplementary information but this is only, of course, if someone died. The major problem with using the documents produced by all these courts, both civil and criminal, in England and Wales is that, because colour and/or ethnic origin had no legal significance, these factors are rarely stated except where they had some bearing on the case, either in matters of settlement or for identification purposes, to distinguish one person from another. Nor are provincial trials covered in the detail provided by a contemporary publication, *The Whole Proceedings on the King's Commissions of the Peace, Oyer and Terminer, and Gaol Delivery held for the City of London, etc.*, which covered trials at the Old Bailey in London. Cases outside London and Middlesex therefore have to be recovered from newspaper reports in provincial newspapers, which do not usually provide a complete transcript of evidence. Because court papers rarely mention colour, it is impossible to determine just how many Black people were involved in cases outside London. It is therefore only from the *Proceedings* of the Old Bailey that some idea of how Black people were perceived both by the authorities and by their white contemporaries can be gained. The full title of the published Old Bailey proceedings is sometimes abbreviated as *OBSP* (*Old Bailey Sessions Papers*), but this is misleading. They are not sessions papers, but transcripts of shorthand accounts of the court proceedings, originally published as a commercial venture but accepted as an official record from 1748. I therefore prefer to use the abbreviated title *Proceedings* because this is a more accurate description, and in order to distinguish them from official court documents and thus avoid confusion between the two sources of information.

The *Proceedings* are an invaluable guide to what was said in court but they have limitations. They record only those who were actually brought to trial at the Old Bailey, not the total number of crimes. Modern statisticians are able to draw on crimes *reported* to the authorities, but at this period no records were compiled of crimes that did not result in the appearance of a defendant before a court . Some appear in JPs' notebooks or in the form of informations deposited at Quarter Sessions or Sessions of the Peace but few of these have survived. If no one was apprehended, there could be no trial. Joseph Mountain, a Black American who came to England in 1775, was, by his own account, involved in a number of crimes around the country and in France but always escaped capture and appears in no court records here.[2]

A prisoner might die or abscond before coming to trial. In 1784 a newspaper carried an item about a Black man who had hailed a boat at Wapping. The boatman refused to take him and the two fought. The boatman died and his assailant was taken to the lock-up at Whitechapel in Middlesex. This was plainly a case of murder or manslaughter, so should have been heard at the Old Bailey, but no trial appears in the *Proceedings*. What happened to the Black man is therefore not known. He may have absconded, or even died. Another newspaper report in 1784 said that 'a Negro youth' from Nevis was committed to the New Prison in Clerkenwell, Middlesex following an incident when a seaman who had 'rendered himself extremely obnoxious to the rest of the crew' was tarred and feathered. The captain of the ship had bailed the mate and four of his men. Why he did not do the same for the Black man and what subsequently happened are unknown. According to the newspaper report, the obnoxious one did lay charges for assault but he may, on further reflection, have decided not to proceed further or may not have been able to pursue the matter because he had to go back to sea.[3] In 1783 Edward Coffee was accused of assault and theft from John Baptiste Benedick but the case collapsed because, by the time it reached the Old Bailey,

Benedick had gone to sea. It is possible that one or both of the parties was Black: their names do not appear to be of English origin.[4]

Minor matters might be resolved at a lower court. However, few records of Petty Sessions survive. The notebook of Henry Norris, a JP in Hackney, records a case in 1737 when a local woman, Ann Godfrey, said that three men, one of them Black, had stolen washing from her garden. She was informed that the Black man's name was George Scipio and Norris issued a warrant to arrest him. Both Godfrey and Scipio came before Norris with witnesses and Scipio's gave him an alibi. Although recognisances to appear at the next Sessions of the Peace for Middlesex were taken, Ruth Paley, who edited the notebook for publication, found no indictment in a higher court and concluded that the case had been 'compromised', i.e. settled out of court.[5] Alternatively, Norris may have decided that there was not enough evidence to proceed.

The injured party might not proceed with a prosecution, perhaps thinking that the time, trouble and expense involved were out of proportion to the likely outcome. This is particularly true of minor pilfering by an employee. Where the traditional perquisites of a job, e.g. selling a master's old clothes, shaded into theft was a grey area. In such cases an employer might confront and punish the employee, dismiss him or her or take steps to prevent further theft by, perhaps, locking away possessions. Alternatively, the injured party or parties might decide to inflict summary punishment on the perpetrator of a crime without involving the authorities. In 1744 a newspaper reported that two sailors had been drinking together when one stole half-a-crown from the other. Although the victim got his money back, he 'then deliver'd him [the thief] up to the Populace, who gave him the usual Discipline of Ducking'.[6] It seems likely that an unnamed Black boy who passed goods out of his master's house to John Lawrence (who was also Black) was punished by his master rather than by the court, as he was not charged, although there was no doubt that he was implicated in the crime.[7] In 1786, John Thomas, a Black labourer on the quays at Queenhithe, was caught stealing from John William Goss. Two men suspended him by his arms from a crane, at Goss's instigation. The matter might have ended there but Goss also decided to proceed with a prosecution. Although the value of the goods Thomas had stolen meant he was charged with a felony, the jury reduced the sum involved to the level of a misdemeanour and he was punished with a whipping rather than execution or transportation. The judge remarked that he 'would have punished him more if Mr Goss had not taken the punishment into his own hands'.[8]

Appearances by Black people at the Old Bailey

London and Middlesex are the only areas where any valid statistical data can be generated about Black people and how they were treated under criminal law. This is partly because of the published transcripts of trials and partly because the London area had a substantial Black population. In the rest of the country, occasional cases involving Black people are found but no justifiable conclusions about official or unofficial attitudes towards them can be drawn because the numbers are, apparently, so low. The digitisation of the *Proceedings* and their availability on the internet has made it possible to produce statistics on cases between 1674 and 1812. The site also contains statistical information which makes possible comparison of the treatment of Black and white people by the courts at the Old Bailey during a large part of the period covered by the British slave trade.[9] Whether all Black people have been identified in the transcripts of these trials is impossible to say. There is, for example, a period of ten years from 1755 to 1764 in which no Black person is stated to have appeared in any capacity at the Old Bailey. Given regular appearances both before and after these dates, it is almost impossible to believe that no Black person was involved in any crime during this decade, especially as the Black population was apparently increasing. There are shorter periods between 1737 and 1743 and 1746 and 1751 when there also seem to have been no Black participants in trials. Although it is possible, by a statistical freak, that none did appear in court during these years, it is more likely that Thomas Gurney, the first official transcriber, did not routinely identify ethnic origin. He was appointed in 1748 (although he may have been practising unofficially from 1737) and was still working when he died in 1770.[10] Towards the end of his period of office a description in brackets that mentions colour is given in some trials after the participants' names.[11] There is another period at the beginning of the nineteenth century when neither the colour nor ethnic origin of trial participants seem to have been noted regularly.

The *Proceedings*' descriptions of colour and/or ethnic origin cannot be conclusive, since someone described as 'black' might be a dark-skinned British or mainland European person who had spent a great deal of time outdoors, like a sailor or agricultural labourer, or someone with gypsy ancestry. For a long time Sarah Lyons, described in the *Proceedings* as 'a short, black girl', was included on the database but she was later discovered to be Jewish.[12] Sometimes there is a note, either at the foot of the page or in parentheses, recording colour or ethnic origin when this is important to understanding the evidence. In 1767 Thomas Windsor was indicted for stealing a brass mouthpiece from John Shropshire. A witness said: 'I went to the Red Lion, there I saw these two Blacks sitting in a box together.' After 'Blacks' the words 'note, the prosecutor and prisoner were both Blacks' was inserted in brackets.[13] In other cases, colour or ethnic background might emerge from the evidence. At the trial of Elizabeth Gift in 1755, a witness said, 'we asked the woman of the house if a Black woman had sold or pawned two aprons'. James Turner, indicted for theft in 1765, was referred to by a witness as 'this Black'. In both cases, the witnesses' testimonies were the only indication of colour.[14] The case of Joseph Curry and Thomas Riley shows that deducing colour is sometimes more problematic. Joseph Curry, accused of theft, was pursued into a public house in East Smithfield where there were already some forty Black people. This suggests that Curry was Black himself (although it is never explicitly stated anywhere), because if he were white it would have been impossible to hide himself there, which is presumably what he was trying to do.[15] In two cases, the fact that witnesses, though adult, were asked about baptism suggests that they were Black, in the absence of an explicit statement or any other evidence.[16]

Occasionally the reference is ambiguous because the person concerned is nicknamed 'Black', like John Wallis, alias Black Jack, tried for theft in 1741. Others are more clearly identified, like Joseph Black, otherwise 'Joe the Black'.[17] In 1804, Rebecca Stanforth and Mary Smith were tried for theft. Both were from Boston, North America. One witness identified Mary as 'the prisoner in the blue gown' and another said: 'I knew it was the prisoner Broad; she went by the name Birmingham Beck; I found her going into a gin shop along with this little Black Pat, as they call her.'[18] Another case shows how widely and imprecisely the term 'Black' was applied. In 1804 James Franks was indicted for stealing a £10 bill from Lochlan McDonald. McDonald testified that the two men slept in the same room in a lodging house, but did not mention Franks's colour. Barnard Moses, a shopkeeper, was asked if 'a Black man' had come to him. Other witnesses mentioned 'a Black man'. The defendant claimed that he had been given a waistcoat by 'a Black man, a Greek' and later said 'I went to my comrade, a Black man, a Greek'. Whether Franks was a very dark European or someone of African origin or mixed race, perhaps from Greece, never becomes clear.[19]

In some cases, however, there is no indication. George Francisco, for example, was tried at the Old Bailey in 1784. His colour and ethnic origin are not mentioned in the *Proceedings* but he is called 'a Black' in the records of the *Ceres* hulk to which he was sent to await transportation.[20] Scipio Africanus was tried in 1787. Again, there is no indication of his colour or ethnic origin in the trial transcript but, given his name, he must have been Black.[21] Ann Calabar's name suggests that she might have been Black and had been named after the port from which she was shipped, but there is nothing to confirm or refute this in the account of her trial for theft from a merchant in Mincing Lane.[22] William Lion was tried for theft in 1758. A witness said: 'He is not one of our countrymen, he is a *Barbarian*' (italics in original). Understandably, he was asked, 'What is a Barbarian?' to which the reply came: "That is, he is a man from Barbadoes.' Lion was most likely Black or mixed race, but might have been white.[23]

Roles

Black people appeared as defendants, prosecutors and witnesses. One hundred and twenty-six (109 men and 17 women) were accused of a crime, but a few defendants made multiple appearances. There were forty-six prosecutors (forty-one men and five women) and twenty witnesses (nineteen men and one woman). Two young Black boys, Adam Stanton and William Coffe, were involved in thefts and then turned King's evidence against their fellow thieves, so are included in the witnesses' category. Guardaloup, a Black boy, was called as a witness but was not allowed to testify because he could not give satisfactory evidence of a religious faith, and is therefore not included in these figures.

As poverty is a strong predictor of involvement in crime, the greater number of defendants may suggest that Black people were poorer than the general population. As Table 3 shows, the majority of crimes for which they were committed to trial in London and Middlesex were theft or housebreaking/burglary, but this was also the most frequent crime among the general population. Almost 83 per cent of cases tried at the Old Bailey between 1674 and 1812 were for theft, including housebreaking/burglary. Just over 6 per cent were for theft and violence. These figures are comparable to the percentages of crimes involving Black people.

To judge by the cases before the Old Bailey, personation by one sailor in order to claim the wages and any extra money due to another was fairly common, but there was only one case of personation involving a Black man, John Moseley.[24] In another case, Joseph Scott was accused of forgery of a document in order to claim wages due to a sailor called Alexander Scott. He did not actually write the document in question but persuaded

Table 3 Crimes for which Black people were tried at the Old Bailey, 1674–1812

Crime	Male	Female	Total
Theft	70	10	80
Housebreaking/burglary	15	0	15
Aggravated theft	8	6	14
Assault	3	0	3
Riotous assembly/riot	2	1	3
Assault with intent to murder	2	0	2
Arson (and theft)	1	0	1
Forgery	1	0	1
Horse-stealing	1	0	1
Murder	1	0	1
Perjury	1	0	1
Personation	1	0	1
Rape	1	0	1
Totals	**107**	**17**	**124**

an attorney to produce it, so was charged with forgery rather than personation, which was his intention.[25] There was also one case where Mary Leak, a white woman, prosecuted William Smith, a Black man, for theft and suggested in evidence that he had attempted to rape her before stealing a ring, but this was not included in the indictment.[26]

No Black person appeared before the courts in cases of counterfeiting coins or banknotes, infanticide, sodomy or buggery. The last three were rare crimes (or at least, rarely appeared before the courts), so statistically it is not surprising to find no Black people involved in them. Myers also notes that in the periods she studied after 1780, none was accused of a crime connected with African cultural practices, like scarification of children, polygamy, or the practice of voodoo rituals.[27] She might have added female circumcision and human sacrifice. Nor do any of these apparently occur outside her period of interest. The absence of any distinctive cultural practices may be evidence that there was no separate Black community or that these practices were well concealed. There was also no law about cohabiting with more than one woman: it was going through a ceremony of marriage while a previous spouse was alive that was illegal. There may be examples of cohabitation by Black men (as there are among white men) with more than one woman, so how many had effectively practised polygyny in this country without going through a

The criminal justice system

Table 4 Verdicts passed on Black and all defendants at the Old Bailey 1674–1812 (percentages)

	Black males	All male defendants[a]	Black females	All female defendants[a]
Guilty as charged	62.03	47.03	35.29	34.84
Guilty (reduced)	12.04	16.76	17.65	22.59
Acquitted	25.00	35.21	47.06	42.43
Totals[b]	**99.07**	**99.00**	**99.08**	**99.86**

Notes:
[a] These figures are for all cases. They therefore include the Black defendants, but these are such a tiny proportion of the total number of trials that their inclusion is not significant.
[b] There were insignificant numbers of other types of verdict, no verdict at all or respited.

ceremony and thus falling foul of the law is not known. Counterfeiting was, however, more common. It is likely that Black people were not involved in this type of crime because their level of literacy was likely to be low, and the majority must also have lacked an educational background which included drawing, engraving or generally making visually identical copies of documents or Western handwriting. Another factor might be that they were remarkable: their colour would make them especially notable and people would therefore be able to identify the person who passed forged documents or coins more easily.

Verdicts

The great severity of the sentences for even minor crimes led juries, whether they were trying Black or white people, to reduce the value of the goods stolen or to ameliorate the crime in some other way. It is in this area where the experiences of Black and white people before the Old Bailey seem to be different.

It seems that Black men were significantly more likely to be found guilty of the crime with which they were charged and not have the charge reduced or be acquitted. There is a difference between the treatment accorded to Black men and women, although the small number of women involved makes any firm conclusion doubtful. The very high acquittal rate among women is mainly accounted for by one individual, Ann Duck, who was acquitted on four separate occasions and against whom there were no further proceedings on a further charge because she had already been sentenced to death.[28] There are, however, many variable factors during this whole period. There were periods of what is called 'moral panic', when fear of crime caused jurors not to acquit or reduce a crime. The degree of severity involved in the crime was also not uniform. Some Black people were charged with assault and theft, but the assault component covered a wide range from simply pushing a victim to inflicting life-threatening injuries. The value of the goods stolen also varied widely and it is likely that this also influenced the severity of the sentence.

This apparent difference between verdicts passed on Black and white defendants may in part be due to jurors' prejudices, but there are other factors. Studies outside London have shown that testimony by character witnesses played a large part in determining whether or not discretion was exercised in reducing the verdict.[29] As some of the cases at the Old Bailey were summarised, rather than given in full, it is impossible to know exact figures, but only fourteen male defendants seem to have been able to call people to give them a good character. Some of these had only known the person for a few months but, overwhelmingly, these people did receive more favourable treatment. At least fifty-nine, however, called no character witnesses. As John Moseley sadly said, 'I have nobody to call.'[30] Two of those who did not call character witnesses, Benjamin Bowsey and John Glover, were found guilty and sentenced to death for their parts in the Gordon Riots of 1780 but were pardoned following strenuous efforts made after their trials by former employers.[31] In another case, John Thomas, the ex-slave of a family with estates in the Caribbean, called a member of that family to bear witness to his character. His testimony was favourable and Thomas was spared the death penalty.[32] This both shows how important support from respectable and influential people was, and suggests that the support system existing between master and servant extended beyond their period of service.

At least five made confessions before a JP and therefore admitted guilt. All these confessions were before 1730. Presumably Black people soon realised that a confession would end any hope of discretion or pardon. A third possible factor is not quantifiable. Even today, cultural differences can unconsciously prejudice people against those from a different background. In many cultures it is a mark of disrespect to look a person in authority in the eye, but in British culture this signifies trustworthiness and honesty. In some African cultures people of lower social status must crouch before a senior or older person.[33] To the British this looks like shiftiness. How much prejudice on the part of the jury was due to such factors cannot now be recovered, partly because British attitudes and behaviour towards those of higher and lower social status have changed and partly because no eighteenth-century comparison of paraverbal factors in Black people's behaviour seems to have been discovered. As well as body language, there are sociolinguistic conventions that must also have changed over the centuries.

One man, Peter Bristow, was found guilty of theft but died before sentence was passed.[34] Another, William Bristow, found guilty of a misdemeanour, was offered a choice: twelve months' imprisonment or transportation before the end of that time. He apparently chose transportation, because he was sent to Maryland in October 1722.[35] Sadi, also known as George Horne, was convicted of theft and sentenced to death. He was pardoned on condition that he gave evidence against Robert Atkins, also thought to be involved in the crime, but Sadi died in Newgate before Atkins, who had absconded, surrendered himself.[36]

Death sentences, commutations and pardons

The whole subject of crime and punishment is still a matter of debate. Theories about the causes of crime range from social to genetic, and the purposes of punishment from pain (either physical or mental) to rehabilitation. What is beyond dispute is that throughout the long eighteenth century more and more crimes, punished with harsher and harsher sentences, were created. This did not, however, lead to an increase in executions, except in periods of moral panic. Judges, juries and even prosecutors regularly recommended criminals to mercy. The monarch, equally regularly, reprieved those condemned to death and substituted transportation. In some cases a free pardon was granted. Reprieves can also be seen as a way of sorting out those who were thought to be capable of reform and giving them an opportunity to do so. The chance to begin a new life in Australia was one that many people grasped, as various biographical works dealing with transportees have demonstrated. Transportation to America may have had similar effects, but as far as I know no study on the subject has been undertaken. The main problem here is that, during the period when the Americas were a destination for transportees, they were simply sold like slaves to local inhabitants and no further official interest was taken in their welfare. Some did manage to escape or to return, often illegally, but a statistical study would seem to be impossible. Sending criminals overseas had the additional benefit of removing a source of crime from the community. This last is a fourth theory of sentencing that has not been much considered by historians, who concentrate on punishment, deterrence and rehabilitation.

There is no official list of prisoners executed in London and Middlesex in the archives. Newspapers, the *Newgate Calendar* and the Ordinary of Newgate's *Accounts* are the best sources of information, but the first two do not cover every execution and the Ordinary's *Accounts* were published only between 1690 and 1772. In the first part of the eighteenth century newspapers, even though they were smaller and had less space than later publications, usually listed those hanged. In the second half of the century only the executions of infamous people or executions where there had been some remarkable occurrence were covered. What might be called more routine hangings were generally omitted when a more newsworthy story was occupying the columns. The official transportation records and reprieves are incomplete, but reprieves are usually mentioned in at least one of the contemporary newspapers and it must be presumed they were granted on condition of transportation. It is possible that in some cases a last-minute reprieve was obtained after the death sentence had been confirmed, but this is rare and appears more in fiction than in fact.[37] Published research on transportees to America and Australia has also revealed the fate of other Black criminals. I used all these sources to try to discover how many of the Black people sentenced to death were actually executed.

A total of twenty-three Black people (twenty male, three female) were sentenced to death between 1684 and 1812. In addition, James Franks (described as 'a black man' and also as a Greek) and Francis Fernandez, who was probably, though not certainly, an East Indian, were sentenced to death in 1804 and 1811 respectively (Table 5). It is not known what happened to either of them. Except at times of moral panic, about one-third of those sentenced to death were executed. Eight out of the twenty-three Black people sentenced to death were executed. Two died in Newgate[38] and the fate of another is unknown, although he was probably reprieved.[39] From this it seems that Blacks were as likely as white people to be executed, but with such a small sample it is impossible to draw a firm conclusion. On examination of the individual cases, it seems that whether Black people were executed or reprieved reflected both the nature of the crimes they committed and their ability to call character witnesses, as it did in the white population. Julian, for example, had stolen from his master and then, in an attempt to conceal his crime, set light to their house.[40] In a patriarchal and hierarchical society, the head of the household was regarded as representing the monarch and, ultimately,

Table 5 Sentences passed on Black people at the Old Bailey, 1674–1812

	Male	Female	Total
Transportation	44	4	48
Death	22	3	25
Mixed	5	0	5
Whipping	3	1	4
Imprisonment	2	1	3
Respited – no further information	2	0	2
Burned in the hand	1	0	1
Totals	**79**	**9**	**88**

God: women who killed their husbands were regarded as having committed petty treason, and crimes by a servant against his or her master were similarly regarded. Arson, too, was particularly feared in a crowded city where wood formed a major part of the structure and internal furnishing of houses[41] and the fire services, particularly in the earlier half of the century, were rudimentary. In 1724, when Julian committed his crimes, this would have been just within living memory of the Great Fire of London in 1666, so it is not surprising, combined with the lack of anyone to act as a character witness, that he was hanged.

The mythology, glamour and literature that surrounded highwaymen has been explored in a number of studies, but, however fascinating the public found it, it was another crime which attracted few reprieves. Fear of highwaymen and footpads limited personal freedom to travel. Isaac George and John Cross were footpads who threatened to assault or did assault travellers;[42] Joseph Guy was on horseback. The first two were executed. One of the witnesses at his trial said Guy was in a regiment, and a newspaper reported that, at his appearance before the JP Sir John Fielding, he said he was a drummer at Portsmouth.[43] Presumably, as a member of the army or a marine, he was reprieved on condition of rejoining, because he does not appear in newspaper reports of executions, nor in transportation records. Although he was convicted of horse theft, a crime which attracted a high percentage of executions, John Edinburgh was reprieved and transported. The testimony of his previous employers displayed shock and surprise that so exemplary a servant could have committed such a crime: one of them had recommended Edinburgh to another man and to his own brother.[44] Presumably their efforts on his behalf led to the commutation of his sentence, as in the cases of Benjamin Bowsey and John Glover.

The age, sex, number of previous offences and social situation of the offender also influenced the outcome.[45] The age of defendants is rarely given in court papers or the *Proceedings* before the nineteenth century. However, transportation records in the last quarter of the eighteenth century show that most of the men, of whatever colour, were between 19 and 30 and unmarried.[46] It has already been demonstrated that the majority of Black people in this country were young men at the time of their baptism, which probably took place relatively soon after their arrival in England, and this was the section of the population most likely to suffer the full penalties of the law. The Ordinary's *Accounts* confirm that Jeffrey Morat was 16 or 17; Thomas Wheeler was about 17; Isaac George was 22 and John Cross was 25.[47] Ann Duck, who was about 25, was a persistent criminal. One of her relatives did petition the king but this was in vain.[48] This relative was unlikely to be of any great influence: the social status and respectability of those petitioning the king were of great importance in securing pardons or reprieves. Some thirty-five years later Lucy Johnson, who committed the same kind of crimes as Duck (and, incidentally, lived in the same notoriously criminal area), was reprieved, presumably because it was her first crime, or at least the first time she had been caught. By the time Johnson was tried, the law inflicted harsher penalties for theft, which may explain why the jury did not acquit for what was apparently her first offence.[49] Joseph Scott, a man 'without feet', who attempted to claim money due to a sailor by means of a forged document, was recommended to mercy by the jury. His disability, acquired in the King's service, was undoubtedly a factor. Their recommendation, however, was in vain. There were four other cases of forgery or personation to claim sailors' wages made by white men at the same sessions and none of those was reprieved.[50] John Moseley, reprieved, was a sailor who had served his country. Either his service or the efforts of his companions in arms made the difference.[51]

The sole case in which a Black person was convicted of murder occurred when John Hogan was indicted for killing Anne Hunt. Hogan seems to have been of mixed race, as he is described as 'a mulatto'.[52] The events that led to his trial and sentence are worth setting out in full because they refute Folarin Shyllon's assertion that the case was given such detailed coverage in the newspapers and Hogan was condemned to death simply because of his colour.[53]

On the afternoon of Sunday 26 June 1785 Mr Orrell, an attorney, and his wife left their servant Anne Hunt alone in their house in Charlotte Street. When they returned, they discovered that Hunt had been brutally attacked. She was taken to the nearby Middlesex Hospital, where she was examined and found to have a fractured skull, a broken arm and finger and cuts to her chest. Her throat had also been cut and it was this last injury that caused her death some eight hours later. During this time, Orrell questioned her. Some of the replies she gave were lucid, but generally she was too confused to give the name of her attacker. A number of spoons, as well as Mrs Orrell's cloak, were found to be missing and a razor was discovered in the fireplace. Orrell made enquiries which led him to John Hogan, a porter. There was some evidence against him – he had recently delivered chairs to the Orrells' house; his clothes had been washed and cuts on his hands were more recent than he claimed and could not have been caused in the way he said. Hogan also gave contradictory statements about how well he knew the dead woman and about where he lived and how long he had lived there. Orrell took Hogan to Bow Street to be examined before a magistrate who decided there was not enough evidence to commit him for trial, and he was released. Further enquiries by Orrell found a witness who had seen a mulatto man near the house at the time of the murder and he took the witness and Hogan before two JPs who decided, because the witness could not positively identify him, that Hogan should again be released. Orrell went before another magistrate with the same result.

There was no further action for several months, during which time Orrell had handbills printed and distributed. Newspapers also continued to mention the case. Some time in August, a month or five weeks after the murder, Elizabeth Pugh, the woman with whom Hogan lived in Southwark, read aloud a newspaper account to Hogan, who confessed that he had killed Anne Hunt because she resisted his sexual advances and that he had thrown the spoons he had stolen off London Bridge. Pugh did not turn him in, perhaps because she did not want to see him hanged or perhaps because she was afraid that she would be made an accessory to the murder. Hogan had given her Mrs Orrell's black silk cloak but Pugh had pawned it the day after the murder. Pugh may not have turned him in, but she did turn him out of the room she rented. What happened to Hogan, where he lived or what he did for the next few weeks is not known, but on 26 October he stole five linen sheets and was committed for trial at the Old Bailey in December. Whether the theft was a ploy to get himself transported or whether he needed money now that he was no longer supported by Pugh, this case was to prove his downfall. He asked to be sent back to his own country, which he said was Bengal. Plainly he did not understand that transportation did not mean repatriation.[54] As this was in 1785, during the gap between the ending of transportation to America and the beginning of the period when convicts were sent to Australia, he remained in Newgate. Orrell, meanwhile, saw newspaper coverage of this case and obtained a copy of the *Proceedings*, where he read the details of the trial, which included the name of the pawnbroker with whom Hogan had pledged the sheets. He went there, taking his wife, who identified her cloak. A neighbour who had cleaned it also recognised the marks produced by the cleaning fluid. Finally, Orrell had the piece of evidence he needed to link John Hogan to the murder of his maid servant. When John Hogan was brought before the Old Bailey in January 1786, Orrell hired an attorney to put the prosecution case. The case the two men built was solid. In his summing up the judge warned the jury not to be influenced by Hogan's colour or nationality:

> I am sure you will suffer yourselves to have no impression from the difference of complection [*sic*] or country, but that you will try this man that stands at the bar, just as you would a man of your own country and complection, and whose character before this stood unimpeached . . .

This last phrase was a warning to the jury not to be swayed by the evidence of the theft for which Hogan had already been sentenced to transportation. Ordinarily evidence of previous crimes was, and still is, not referred to at a trial unless there are special circumstances. It was integral to this case because Orrell had been led to the pawnbroker who had his wife's cloak by reading about Hogan's trial for theft. The judge continued by telling the jury that Pugh was not an entirely reliable witness, since she had not volunteered her knowledge of Hogan's guilt. He then summarised the various witnesses' sometimes confusing testimony in a clear and succinct manner and concluded:

> if you can find in the whole case, any reasonable ground of doubt, though you are not to go to conjectures and probabilities, to let a man escape justice, yet unquestionably, if you find any reasonable ground of doubt, you ought to acquit the prisoner.

The jury found Hogan guilty; he was sentenced to death and hanged.[55]

In the course of a burglary, Jeffrey Morat also assaulted a woman, but she survived. Morat was found guilty of theft and assault and sentenced to death, but died, unpardoned, in Newgate before he could be executed. His crime was a particularly nasty one: there was an element of sadism in his treatment of Hannah Emberton, a servant in the house he burgled. Morat was a servant of the Duchess of Manchester and it must be significant that no member of the noble family would either testify for him or petition the king for a reprieve.[56]

The conclusion must be that most of the Black people who were actually executed had either committed crimes that were regarded as exceptionally serious and/or lacked the influential friends necessary to obtain a reprieve. Comparison with white people committing similar crimes to Joseph Scott's shows that he was not treated more harshly than white men who had committed the same crime during the same period.

Transportation

In addition to those reprieved from a death sentence on condition of transportation, a number of Black people were transported for the crime they had committed. Until the American War of Independence started in 1775 most transportees were sent to America, but at least one, John Gibbons, went to either Nevis or Jamaica.[57] In 1788 transportation to Australia began. During the intervening thirteen years there were schemes to send criminals to West Africa, but they came to nothing.[58] The conditions and experiences of those sent to the Americas and of those who went to Australia were very different. Both Black and white convicts sent to the Americas were shipped as a commercial venture. Agents tendered for a contract to deliver them and on arrival they were sold like slaves to provide labour there. The experiences of the Black transportees cannot have been much different from those of slaves brought directly from Africa. For some Black people this might be their second experience of transportation across the Atlantic and enslavement. It is impossible to know whether they were freed at the end of their sentences or whether their masters ignored this because they were Black: there are no official records about their fates.

The transportees who went to Australia, however, were sent to populate the continent. There was a government scheme to give people their liberty (and a grant of land) at the end of their sentences. Three Black men sentenced to transportation in the years 1775–88 do not appear in the record of the first fleets to Australia. They may have been among the few sent to West Africa as soldiers, or they may have died in the noxious conditions of the hulks where convicts were sent to await transportation. It is noticeable that the books detailing the descendants of those who sailed with the first three fleets seem to include none of the Black transportees, although, since several had common names which they shared with white transportees, it is impossible to be categorical. This may be due to reluctance on the part of modern-day Australians to admit to Black ancestry: it is only comparatively recently that convict ancestry has not been a source of shame, and a Black convict as an ancestor might be a step too far. Alternatively, they may not have had, unlike the white transportees, a commitment to recreate a society on a British model. Ian Duffield, for example, sees John Caesar's decision to take to the bush as recreation of the marronage that existed in Jamaica.[59]

Twenty-seven Black people were sentenced to transportation before 1775, either because their death sentence had been commuted or because that was their sentence. Twenty-one were transported; one, John Hogan, was sentenced to transportation but tried for another offence before this could be carried out; two, possibly three, died in Newgate[60] and the fates of the remaining two or three are not known. They may have died before they could be put on a ship or may have been on ships for which records do not survive. Alternatively, their masters, unwilling to lose the services of an expensive and otherwise good servant, may have been able to keep them in this country by giving sureties for their good behaviour but the pardons have not survived. A man who had been about to take Paul Lewis Zafier into his employment when Zafier broke into a house undertook to return him to his Pondicherry, his home.[61] John Thomas, mentioned previously, was returned to his masters in Jamaica after one of the family appeared as a character witness. These men were therefore not so much transported as repatriated.

Black prosecutors

There are far fewer instances of Black people prosecuting crimes committed against them than as defendants. Although some may have felt themselves vulnerable and not wanted to come to the attention of the authorities, what is surprising is the willingness of Black people to prosecute crimes and the confidence they displayed in court. In many cases, especially those involving lascars who did not speak English, they must have had help to negotiate their way through the process. It would be reasonable to presume that masters helped their servants to bring prosecutions, but there are a number who did not have this kind of assistance. Several said they were servants 'out of place'. Whether they approached previous employers or were simply familiar enough with the process and confident enough to undertake it themselves does not appear. Some probably had help from fellow servants. By the mid eighteenth century Black servants were organised enough to belong to associations to help the temporarily unemployed and these may well have provided the necessary support and expertise.[62] In one case, that of Edward James, who was assaulted and subjected to a demand for money, there is explicit testimony that he was supported in his complaint against John Sommers, or Sommerville, an Irishman. James said that Justice Hole, who was walking in the vicinity where he was attacked, encouraged him to report the crime, and he may well have told him how to go about it.[63]

Crimes committed against Black people were overwhelmingly theft, sometimes involving assault. Two were assaulted without being robbed. There are no records of burglaries, which suggests that few Black people had houses or businesses to break into or were involved in dealing with large sums of money (forgery and counterfeiting were common crimes among the white population). Nor were any rich enough to be owner or hirer of a coach which was held up, although a couple of servants were involved as witnesses in such cases. The small number of Black prosecutors is therefore an indication of their comparative lack of wealth. To judge by the *Proceedings*, cases of rape were not uncommon, but in the sole rape case involving a Black man, John Sutton, the alleged victim, Mary Swain, was 'a mulatto'. They seem to have had some kind of previous relationship and Sutton was acquitted.[64]

Indictments on coroners' warrants

Until 1977, the jury at a coroner's inquest could name the person they believed to be responsible for the crime that caused the death, like murder or manslaughter. The person was then committed to trial on a coroner's warrant. In the 148 years of trial reports covered by the *Proceedings* between 1674 and 1812 there were only five trials arising from inquests that involved Black or Asian victims: the murder of a Black man by a white man; a trial resulting from the death of a lascar through neglect; the death of a Black man at the hands of his white cohabitee; the murder of a mixed-race woman by her white husband; and the case of a Malay man killed by three of his compatriots.

Neither Henry Oliver, a Black man, nor John Burnham had a good day on 7 March 1741/2. Both had already had unpleasant experiences when they encountered each other. Oliver had been robbed in an alehouse by two women, one Black and one white, after he had bought them three half-crowns' worth (7s 6d) of punch. Oliver made a fuss and was ejected, along with the women. In the street, Oliver and the Black woman fought and the woman scratched Oliver's face above his eye. The wound bled profusely. Despite being advised to go home, Oliver hung around for another hour and a half, presumably planning what to do. Some time after Oliver's experience, in a completely unrelated event, a woman picked the pocket of a sea captain. Unfortunately for her, he was leading a press gang, who captured her and took her to the watch-house. John Burnham was running down the street at the time, carrying a stick and a dagger. One of the press gang snatched the stick and punched Burnham, who fell over. Oliver watched the woman being arrested and, seeing someone who was, like him, apparently a victim of theft, remarked to Burnham that the woman was a whore who deserved to be hanged. Although Oliver could not have known this, it was not the most tactful thing to say to Burnham: the woman being arrested was his wife and she was a prostitute.[65] Unexpectedly, Burnham lashed out, striking Oliver in the eye and then on the shoulder with his dagger. A bystander shouted, 'The Fellow has kill'd the Black!' Burnham fled but was pursued and captured by a crowd of people. At the trial Burnham tried to suggest that it was the first injury to Oliver's forehead caused by the woman who robbed him that had led to his death, but a surgeon who had carried out a post-mortem testified otherwise. Burnham was found guilty of murder, sentenced to death and hanged.[66]

Although the account of the trial of Jacob Jeggett in 1783 did not explicitly say that he had been indicted on a coroner's warrant, the mention of jurors in the charge and witness evidence makes it clear that this was the case. The phrasing of the charge is also typical of the careful and exact wording employed by Thomas Phillips, then the County Coroner for the Eastern Division of Middlesex:

> that he, on the 6th of November, about the hour of eleven at night, on John Dullen, then and there lying on a certain bed in a certain dwelling house, then and there being situated, and being there and then ill, and languishing, and unable to walk and support himself, feloniously, wilfully, and with malice aforethought, did make an assault, and did take, remove and carry him, at a late unreasonable hour of the night, into a certain street or lane of the King's highway called Rose Lane, and he, the said Jacob Jeggett, the said John Dullen did take, carry, remove, drive, and force into the said street, and then and there did leave the said John Dullen against his will and consent, whereby the said John Dullen, through cold and for want of due necessaries for a person in such sickness, did remain and languish for three-quarters of an hour, and then and there died, and so the jurors on their oath did say that he the said John Dullen did kill and murder.

The coroner's papers seem not to have survived, but the evidence at the inquest was almost certainly substantially the same as that given at the Old Bailey and the testimonies there are the only way of knowing Dullen's ethnic origin, which was not given in the inquest verdict. Jeggett was found not guilty of murder but the judge did not leave the matter there. Although he found that the verdict was legally justifiable, he added, 'A more barbarous and inhuman thing I never heard', and detained Jeggett to see if there were grounds for proceeding with a charge of assault.[67] Presumably there were not, because there is no other case involving Jeggett in the *Proceedings*.

In 1789, William Woodcock was charged with the murder of his wife, Silvia. She was described as a mulatto, but witnesses did not know from where she came, although *The Times* reported that she had been brought to England from India and worked for 'a respectable family' for thirty years.[68] The couple, both then servants, had married in Cheshunt, Hertfordshire in 1779.[69] They lived together until 1787, when William got a job working for a gentleman in London. His wife lived in Enfield, in North Middlesex, and he visited her regularly. Then, in 1789 he had banns called in Westminster to marry another woman, claiming to be a bachelor. The day after the banns were called for the second time, Silvia was found dying in a ditch in Chelsea, horrifically wounded. She was taken to the workhouse, where she deposed to a magistrate that her husband had attacked her. Despite receiving medical care, she died four days later. The parish authorities offered a substantial reward and William, by now married to another woman, was arrested. In his lodgings were found a bundle containing a handkerchief he had purchased when in Enfield; a bludgeon which had blood on it and a black satin cloak, also stained with blood. At the trial, evidence was given that William had gone to Enfield to take his wife to London under the pretext of having work for her to do cleaning a house in Holborn. He was found guilty, sentenced to death and executed.[70]

The death of Joseph Walker in 1808 was also a domestic killing. Walker was, like Dullen, a seafarer, but whether he was a lascar or of African origin was not revealed. He lived with Ann Thompson in Denmark Street, East Smithfield, where there were a number of lodging houses for mariners. On 26 December 1807, Walker came home drunk. Thompson refused to let him in: he seems to have had a history of assaulting her, but he managed to gain entry and the two fought. Thompson defended herself with a lighted candle, burning Walker's face. He beat a hasty retreat but returned later. This time, Thompson defended herself with a knife and Walker was stabbed in the left side. He was taken to the London Hospital in Whitechapel but died. Although Ann Thompson was indicted on a coroner's warrant for murder, she was found guilty of manslaughter and sentenced to three months' imprisonment in Newgate and a one shilling fine.[71] Later in the same year three 'Malayans', Sacchar, Glosse and Savau, were accused of assaulting Imambacchus, who died of his injuries. They too were found guilty of manslaughter and sentenced to a year in Newgate and a fine of one shilling each.[72]

In none of these cases involving death or murder was there any suggestion that the victim had been targeted because of colour or ethnic origin. Elsewhere in the country there are a few trials resulting from the murders of Black people, where the motive was theft, like the killing of George Harford, a Black sailor,[73] but these are few and again seem not to have been the result of prejudice. Nor have any inquest records on a Black person where no murderer was brought to justice yet been found. It is possible that one or two of the unknown Black people 'found drowned' in rivers and ports were the victims of murder or manslaughter, but there is no evidence for this, nor of the killers' motives, which, on the evidence from cases where people were brought to trial, are more likely to be theft or a quarrel than racial reasons.

Verdicts passed on people who committed crimes against Black people 1674–1812

Only five people were brought to trial for crimes committed against Black women. Three were found guilty and two were acquitted. This small number makes any statistical conclusion unreliable. It is therefore only possible to look at the treatment of Black *men* who were victims of crime (Tables 6 and 7).

It looks as if those who committed crimes against Black men were more likely than on average to be found guilty and less likely to have the charge reduced, and the acquittal rate is slightly lower than for all

Table 6 Verdicts passed on men committing crimes against Black men

Verdict	No. of cases	Percentage	Percentage of all cases at Old Bailey
Guilty as charged	16	61.54	40.55
Guilty (reduced)	4	15.38	20.08
Acquitted	6	23.08	38.26
Totals	**26**	**100.00**	**98.89**[a]

Note: [a] In some cases there was no verdict or the sentence was respited.

The criminal justice system

Table 7 Verdicts passed on women committing crimes against Black men

Verdict	No. of cases	Percentage	Percentage of all cases at Old Bailey
Guilty as charged	10	37.04	35.53
Guilty (reduced)	4	14.82	20.29
Acquitted	13	48.15	42.28
Totals	**27**	**100.01**	**98.10**[a]

Note: [a] In some cases there was no verdict or the sentence was respited.

crimes tried at the Old Bailey. As noted earlier, it appears that Black men who committed crimes were treated more harshly than their white counterparts, but those who committed crimes against Black men were also disproportionately penalised. Beyond these crude figures, an interesting picture emerges. There were twenty-six cases of men committing crimes against Black men and the verdicts passed on them were substantially different from the rate for all cases tried at the Old Bailey. These men were overwhelmingly more likely to be found guilty as charged, and slightly less likely to have the charge reduced or to be acquitted. It would be expected that considerably fewer women than men would be indicted for crime against Black men: only 39.79 per cent of the total number of defendants at the Old Bailey were female. There were, however, more cases (27) of women committing crimes against Black men. This is explicable by looking at the nature of those crimes, which were overwhelmingly committed by one or two women stealing from a man, often after getting him drunk. The men were mainly mariners or servants out on errands, and the naivety displayed by some of them was marked: they seem not to have suspected any ulterior motive on the women's part beyond their own personal attractiveness (Illustration 7). It was an extremely common kind of theft and the courts probably took the view that men who were that stupid deserved what they got. Beattie noted that judges and juries in Surrey had little patience with men who allowed themselves to be duped like this.[74] Ann Duck, the mixed-race serial criminal mentioned above, preyed on white men in this way and was acquitted four times. There is less difference in the verdicts passed on women. Although the guilty-as-charged rate was effectively the same, it seems that women who committed crimes against Black men were less likely to be found guilty on a lesser charge and slightly more likely to be acquitted. This may be explicable in terms of the type of crime, which

7. A potential typical crime involving a Black person, attributed to Thomas Rowlandson (1756–1827). Black sailors were frequently the target of two women working together to relieve them of their wages and prize money.

was generally simple theft, or it may be evidence of a belief that Black men were less deserving of the court's protection where women were concerned. If the latter were true, however, a much higher acquittal rate would be expected.

Witnesses

At least seventeen Black people were called as witnesses to a crime. In most cases, they were one of a number of witnesses: the jury did not decide on guilt or innocence on their testimony alone, so it is impossible to draw any conclusions about the attitudes of the courts towards evidence given by Black people, beyond noting that it was accepted, unlike the situation in the Americas, where Blacks were not allowed to testify against white people. Only two Black people, both men called in the same case, seem to have acted as character witnesses.[75] Most character witnesses seem to have been, where their circumstances can be determined, householders or people with some social standing, so this is probably further evidence of the scarcity of Black people in positions of relative authority, although there was a Black parish constable in Clerkenwell in 1746 who gave evidence against a woman accused and convicted of theft.[76]

Black prosecutors and witnesses were routinely questioned about their religious beliefs, asked if they had been baptised and/or whether they understood the implications of lying on oath. In 1727 Richard Rose, a white defendant '(being a good Christian)', begged the court to consider 'the Prosecutor was but an Infidel'. As the *Proceedings* noted with some asperity 'but he [John Humphreys] proving a Form of Baptism had been administered to him, this Artifice was but of little Effect, for the Jury found him guilty'.[77] Another defendant accused of theft from a Black man demanded that his prosecutor be asked if he was baptised. He probably regretted this: Thomas Farrow replied that Lord Grantham was his godfather, which, in a status-conscious world, must have added to his credibility.[78] When Guardaloup, 'a Black boy', was called to give evidence he was asked how long he had been in England. He said three years. 'Have you', was the next enquiry, 'been taught any principles of religion?' Guardaloup's reply, 'No: I know nothing of religion,' meant that he was not sworn and therefore not allowed to testify.[79] The issue is a more complex one than simple racial or cultural prejudice. Another Black boy, who was one of a party robbed by a highwayman, said he had been baptised and did give evidence.[80] In the case of John Thomas, a Black man accused of theft, one of the witnesses was a white boy, aged 9, who was asked if he knew his catechism, understood the nature of an oath upon the Bible and what the consequences would be if he lied.[81] There is further evidence that questioning about beliefs was not simple prejudice against Black people. The court seemed to be concerned to establish whether those testifying recognised a higher power that would punish them if they lied, because at least one Muslim was able to swear on the Qu'ran. In 1764, John Morgan from Bengal was robbed of various possessions by the family with whom he was lodging and he took them to court. The trial was delayed while the judges considered whether he could be 'sworn on the Alcoran'. They agreed unanimously that he could, but checked what this meant to him:

> John Morgan: I am a Mahometan.
> Q: In what manner are people of your profession sworn?
> Morgan: I touch the book, the Alcoran, with one hand, and put the other hand to my forehead: then I look upon it I am bound to speak the truth.[82]

He was not the first Bengali to appear at the Old Bailey: presumably the previous ones had sworn on the Bible, the Qu'ran had been accepted without any further discussion, or they had been allowed, as Quakers were, to affirm. Many, however, were apparently not asked about their beliefs (it is impossible to give exact figures because some accounts are simply summaries of the trial rather than full transcripts). It may be that only minors and those who did not speak English very well provoked this kind of question. Some of those described as 'Black' may have been of mixed race and therefore assumed to have been baptised. Defendants were not asked about baptism or the consequences of lying on oath; presumably because it was thought they would lie in any case.

Black women at the Old Bailey

There are relatively few studies of women involved in criminal trials. In most studies the emphasis is on men: women are discussed only in terms of not being men or in terms of the crimes where the majority of offenders would be female, such as infanticide or prostitution. Between 1674 and 1812 apparently only twenty-three cases involving Black women were heard at the Old Bailey. Five of these cases involved the same person, Ann Duck, so in fact only nineteen women appeared. This strikingly low figure could be due to a number of factors. The first is that fewer women were taken into slavery outside Africa. The proportion of men to women transported overseas is generally taken as approximately 2:1. In addition, even fewer came to Britain from the Americas and Caribbean. Even when adjustment is made for this imbalance, Black women seem to have been significantly more law abiding than either their white sisters or Black men. Whether or not women were indicted as often as men in comparable circumstances remains a moot point. As women were perceived as being the weaker sex, it is possible that their crimes were treated with more leniency at a lower level and cases involving them simply did not reach the higher courts. They may never have come before a magistrate: employers who would have brought a male employee to justice may have dealt with a female directly, either by dismissing her or by beating her. This may also be a factor in the small number of prosecutions brought by women. Domestic violence has only comparatively recently been taken seriously by the authorities: the right of a man to apply corporal punishment to his wife (and children and, at this period, servants, apprentices and other employees) was questioned only if it resulted in serious injury or death.[83] The distress shown by a Black servant, Pamela Clarke, when her employer's box was stolen while in her care may have been due to fear of such punishment.[84] Silvia Woodcock was murdered by her husband, but did not die as the result of domestic violence; she was murdered because he wished to marry another woman.[85]

Poverty is generally assumed to be a major factor contributing to crime. Black servants were in a relatively privileged position: their food, shelter and clothing were provided. During this period, three women who appeared at the Old Bailey were servants but only one of them had stolen from her employer.[86] Of those women whose occupation was given at the trials most were outside the support system supplied by an employer. Elizabeth Gift was a workhouse pauper.[87] Three were or appear to have been prostitutes: Mary Holliwell was robbed by a client who was, on her evidence, sentenced to transportation for seven years;[88] Ann Holman claimed she was assaulted by the keeper of a bawdy house where she took clients, but in this case the defendant was acquitted;[89] and Esther Allingham was acquitted of theft from a client.[90] In addition, Ann Duck had been a prostitute before she turned to theft.

Of the remaining women in this study, Mary Swain, who was mixed race, was a prosecutor in a case of rape and the defendant, a Black man, was acquitted. This, however, had little to do with race. As many studies have shown, it was rare for men to be found guilty of rape, even on children. The fact that the two seem to have had a relationship in the past may have been a contributory factor in the defendant's acquittal.[91] Hannah Bowling, a witness and co-prosecutor with her husband, was the wife of Thomas Bowling, said to be a captain in the West Indian Army, though this was before the West Indian Regiments were formed.[92] He was defrauded of money he had paid to a man in order to secure his release from a sponging house. Her colour may be deduced from the testimony of one of the witnesses in the case, who remarked that he had known Thomas 'in his white wife's time', which suggests, by contrast, that Hannah was Black, although this was not directly stated. The defendant in this case, a Jew, was found guilty and the judge had harsh words to say about his conduct.[93]

Nothing further is known about the remaining women. Elizabeth Mandeville was sentenced to transportation for theft in 1808.[94] Lucy Johnson was in Newgate awaiting transportation when the prison was broken open in the Gordon riots of 1780. She disappeared. Charlotte Gardiner was condemned to death and hanged for her part in these riots but, unlike Benjamin Bowsey and John Glover, Black men who were also involved in the riots and received the same sentence, Gardiner had no employer or former employer prepared to petition the authorities for a reprieve.[95]

Accounts of trials at the Old Bailey given in the *Proceedings* seem to show that Black people were not treated substantially differently from the general population. It must be emphasised, however, how few Black people there are among the cases tried there. Between 1674 and 1812 there were 66,282 trials but only around 200 (making a generous allowance for cases where colour/ethnic origin were not mentioned) involved Black people. There are apparently small variations, but this may be due to statistical factors: the small numbers involved may have distorted the results. The major interest in these trials therefore lies less in the treatment accorded to Black people than in the incidental information revealed about their lives that emerges from the evidence given both by them and by other people, which is indicated elsewhere, as in Chapter 3, where the status of servants is explored, and in Chapter 9 on working lives.

Notes

1. *Gazetteer or Daily Advertiser*, 9 March 1767, p. 2b and 11 March 1767, p. 2.
2. Mountain, J., *Sketches in the Life of Joseph Mountain compiled by David Daggett* (New Haven, CT, 1790). He was executed for rape in New Haven after returning to America.
3. *Parker's General Advertiser and Morning Intelligencer*, 4 September 1784, and *Morning Chronicle*, 12 October 1784, quoted in Sprott, D., *1784* (1984), pp. 208 and 241–2.

4. *Proceedings* 1782–3, VII, no. 656. Alternatively, Coffee might be Irish (Coffey is the usual spelling) and Benedick Dutch or German.
5. Paley, R. (ed.), *Justice in Eighteenth Century Hackney: the Justicing Notebook of Henry Norris* (1991), pp. 38–9. George Scipio's colour was important because the case hinged on identification by his appearance, since none of the Hackney witnesses said they actually knew him. It is possible that other cases in Norris's notebook involve Black people without mentioning their colour.
6. *Daily Post*, 18 March 1743/4, p. 3.
7. *Proceedings*, 1783–4, VII, no. 813. Lawrence was found guilty and sentenced to seven years' transportation.
8. *Proceedings* 1786–7, I, no. 28.
9. The website <www.oldbaileyonline.org> has cases from 1674 to 1913.
10. *Oxford Dictionary of National Biography*, XXIV, p. 295.
11. It is worth noting that during and after Gurney's period of office, Jews and Irish people were not routinely identified either. Gurney's predecessors and some of his successors did identify them.
12. *Proceedings* 1787–8, VI, no. 406; Rees, S., *The Floating Brothel* (2001), p. 127.
13. *Proceedings* 1766–7, VIII, no. 575.
14. In all the following cases, witness evidence is the only source of such information: *Proceedings* 1766–7, VIII, case no. 575; *Proceedings* 1754–5, no. 66; *Proceedings* 1765–6, I, no. 26. Similar cases appear in *Proceedings* 1745–6, nos 88 and 89; *Proceedings* 1751–2, nos 376 and 377; *Proceedings* 1751–2, nos 93 and 94; *Proceedings* 1764–5, no. 258; *Proceedings* 1764–5, no. 32; *Proceedings* 1765–6, no. 26; *Proceedings* 1765–6, nos 442 and 443; *Proceedings* 1765–6, no. 115; *Proceedings* 1766–7, no. 128; *Proceedings* 1766–7, no. 172; *Proceedings* 1768–9, no. 432; *Proceedings* 1771–2, no. 679; *Proceedings* 1779–80 nos 196 and 197; *Proceedings* 1785–6, no. 122; *Proceedings* 1793–4, no. 45; *Proceedings* 1804–5 no. 614; *Proceedings* 1807–8, no. 100.
15. *Proceedings* 1786–7, VIII, no. 559.
16. *Proceedings* 1784–5, I, no. 31.
17. *Proceedings* 1740–1, IV, no. 66; *Proceedings* 1747–8, III, no. 156.
18. *Proceedings* 1803–4, II, nos 106 and 107. It seems likely from her nickname that Mary Smith was a Black woman from America, but whether Rebecca Stanforth also was is not stated. Nor is it known how she got the nickname 'Birmingham'. I have omitted this case from my analyses because there is even less evidence of their colour than in the case of Sarah Lyons.
19. *Proceedings*, 1803–4, VIII, no. 558. The name is no help: foreign names were regularly translated or transliterated.
20. *Proceedings*, 1784–5, I, no. 101; Gillen, M., *The Founders of Australia: a Biographical Dictionary of the First Fleet* (Sydney, NSW, 1989), p. 134.
21. *Proceedings*, 1786–7, VI, no. 655.

22. *Proceedings* 1747-8, I, no. 141. Members of a family called Calabar also appear in the parish registers of St Edmund the King and Martyr in the City of London, GL, Ms 20,204-5. Possibly Ann was a second- or even third-generation descendant of a Black man.
23. *Proceedings* 1757-8, VII, no. 305.
24. *Proceedings*, 1783-4, IV, no. 392. Personation is the crime of representing oneself as someone else for fraudulent purposes. Impersonation is what entertainers do for comic purposes.
25. *Proceedings*, 1782-3, no. 626 and *Whitehall Evening Post*, 20-23 September 1783, p. 2. Although Joseph Scott, the defendant, was called 'a Black', it is unclear whether the sailor he intended to impersonate was also Black: the evidence is ambiguous.
26. *Proceedings*, 7-12 September 1722, p. 5. The two had known each other from previous service. Smith said 'he had no occasion to throw her down, for she was always willing' and claimed he was being prosecuted out of spite because they had quarrelled. He was acquitted.
27. Myers, *Reconstructing the Black Past*, p. 85.
28. *Proceedings* 1742-3, II, nos 77 and 297; *Proceedings* 1742-3 VI, no. 448; *Proceedings* 1742-3 VIII, nos 435 and 459.
29. King, P., *Crime, Justice and Discretion in England 1740-1820* (Oxford, 2000), pp. 309-10.
30. *Proceedings*, 1783-4, IV, no. 392.
31. Sherwood, M., 'Blacks in the Gordon Riots', *History Today* 47 (12) December 1998, pp. 24-8.
32. *Proceedings* 1782-3, VIII, no. 766. He was transported to the West Indies, presumably back to slavery in the family. However, it should be noted that he had left them to go to sea with their consent, and they were willing to testify for him at the Old Bailey, which suggests he had a privileged position in the household.
33. I have come across many examples of this in workshops I run on job-hunting skills. Barley, N. *The Innocent Anthropologist* (1983) and *A Plague of Caterpillars* (1986) are accounts of field trips among a West African tribe, the Dowayo, and provide many examples of differences in cultural practices.
34. *Proceedings* 1786-7, VI, no. 31.
35. *Proceedings* 7-12 September 1722, p. 6; Coldham, P.W., *The Complete Book of Emigrants in Bondage* (Baltimore, MD, 1998), p. 99.
36. *Proceedings* 1786-7, VI, no. 600 and *London Chronicle*, 16-18 September 1788, p. 2.
37. Official records are found in two record offices. TNA contains the fullest records of those transported by the national government, but people could also be sentenced at Quarter Sessions, in which case the county would make arrangements and bear the costs. LMA has documents detailing pardons and commutations from 1667 to 1826 but relatively few years are represented. Those for

The criminal justice system

1785–96 are missing altogether and in most cases not all the reprieves/pardons for a particular year survive. Only two pardons in the period 1700–1812 survive. The extant transportation records there are also incomplete.

38. Jeffrey Morat, Ordinary's *Account*, 3 March 1736/7, and Thomas Cesar, bur. 12 April 1726, HS 21 *The Registers of Christchurch Newgate*.
39. Thomas Robinson, *Proceedings*, 17 January 1723–4. There is no newspaper account of an execution, nor an Ordinary's *Account* mentioning him. Nor is there a burial entry relating to him in the registers of Christchurch Newgate.
40. *Proceedings* 14–21 October 1724; Ordinary's *Account* , 11 November 1724.
41. McLynn, F., *Crime and Punishment in Eighteenth Century England* (1989), pp. 83–7, details other arson cases.
42. *Proceedings* 1737–8, VI, no. 7; *Proceedings* 1748–9, VIII, no. 528.
43. *Proceedings* 1766–7, III, no. 172; *Gazetteer*, 11 February 176, p. 2.
44. *Proceedings* 1763–4, I, no. 22; Coldham, P.W., *The Complete Book of Emigrants in Bondage*, p. 257.
45. King, *Crime, Justice and Discretion*, pp. 298–9, examines and quantifies the many factors.
46. Shaw, A.L., *Convicts and the Colonies* (1998), pp. 164; Gillen, *The Founders of Australia*, pp. 453–535, contains an abstract of those transported, including the age at which they were sentenced.
47. Ordinary's *Account*, 3 March 1736–37(Morat died in Newgate); 19 July 1739 and 18 October 1749.
48. Ordinary's *Account*, 7 November 1744, pp. 6ff.
49. *Proceedings* 1778–9, IV, no. 312. Johnson escaped from Newgate, where she was awaiting transportation, when it was broken open in the Gordon Riots: *Morning Chronicle*, 8 July 1779, p. 3.
50. *Proceedings* 1782–3, VII, no. 636; *Whitehall Evening Post*, 20–23 September 1783, p. 2.
51. Gillen, M., *The Founders of Australia*, pp. 165, 225 and 298.
52. He said he was from Bengal. The *Newgate Calendar* said he was from the Madeiras. Whether he was a fair-skinned or mixed-race Asian or of African origin (the Portuguese had African slaves in Maderia and in India) was never specified.
53. Shyllon, *Black People*, pp. 89ff.
54. Although, as mentioned previously, John Thomas was returned to his country of origin, and another, Paul Zafier, mentioned later, was also returned to his native country, this was because people were willing to be sureties for their good behaviour there. There was no one to make such an undertaking for Hogan.
55. *Proceedings* 1785–6, I, no. 122 and Knapp, A. & Baldwin, W., *The Newgate Calendar* (1824), pp. 37–8.
56. *Proceedings* 1736–7, III, no. 21; Ordinary's *Account*, 3 March 1736–7, p. 10; *Daily Gazetteer*, 4 March 1737, p. 2.

57. Coldham, P.W., *Bonded Passengers to America* (Baltimore, MD, 1983), p. 105.
58. Oldham, W., *Britain's Convicts to the Colonies* (Sydney, NSW, 1990), pp. 95–108.
59. Duffield, I., 'From Slave Colonies to Penal Colonies: the West Indian Convict Transportees to Australia', *Slavery & Abolition* 7 (1986), pp. 29–45, at p. 30. John Caesar committed his crime in Deptford. Duffield seems surprised that he was tried at Maidstone Assizes, rather than in London, but this is because, until the 1888 Local Government Act, Deptford was, for administrative purposes, in Kent and the county assizes were held in Maidstone. John Caesar is the only pre-1831 Black transportee he mentions in this article, but there were many others.
60. HS 21, *The Registers of Christ Church Newgate 1538–1754*: Thomas Casar, bur. 'from Newgate', 12 April 1726; John Nichols, bur. 27 June 1737, and Robert Cadogan, who may be the Robert Cadoy 'prisoner' bur. 18 September 1732.
61. *Proceedings* 1791–2, IV, no. 195.
62. Fryer, *Staying Power*, p. 69.
63. *Proceedings*, 1744–5, IV, no. 206.
64. *Proceedings* 1774–5, IV, no. 24.
65. Ordinary's *Account*, 12 July 1742.
66. *Proceedings* 1741–2, IV, no. 45; Ordinary's *Account*, 12 July 1742; The *Country Journal*, 17 July 1742, p. 2.
67. *Proceedings* 1793–4, I, no. 45.
68. *The Times*, 6 November 1788, p. 3c. It never emerges whether she was of Indian or African origin or which parent was white. Though she is most likely to have had Indian parentage, the presence of African slaves in Asia means she may have had African ancestry.
69. SoG, unpublished transcript, HT/R 62, Registers of Cheshunt, Hertfordshire, 12 January 1779. Her name appears in the entry as Silvey Sidley.
70. *Proceedings* 1788–9, II, no. 98. His body was given to the anatomists, a sign of the opprobrium his crime attracted.
71. *Proceedings* 1807–8, II, no. 100.
72. *Proceedings* 1807–8, V, no. 395.
73. *Gloucester Journal*, 4 June and 20 August 1764. In this case, the murderer confessed to at least three other killings, presumably of white persons, since their colour is not mentioned. I am grateful to Roger Jaques, a descendant of a collateral branch of the murderer's family, for this information. The Gloucester Gaol Book, incidentally, does not mention Harford's colour.
74. Beattie, J.M., 'Crime and the Courts in Surrey 1736–1753', in Beattie, J.M., *Crime in England 1550–1800* (Princeton, NJ, 1986), p. 168.
75. *Proceedings* 1766–7, II, no. 128.
76. *Proceedings* 1745–6, II, no. 100.
77. *Proceedings* 17–18 May 1727, p. 2.

78. *Proceedings* 1735-6, II, no. 35.
79. *Proceedings* 1764-5, I, no. 1.
80. *Proceedings* 22-25 February 1727/8, p. 1.
81. *Proceedings* 1782-3, VIII, no. 766.
82. *Proceedings* 1764-5, II, nos. 154, 155 and 156.
83. On 7 May 1822 the *Manchester Guardian* carried an account of the trial of a cotton spinner who flogged a 12-year-old boy he employed, giving him between twenty and thirty blows with a birch rod. He was acquitted, mainly because the boy had previously assaulted other workers in the factory. Reproduced in the *Guardian*, 7 May 2007, p. 26.
84. *Proceedings* 1785-6, VII, no. 746.
85. *Proceedings* 1788-9, II, no. 98.
86. In addition, one servant was not called because she did not speak English well enough. The defendant (almost certainly white) claimed that this girl had either lost or stolen the goods she herself was accused of stealing. *Proceedings* 1798-9, I, no. 4.
87. *Proceedings* 1754-5, II, no. 66.
88. *Proceedings* 1794-5, IV, no. 189.
89. *Proceedings* 1800-1, VI, no. 646.
90. *Proceedings* 1781-2, III, no. 372.
91. *Proceedings* 1774-5, IV, no. 24.
92. He may have served in the regular army with a regiment stationed in the West Indies. This must await further research.
93. *Proceedings* 1794-5, VI, no. 362.
94. *Proceedings* 1807-8, IV, no. 312.
95. *Proceedings* 1799-80, VI, no. 361.

Chapter 5

Black people, settlement and the poor laws

The third area of the law which had particular application to Black people was that surrounding the continuing problem of caring for the poor and destitute. Poverty among Black people does not seem to have caused particular problems before the end of the American War of Independence, when many came to England, particularly London. Their plight led to a Committee for the Relief of the Black Poor and then to the establishment of the Sierra Leone project. However, the way the poor laws were implemented has implications for how Black people and other ethnic groups are recorded in official records. One of the difficulties of identifying Black people is that colour or ethnicity are not always entered, as has already been seen in the court records. Black people are most often identified in the parish registers recording baptisms of adults, but there are also baptisms of a few children with Black parents. There are considerably fewer burials than baptisms: on the database between 1660 and 1812, for every burial there are there are five baptisms. There are even fewer entries in marriage registers where colour is mentioned: only forty have so far been found, plus one marriage licence, and a marriage that did not take place because the groom was not baptised.[1] The first marriage where a Black person was mentioned occurred in 1613, when Samuel Munsur, 'Blackamore', married Jane Johnson in Deptford, Kent.[2] Given his surname, he may have been an Arab, from the Indian subcontinent, or a Muslim Black African. The small number of Black people mentioned in marriage registers may not be because few married: it is often the record of the birth of a child to a Black person that alerts the researcher to look for and find a marriage. For example, Christopher, the son of Christopher and Harriot Stokes, was baptised on 4 September 1789 in Fowey, Cornwall, when his father was described as a 'Negro'. The couple had married nineteen months before, also in Fowey, on 15 February 1788, but colour was not recorded in that particular official record. Christopher Stokes Senior was simply noted to be 'of HM Ship Sprightly'.[3] In 1737, in Lowestoft, Suffolk, John Juba was christened and married by licence on the same day, but his colour was given only in the baptism entry.[4] The immediate question is, therefore, why colour or origin were so important for baptisms, less important for burials but of much less significance than either for marriages. The answer seems to lie in the administration of the poor laws, for which the parish authorities were responsible. Information given in entries in baptism and burial records seems to be primarily related to settlement under the poor laws, not to ethnic origin. Birth and residence in a parish, but not marriage, had implications for an individual's status. The two marriages mentioned above where one of the parties' colour is recorded took place before the concept of settlement was introduced in 1662. This has implications not just for historians working on Black history but also for those studying all ethnic minorities and for demographers looking at mobility, migration and assimilation/integration.

The poor laws 1660–1812

Before the Reformation and the dissolution of the monasteries, the care of the poor largely devolved upon the church. After the Church of England was established in 1533, the obligation of caring for the destitute, the elderly and the sick fell upon the Anglican parish. The first law mentioning the 'Relief of the Poor' was passed in 1547. The government wanted to make it easy for people to seek work, so the initial aim of the law was to facilitate the free movement of labour. Some parishes complained that they were being swamped by poor people because they were more generous than their neighbours. Regulations to define which parish had financial responsibility therefore became necessary and the concept of settlement was introduced in 1662, coincidentally about the time that Britain's involvement with the African slave trade began in earnest. Settlement was not abolished until 1876, although its operation was greatly altered by the 1834 Poor Law Amendment Act, which set up unions of parishes. In addition to the various poor laws passed between 1660 and 1812, there were statutes relating to individual towns and cities, as well as other amendments and changes produced by such events as the Mansfield Judgment of 1772 on the status of Black servants in England and Wales. There were also laws relating to vagrants and beggars. These, though they may have affected some Black people, had no effect on what was written in parish registers beyond a note that the person concerned was an itinerant.

Before 1662, various Acts had established that the parish had responsibilities for supporting those unable to work and binding orphan children as apprentices. To do this, they collected money from parishioners in the form of rates based on the size of the property they owned or rented. The parish authorities also had to provide work for those who were able to do so but did not have a job. Workhouses were built and administered by individual parishes or by groups of parishes to shelter the indigent and infirm and to provide a place where those fit enough could work. In addition, each county had at least one House of Correction for beggars, idle persons and mothers of bastards, who were largely punished by whipping, either there or in public, and by hard labour. By an Act of 1653 passed during the Commonwealth period, registrars (called 'registers') were appointed to maintain the records. This Act was not repealed after the Restoration, so the position remained. Although ministers were expected to keep their own registers, in many parishes the task was delegated to the parish clerk. I use the word 'clerk' to describe whoever made the entries in the registers, whether minister, curate or parish clerk.

As the Anglican church was also part of the government, its records were a mixture of the religious and the legal and they were used in court cases. It is often assumed that descriptions of people in registers 'were entirely at the whim of the parish clerk',[5] and to an extent this is true, because there were no mandatory rules about what information had to be given before the introduction of printed registers. The Marriage Act of 1753 introduced preprinted registers which required the parishes of the two parties (not colour or ethnic origin) to be recorded. After this date only marriages carried out in the parish church or by Quaker or Jewish ceremonies were legally recognised.[6] When printed registers for baptisms and burials were brought in by the Parochial Registers Act of 1812 these too required 'abode' to be entered. In the centuries before printed registers, however, patterns of what information was generally recorded changed in line with the law. Parish authorities had to keep up with significant modifications. The *London Gazette* and county newspapers covered Parliament extensively, so presumably officials relied on them to keep abreast of legal initiatives which would affect their work, supplemented by legal advice and numerous published guides to parochial authorities' legal obligations, like *The Compleat Parish Officer*.[7] These contained summaries of the law and legal cases related to settlement which had established precedents. All laws, however, have to be interpreted, and the quality of the advice clerks received or their own understanding of the implications must account for variations in what was entered in different parishes' records. The authorities who used the numerous guides to parish law that were published in the long eighteenth century would find no mention of slaves or slavery there. Although these guides usually had a section dealing with people from other countries in the British Isles, like Scotland and Ireland, there was no mention of people from the American or Caribbean colonies, whether enslaved or free. There was therefore no category in which to fit the rare destitute Black person who came to the notice of the parish authorities and they had to make their own interpretation about his or her status.

The 1662 Poor Relief Act introduced the concept of settlement: the definition of which parish had responsibility for an individual. People could be removed to their parish of settlement within forty days of their arrival in a parish if they did not rent a house worth more than £10 per annum, whether or not they were destitute. Legitimate children took their father's parish of settlement. If that could not be determined (because, for example, he had absconded or died), they took their mother's settlement status. Illegitimate children became the responsibility of the parish where they were born and their position is discussed later. People gained settlement in a parish, and thus the right to be supported in a number of ways – should they become unable to look after themselves and their families – which changed over the centuries. Those that affected the majority of Black people were being born in a parish (the majority, of course, were not) or working for at least one year for a master who had settlement in a parish and, crucially, receiving wages. Others, like being bound as an apprentice, owning or renting property worth a certain sum or serving as a parish official, were less applicable to the majority of Black people, though they included some. Marriage in a parish had no significance under this system.

Conscientious clerks seem to have ensured that anything which could be used as evidence should there later be any dispute about a person's settlement status was included in the entries, primarily because of the financial implications for the parish. In terms of proving settlement, baptism was the most important event because birth was the primary way of gaining it. A person's settlement might also depend on the mother's or father's status, so details of origin were sometimes included in burial entries, presumably in case many years later a claimant requested assistance because of his or her father's or mother's settlement. This is probably why ethnic origin was included in the baptismal entries for some babies, but not in the record of their burial. Millicent, daughter of Eliz. Thompson by John Giffin 'a negro', was christened in 1771 in Birchanger,

Essex. When she was buried the following year, only her name 'Millicent Giffin alias Thompson' was given.[8] She was too young to have had children who might have some claim on the parish. The son of Christopher Stokes, mentioned above, was buried two years after his baptism and his name was simply annotated 'an infant' without any mention of his or his father's colour.[9] Legally, however, burial entries required only the name of the deceased, and that is as much as some parishes included up to 1812.

Whether the Black servants (as they are almost invariably called) who came to Britain from the colonies with their masters were paid or not as a matter of course is still a moot point, but if they fell on hard times this was critical to decisions about their welfare made by parish officials. The essential factor in deciding a servant's place of settlement was whether or not he or she was paid. Those Black people who were not paid were outside the law requiring parishes to support them, as were white people who were not receiving wages. Some parishes, however, do not seem to have enforced the laws rigidly, but showed generosity to poor people who, strictly speaking, had no claim on them. In 1765 the parochial officers of Greenwich, for example, took John English into the workhouse when his master left him behind. The minutes for 2 February noted:

Ordered:
That Mr Everest be desired to write a Letter to Captain Bolton at Harrow on the Hill to take his Black named John English out of the workhouse.
That the s[aid] John English be admitted.

The letter does seem to have been written and a reply received, because on 9 March 1765 it was recorded:

That Mr Everest [be desired, erased] do write to Captain Bolton to acquaint him that the Black Man who formerly lived with him is willing to go abroad and that Capt. Bolton will get a passage for him according to his promises in his letter of the 2 instant and to desire him to pay the Expense of keeping him in the workhouse.[10]

It is not clear whether the unfortunate John English was paid or unpaid. The request for his master to pay for his maintenance suggests three possibilities: first, he was not paid; second, he had worked for Captain Bolton for less than a year, because if he had been employed for more than a year and been paid the parish would simply have accepted its responsibilities and supported him, as seems to have been done elsewhere. In Huntingdon, for example, the workhouse records note distribution of clothes to a 'Black Girl' receiving parish relief.[11] The third possibility was that Captain Bolton did not have settlement in Greenwich: a paid servant's settlement was dependent on the master's.

Before 1662, registers tend to include very little information beyond name and father of the child being baptised, although some included the mother; and for burials, simply the individual's name. After 1662 parishes started to note the parish of origin of strangers. Black people and other 'strangers' were noted, presumably because of the parish's responsibility to support its own poor. How far this extended to non-English people was always unclear.[12] The 1691 Poor Relief Act provided additional ways of gaining settlement. These methods were by paying rates; by serving as a parish official; by being bound as an apprentice to or being the servant of a master settled in the parish. Servants had to work for the same master, who also had to be settled, for a year before they qualified for settlement. Parishes began to note whether those adults who were baptised or buried, whatever their colour or origin, were servants or apprentices, usually with the name of their master. Although the colour of many Black servants was recorded, there are other cases where this may not have been the case before 1691. In 1667, for example, Jonathan Streames, servant to Mr John Streames, was buried in St Sepulchre, London. Whether Jonathan was a relation of John or a Black servant given the same surname as his master is unknown.[13]

The 1693/4 and 1695 Taxation Acts introduced tax on parish register entries for five years. The parish was responsible for collecting the taxes. Fines were levied on people who did not notify the minister of the birth of a child, even if it was not christened. This was relatively easy to do in a small parish, but was more difficult in large towns and cities or where the population was widely spread across remote settlements, and another Act was passed in 1705 to indemnify parish officials from failure to comply. The effect of these Acts continued after the end of the five-year period and clerks continued to note the date of birth of a child as well as its baptism, and also to give the ages of those, like Black people, who were not infants. As many of those born in Africa often did not know the year of their birth as reckoned by the Christian system, where only an approximate age is given it may suggest that a Black person had been born there. Those from North America and the Caribbean, where a European system of bureaucracy and a legal system that depended on age prevailed, mainly knew at least the year, and quite often the day and month of their birth, like Thomas Clements, 'a Black from Jamaica Aged 17 Years', baptised in 1776 in Westminster.[14]

The 1696/7 Relief of the Poor Act introduced settlement certificates. Parishes agreed to indemnify people from their own parish if they became chargeable to another and issued certificates to those intending to move elsewhere. People with certificates could not be removed to their home parish until they became chargeable. This made some parishes reluctant to baptise anyone without a certificate whose status they were not sure about, in case it gave them rights. Annotations like 'stranger', 'traveller', 'sojourner', 'Dutch', 'French' become more frequent. In some cases the reasoning behind decisions to baptise or not was added. The gap between what the law said and what happened in practice could be wide. Some parishes were relatively lax in enforcing the letter of the law, but an entry in the baptismal register of Wimbledon, Surrey shows to what extent some parish authorities would go to prevent poor people gaining settlement:

> Susanna, d. of Moses and Mary Cooper, Travellers, born in Martin [Merton] and the poor Woman being Desirous to have it Baptized tho' she had lain in but a week carried it in her own Arms to Martin Church to tender it to me to Baptize it there on Sunday last being June ye 30th. But Justice Meriton being Inform'd by the Constable of her being in the Porch with that Intention went out of his seat in time of Service to her, and took hold of her, and led her to the Court of his House, being over against the Church and shut the Gate upon her and her Husband and Let them not out 'till sermon and service were over & I was gone Home and made the Man Mittinus [sic] to send him to the House of Correction if he would not carry his wife and child out of the parish without being Baptized and consequently Registred [sic] there ... .[15]

Other parishes were explicit about the need for people to be able to prove their place of settlement. The records of St Helen Bishopsgate and St Olave Hart Street in the City of London contain several notes about the birth of Jews in these parishes in the late eighteenth century. The clerk of St Olave, for example, recorded that 'Barent the Son of Solomon and Lea Gompertz was born in this parish April 13 1777 which is here noted at the request of his Father as it may be of service to him hereafter, tho a Jew, to know his parish'. The Gompertz' son Lion had been entered in 1766. In the same year, John 'son of Richard and Sarah Butler supposed to be a Romish priest, but is here registered at Mr Butler's request' was noted.[16] I have not yet found a similar entry for a Black person, but it seems likely that they too were regarded as the parish's responsibility, whether baptised into the Church of England or not.

Some parish authorities were careful to discover and record the origins of all those they baptised, both Black and white, and to note the reasons for decisions made about whether or not to baptise someone. Ashtead in Surrey had a series of punctilious clerks and many entries contain addenda. On 3 November 1726, for example, Elizabeth Bulpin, daughter of Alexander and Ann, was baptised, but only after some investigation into her legitimacy. As a note says, her mother 'was a servant to the Lady of the Manor – no father seen or heard of but on 20th mother produced a letter from husband so child was registered'.[17] At this time illegitimate children became the responsibility of the parish, regardless of the parents' place of settlement. As Elizabeth's parents (who were almost certainly white) were married, the infant took the settlement of the absent father, so Ashtead baptised her but gave the additional information, intended to safeguard the parish's position should there be any dispute later. Other parishes were more generous. The register of Chigwell in Essex carried an entry in 1744 which stated: 'Joseph Ricketts base s. of [blank] born in a house in Gravelly Lane disputed between Lambourne and Chigwell. Upon the refusal of the parson of Lambourne christened at Chigwell.' The clerk was, however, careful to record the circumstances of the baptism.[18]

Other parish clerks either were less thorough or the concept was so deeply internalised that they simply noted 'stranger', 'foreigner', 'traveller', 'sojourner', 'Dutch', 'French', etc. It is not just Black and other people of foreign origin who are singled out. Even English people who for one reason or another wanted ceremonies conducted in a different church from their local one had their parish of origin recorded. St George Hanover Square in Westminster was the most fashionable church in eighteenth- and nineteenth-century London. The pages of its registers are scattered with the offspring of lords, ladies, earls, duchesses, sirs and esquires. Despite this grand social standing, the clerks were careful to record their place of residence. For example, in 1758 a daughter of the Earl and Countess of Powys was baptised. The clerk noted that the child had been privately baptised the year before at West Woodlhay in Berkshire.[19] St Clement Danes, also in the City of Westminster, had a large number of parishioners from the West Indies. In 1782, Mary 'the daughter of Nathaniel Morgan Esqr and Mary his wife of St Mary's in the Island of Jamaica aged about 7 years' was baptised.[20] To the casual reader, these entries may look as if the people concerned were boasting about their status and property, but the clerk was actually recording details that would ensure that, should these rich, privileged infants fall into penury, the parish authorities would not be liable to support them. They were in exactly the same legal position as Black servants.

Settlement examinations

There seem to have been very few Black people in settlement examinations and there are a number of possible reasons for this. The first is that the majority of Black people in this country were young men, a group which is generally underrepresented in examinations and any resulting removal orders. As Dorothy Marshall observed:

> In a country district the type of wage earner most likely to fall into distress was the married labourer overburdened with children . . . next came the unmarried woman . . . Unmarried labourers, however, if they had their health and strength, could always earn enough to support themselves without any assistance from the rates. Consequently they were but little molested by the overseers.

She adduced evidence from the Cambridge Quarter Sessions and Dunstable parish records. In urban areas, the practice was different:

> In manufacture the married labourer was rather at an advantage than otherwise, for he could draw on the labour of his wife and children . . . It was the woman following poor trades, and the young children, who were most likely to bring a charge on the parish.

Marshall noted that in Middlesex women were the most likely to be removed. 'Evidently the parish officers were most suspicious of the unattached women, whether they were burdened with children or not.'[21] Women are disproportionately represented in the few settlement examinations relating to Black people that have been found in archives (although there are probably many more, since relatively few have been indexed).[22] Considering the imbalance between the numbers of Black men and women in this country, this is further evidence that it was women who gave the authorities the most concern, because they might become pregnant.

Another reason for the lack of Black people in settlement examinations is that they seem to have been mainly the servants of the well-to-do or, having left service, followed occupations which enabled them to support themselves. Those who lived all their lives with their masters, like Tobias Pleasant, servant of John Lane of Hillingdon, Middlesex, would probably never need to claim poor relief. Pleasant's life seems to have been uneventful until, after thirty-two years of service, a highwayman robbed his master while the two were travelling from Hillingdon into London. Were it not for his appearance as a witness at the thief's trial, where he said how long he had worked for his master, nothing would be known of his life.[23] The same would apply to many other servants. Those Black servants who left their masters' service to set up in business, like Affrick Hunsdon,[24] Ignatius Sancho[25] and Cesar Picton,[26] are not mentioned as Black in registers because their prosperity meant that they automatically gained settlement in their parishes so their origin and that of their children (both Hunsdon and Sancho had offspring) became irrelevant.

A third possible reason for the apparent lack of Black people in settlement and other official examinations is difficult to prove. They may simply not have had their colour recorded. In 1719/20 the parish officials of St Margaret, Westminster, carried out an examination on Esther Roberts, pregnant by a sailor who was now overseas. It followed the standard format then used but, some time after the document was written, the note 'A Blackamoor' was added in another hand.[27] It is impossible to know how many other documents relating to Black people, especially women, do not have such addenda. There are others in Westminster who may be Black, like Kitty Collis of Boston, New England. Her settlement examination in 1785 in St Clement Danes, Westminster, did not say. Her husband was Irish.[28] On marriage his place of settlement became hers, so her colour or ethnicity became legally irrelevant. A further explanation for not recording colour or ethnicity is that those who became parish officials automatically gained settlement, if they did not already have it. As well as John Mills, the churchwarden of Wolstanton, and Thomas Latham, the parish constable of Clerkenwell, previously mentioned, John York, the son of John and Mary York who were both Black, became sexton of the parish of Kirkby Ravensworth in Yorkshire.[29]

Illegitimate children

As well as the poor laws there were regulations relating to bastardy and settlement. Bastardy seems to have been comparatively rare until after 1750 and there are a number of theories about the causes of its increase from the middle of the eighteenth century.[30] There were many laws covering how the parish should or could deal with an illegitimate child. The father (or a member of his family) could put up a bond to indemnify the parish against the costs of its support. Pressure, which might include some financial inducement, to marry was also imposed but this, of course, is not mentioned in parish registers.[31] A woman expecting an illegitimate child was supposed to declare her pregnancy and name the father. A man charged on oath with being the father of a bastard child could be imprisoned until he agreed to indemnify the parish against expense. The effects of these laws are more clearly seen in bastardy and settlement examinations, rather than in registers, although entries are frequently annotated with the name of the reputed father. Occasionally the baptism of an illegitimate child mentioned that one of the parents was Black. In Chiswick, Middlesex, Robert the 'illegitimate son of Jane Leake by Robert Le Cruse – a Black' was baptised in October 1776. The infant was buried less than a month later, so there was no need to set in motion the process needed to determine who was to bear the cost of his upbringing.[32] There are a few bastardy examinations where the mother's colour/ethnic origin is noted. Occasionally, however, these are omitted but can be deduced from other records.

The records of St Martin in the Fields in Westminster contain two settlement examinations relating to Nancy Lynch from Charleston, South Carolina. The first, conducted in September 1786, stops in mid-sentence. Lynch was then pregnant by Alexander Stewart, who had brought her 'against her will' to England in November 1785. Eighteen months later, in March 1788, Lynch and her daughter Ann again came to the attention of the parish authorities. Almost every day one or two people were examined and the records suggest this was done to set formulas following one of two patterns. Either a parish official made a sworn statement that the person was a stranger likely to become chargeable and the person concerned made a statement about their settlement position or the person (probably seeking assistance) made a statement. Nancy's examination falls into the second category. She stated on oath that she was over 25 years old, was born in Charles Town [Charleston] South Carolina and 'never did any Act whereby to gain any settlement in England'. She added that she was

> Delivered in the Month of January 1787 of a female Bastard Child since baptized Ann at the house of Mr Berry, near the Swan in Greenwich in the parish of Greenwich in the County of Kent ... it is not in her Power or Ability to provide for the same but freely & voluntarily relinquishes & gives up the same to provide for herself

She signed with a cross.[33] A few days later a removal order was obtained and Ann Lynch was sent to Greenwich, where the minutes of the workhouse for 8 March 1788 recorded the decision that 'Ann Lynch an infant illegitimate mulatto Child who is sent by order of Removal from St Martin in the Fields in Middlesex be admitted'. Eight months later, the parish register recorded the burial of Ann Linch [sic] on 12 November. The entry is annotated 'w[orkhouse] poor'.[34] Presumably her mother was left to fend for herself. The records of St Martin in the Fields' workhouse for that period have not survived, so it is impossible to find out whether she was admitted. As Nancy's daughter was sent alone to Greenwich, this seems unlikely. Although, by modern standards, the treatment given Nancy and Ann Lynch seems harsh, it was no different from that other destitute people received. It is only through the Greenwich workhouse minutes, which note that Ann was 'mulatto', that it can be deduced, combined with her place of origin and the fact that she was brought to England from America 'against her will', that Nancy was almost certainly the Black parent. Her colour or ethnic origin was not at issue, it was her birthplace. She had no settlement in England, so no parish was under any obligation to support her. Her daughter's birth in Greenwich gave the child settlement there. She became Greenwich's responsibility, which the parish did not contest.

Masterless men

In the hierarchical society of the seventeenth and eighteenth centuries, it seemed especially important to be able establish who had responsibility for every individual member of society. It was a top-down system, with the monarch at the top. Each level of society had obligations to those above and responsibility for those below. Within individual households, men had responsibility for every person under their roof or in their employ: wives, children, servants and apprentices. Those who could not be fitted into this system caused the authorities grave disquiet. They were known as 'masterless men' and their independence, it was thought, needed to be curbed lest they foment rebellion. The 1740 and 1744 Amendment Acts classified vagrants into three kinds: 'idle and disorderly persons'; 'rogues and vagabonds'; and 'incorrigible rogues'. These encompassed just about anyone who was not employed by a master and included actors, unlicensed peddlers and those who gained money by begging or by offering such spurious services as fortune telling of one kind or another. The Acts also covered anyone who left their dependants chargeable to the parish. Few Black people came into this category before the influx of the 1770s and 1780s. William Biznea, a Black beggar, came to the attention of the authorities in Lincoln on 3 April 1788. They conducted a settlement examination and on the following day the local Quarter Sessions granted a vagrancy pass to return him to his last place of legal settlement, Troborn in Fifeshire, Scotland, where he had worked for a year and received £8 wages in 1782. His colour is not given in the documents relating to the case. It can be deduced because he was born in Guadeloupe and was brought to London aged around 7 by a Captain Biznea.[35] It is impossible without considerably more research to identify others that may be in court records, because these did not routinely include colour or ethnicity.

The 1783 Stamp Act (repealed in 1794) imposed a duty of threepence on each register entry of birth or baptism, marriage or burial. As with previous Acts, the parish was responsible for collecting the tax. Like the 1693/4 and 1695 Taxation Acts, this made clerks more careful about keeping records. They entered 'poor' against the names of those whose income fell under the threshold for payment. A number of entries relating to Black people are so annotated, like that of William Morris in St George in the East, Wapping, in 1794.[36] This may suggest they were 'masterless men', not living as servants, because their masters would presumably have paid the tax for them. It would be wrong to think, however, that they were destitute: they were simply not liable to pay the tax because their income was too low.

The 1795 Poor Relief Act forbade removal until a person actually became chargeable to the parish, i.e. was destitute through unemployment or illness. Until this point, parishes could send anyone they thought likely to become chargeable back to their home parish or, as in the case of John English, previously mentioned, to their master. In the case of those born in other countries, including Scotland and Ireland, the expense of removing them might be prohibitive, so it was rarely done,[37] although Lincoln did think it worthwhile to return William Biznea (mentioned above) to Scotland. Places like Bristol which had regular shipping links to Ireland did remove people there. Black people, if they originally came from the Caribbean or from Africa, would have been too expensive to remove.

Effects of the Mansfield Judgment

In addition to these various Acts of Parliament, the judgments which Lord Mansfield made in 1772 in the case involving James Somerset and in 1778 in that on Charlotte Howe[38] seem to have had an effect on how Black people were recorded in parish registers. Before the 1770s most entries relating to Black people carefully noted their status as a 'Black servant'. This was probably in order to establish that they were outside the settlement laws, so may indicate that the person was not being paid or had been in service for less than the statutory year which would confer settlement. This may, incidentally, have led historians to believe that most

Black people in eighteenth-century Britain were servants, because this was the occupation regularly recorded. There are, however, many Black people who were not noted as servants in the registers, or who appear in other types of documents as pursuing another occupation.[39] Indeed, those whose occupation is not given form the majority. Nothing is known about their occupations, presumably because they had no legal significance. From the 1770s onwards it became more common to find that only the occupation and place of birth were entered and colour was sometimes omitted, although many clerks took a belt-and-braces approach, including both colour and place of origin.

After the 1772 judgment clerks recorded place of origin rather than colour, returning to the practice prevailing before 1662. In 1773, Samuel George 'from Calcutta in the East Indies, supposed to be about 14 years old' was baptised in the City of London.[40] Other clerks went on noting 'Black', either considering that this was enough to absolve the parish of financial responsibility or because, like most people, they were not entirely clear about the legal implications of the Mansfield Judgment. This argument is given more weight by the fact that other official records do not mention ethnic origin where this was not pertinent. The 1841 Census asked whether each member of a household was born in the county or not. From the 1851 Census, each person's parish of birth was entered, not ethnic origin. This is an important distinction. It was not until 1991 that the census asked for ethnic origin, rather than place of birth, although giving this information was not obligatory.

Children

Under the poor laws, it was primarily the father's status that determined that of his children, unless they were illegitimate, so it was details related to the father that were noted in the registers. There are several instances of the colour of a father being given for the first baptismal entry of his children but not for those following, suggesting that by the time the second was born the father had been resident and in paid employment in the parish long enough to qualify for settlement and so colour and origin were no longer legally significant. On 3 April 1715, Samuel, son of Michael Kendale '(a Negro Man)' and Catherine was baptised in East Greenwich, Kent. Another son, Michael, was baptised on 7 July 1717 and the names of his parents were given as Michael Kendal 'a Negro Lab[ourer]' and Catherine. There were to be at least three more children, but in their baptismal register entries no reference was made to their father's ethnic origin.[41] In Cambridge in 1677, John George Ostin was baptised in St Michael. The entry reads 'A Blackamore aged about twenti [sic] years was baptizid [sic] . . . son of Edmund and Martha Ostin'. In the same register are entries relating to the baptisms of three other children of Edmund and Martha in 1672, 1674 and 1679. Edmund was buried on 26 January 1696/7 and his wife on 25 February 1711/2.[42] In none of these entries was any mention made of colour or ethnic origin. It looks as if it was only because John George was an adult, perhaps arriving to join his parents after working elsewhere, that his ethnic origin was recorded. His parents must have been accepted as settled in the parish, so their origin and colour and that of their other children were irrelevant. In 1807 John Moor 'a Negro' was baptised in Whitehaven, Cumbria. He is described as being 22 years old and a smith. In 1810 Isaac, son of John and Jane Moor, was baptised, to be followed by two other children, Jane and Isabella. The occupation of all three children's father is recorded as sawyer.[43] Because the name is relatively common, it is not clear whether this is the same person. I would argue that it is; smiths and sawyers made a respectable living, so were unlikely to be regarded as potential paupers and recipients of parish relief. John Moor probably changed occupations, or the first entry noting him as a smith was an error.

Some parishes, however, continued to include the colour of a parent for every entry. These were mainly the small rural ones where Black people were a novelty and regarded with the suspicion of the countryman for the outsider. They stood out as a potential source of expense, and so were described in more detail. The larger, urban parishes, where clerks were hard pressed, tended to include few additional details. In some parishes the Black person concerned may never have gained settlement, so his or her origin was always pertinent, but it is also important to look at the information included in all parish entries to see what is normally recorded. In most cases the children of mixed marriages are not recorded any differently from other infants. Joseph Lisbone married Martha Cradwell in St Katherine by the Tower in London on 19 January 1660. Although this was a church where irregular marriages took place, their son Joseph was baptised there on 31 January 1663/4 so it looks as if they had some connection with it, probably through the hospital there. He was perhaps a patient, because the child's baptism took place the day before Joseph senior's funeral: it is only from the burial record, however, that we know the father was 'a Blackemore'.[44] On a limited study of Huguenot immigrants, clerks seem to have applied the same rules to them as they did to Black people.[45]

It is very difficult to determine how many white men in England had Black wives and mixed-race children. It is rare to find the mother's origin stated, unless the parents were not married. The wording of many entries is ambiguous, like that in 1787 in Lymington, Hampshire relating to Sarah Pitts, 'd[aughter] of Benjamin and Joanna (a Black)', because 'Black' appears at the end of the entry. It is not clear whether it was the father or mother who was Black, but I would surmise that it was the father.[46] As the couple were married, his origin was paramount. The same applies to the baptism in 1771 of Elizabeth Blyden, the daughter of William Blyden and Mary 'a Negro' in the City of London.[47] Generally the Black partner of a white man is a matter for conjecture. In 1798 the two children of Benjamin Hopkinson 'by Johanna' were baptised in the City of London. Benjamin James was born in 1785 in Tobago and John Thomas in 1787 in Demerara.[48] Possibly they were the children of a white couple in the West Indies for business reasons, but in that case, why wait for so long before having them christened? They appear to be the mixed-race children of a white father by a Black, slave mother, especially as the usual wording used by the parish clerk at that time is 'son/daughter of X by Y his wife' and these last two words are omitted in both entries. If their father was white and qualified as settled in the parish, there could, at this date, be no legal problem about his children's settlement, so their colour and that of their mother were irrelevant for legal purposes.

Non-Anglican records

Nonconformity appealed to the lower-middle classes and to the working class, so might be expected to attract Black people. Ukasaw Gronniosaw was converted to the Baptist faith, and shared religion was a factor in his choice of wife, an Englishwoman.[49] There has not yet been time to explore Black adherents of non-Anglican denominations in any depth, but there are a few, like James French, an 'Asian' baptised in the Roman Catholic Chapel in Virginia Street, London and Isaaq Glode, who was baptised in 1698 in the Glasshouse Street Huguenot Chapel and described as 'More de la Coste de g'nee' [Moor from the coast of Guinea].[50] These examples seem to cast doubt on the theory that Black peoples' colour or origin was only relevant in relation to the settlement laws and would therefore not be included in the records of non-established churches, but more evidence needs to be collected. The problems are many. The first is that the survival of nonconformist records before the nineteenth century is patchy. Then there is the problem of negative evidence. As indicated earlier, there are many entries in Anglican registers and other official documents which appear to refer to Black people, but without a definite statement to that effect, especially where only a birthplace is given. Because non-Anglican registers had no legal status there was even less onus on clerks to record information that might be important in settlement cases. Possibly hundreds of Black people in seventeenth- and eighteenth-century Britain may be recorded in Anglican parish registers or nonconformist documents without mention of their colour. This question of settlement confuses the issue of just how many Black people there were in England. Evidence suggests that, if the person had worked and been paid for a year, colour was irrelevant and so was not always recorded. There is a strong argument to be made that the number of Black people in parish registers is considerably underestimated. Beyond the question of Black history, this matter of how and under what circumstances origin was recorded in parish registers has implications for the study of all ethnic minorities: most notably Huguenots, the largest immigrant group, but also Germans, Dutch people, Italians and other 'strangers' who either formed communities within cities and urban areas or settled singly in other parishes. It also has implications for the study of the assimilation of these ethnic minority groups.

Notes

1. A marriage entry in Leicester in 1649, 'Thomas Garrett of Mountstrill and Blacke Bess, Mr Mountney's mayde', may also be of a mixed marriage. Hartropp, H., *The Registers of St Mary Leicester in the County of Leicestershire*, Vol. I (1909). Although 'Black' was often used as a description or nickname for someone with a dark complexion, Bess's lack of surname seems significant. The word 'maid' is also ambiguous. It could refer either to her unmarried status or to her occupation.
2. SoG, unpublished transcript, KE/R 13. Cowell, F.V., Registers of Deptford, Kent, 26 December 1613.
3. SoG, unpublished transcript, CO/R 37, Registers of Fowey Cornwall.
4. Crisp, F.A., *Registers of Lowestoft* (privately publ., 1904), 17 November 1737.
5. BASA *Newsletter* 30, April 2001, p. 23. The editor, Marika Sherwood, informed me that she had been told this by the archivist at Lambeth Palace Library.
6. Steven Wise seems to have misunderstood one of the effects of this law. He said that Roman Catholic children were illegitimate, but there was no Act specifying this. Many Roman Catholics refused to be married by an Anglican, Jewish or Quaker rite (as the law required), so they were not considered to be

legally married and their children were therefore illegitimate. Wise, *Though the Heavens May Fall*, p. 210.
7. Jacob, G. (?), *The Compleat Parish Officer*. There were at least ten editions; the seventh (1734) has been reprinted by the Wiltshire Family History Society (Devizes, facsimile edition, 1990; 2nd edn, 1996).
8. SoG, unpublished transcript ES/R 'Registers of Birchanger, Essex', 5 March 1771.
9. SoG, unpublished transcript CO/R 37, 'Registers of Fowey, Cornwall', 25 December 1791.
10. GHC, Black History Sources: Parish Records file, Minutes of Greenwich Workhouse.
11. Huntingdon RO, HP34/18/1.
12. Shaw, J., *Parish Law* (1750) is one of the many guides to parish law. It discusses Scottish and Irish people, those from Jersey, Guernsey, the Isle of Scilly and gypsies, but does not write about those born in countries other than these (pp. 157–8).
13. GL, Ms 7219/1 8, September 1667.
14. CWA, Registers of St Clement Danes, 16 March 1776. It should be noted, however, that records for adult baptisms of white people often also record only approximate ages: perhaps the clerks were being cautious in case these people were not being truthful, in order to exploit some legal quibble later.
15. Clarke, A.H.W., *Registers of Wimbledon* (1925), 30 June 1723. A few days later, the mother returned and the child was baptised, obviously with the minister's approval, as he entered the names of witnesses to the event. This, incidentally, gives an example of the conflicting demands of religion and law faced by Anglican ministers.
16. GL, Ms 17,818.
17. SoG, unpublished transcript, SR/R 134. Webb, C. et al., *Registers of Ashtead, Surrey* (1990).
18. Crouch, C.H., *Registers of Chigwell, Essex* (1948).
19. CWA, Registers of St George Hanover Square, 16 July 1758.
20. CWA, Registers of St Clement Danes, 19 March 1782.
21. Marshall, D.M., *The English Poor in the Eighteenth Century* (1926), pp. 164–6.
22. Between 1708 and1795 some 30,000 settlement examinations were carried out in the parish of St Martin-in-the-Fields, Westminster. They are being indexed by CWA and so far thirty relating to Black people or of white women married to Black men have been found. One of these was of a child whose mother had died and whose father was at sea. Only twelve relate to men, two of whom were beggars, not apparently seeking relief but picked up by the authorities with the intention of removing them. CWA, *Sources for Black and Asian History*, pp. 56–64.
23. *Proceedings* 1780–1, I, no. 3. Pleasant may also have been the unnamed Black

boy mentioned in the trial of another highwayman who held up John Lane in 1731, *Proceedings* 1730-1, VII, no. 508. There is no baptism or marriage entry relating to Pleasant in the Hillingdon registers, but Pleasant's burial took place there on 6 May 1784, when he was described as 'a Black servt to J. Lane'. SoG, unpublished transcript, MX/R 274.

24. The registers of Hunsdon, Hertfordshire, record Affrick's baptism on 1 April 1711, when he is described as 'a native of Africa servant to Mathew Blucke of Hunsdon House'. He married Dorothy Jordan in Hunsdon on 1 December 1724. There is no reference to his colour in the marriage entry, nor in the baptism record of his son, also Affrick, on 8 September 1727, when Affrick senior is simply described as a 'victualler'. I am grateful to Dr Jill Barber of Hertfordshire RO for these references.
25. Sancho appears in *A Correct Copy of the Poll for Electing Two Representatives in Parliament for the City and Liberty of Westminster* (1774), p. 15. He rented property worth more than a certain amount, so he automatically gained settlement in the parish of St Margaret and also qualified for the franchise.
26. Leaflet produced by Kingston Record Office (nd,) sent to me by Marian Bone.
27. CWA, E2574, p. 46.
28. CWA, B1187, p. 34.
29. Bogg, E., *Richmondshire* (1908), p. 182. The entry recording his burial at the age of 84 on 21 May 1885 did not mention his colour, but did note his occupation. I am grateful to Audrey Dewjee for this reference.
30. Laslett, P., *The World We Have Lost Further Explored* (3rd edn, 1983), pp. 151–73, examines the changes in the illegitimacy rate and discusses theories about them.
31. The diary of James Woodforde, minister of Weston Longville in Norfolk, contains a number of examples. Woodforde, *Diary*, pp. 54, 164 and 294.
32. SoG, unpublished transcript, Mx/R/108. Hill, J.P., Register of Chiswick, 29 October and 25 November 1776.
33. CWA, F5071, p. 289. Why the first examination was not completed in unknown.
34. GHC, Black History Sources, Parish Records File, Minutes of Greenwich Workhouse and Burial Register.
35. *Lindsey Quarter Sessions Poor Law Documents 1702–1800*, p. 116. I am grateful to Dr Joan Kemp for this reference.
36. LMA, Registers of St George in the East, 24 January 1794.
37. Powell, W.R., *Victoria History of the County of Essex*, Vol. VI (Oxford, 1973), p. 99.
38. Charlotte Howe was a slave brought to England from America in 1781. She applied to the authorities of Thames Ditton for parish relief, but was refused because she had not been paid as a servant. The case went to the court of King's Bench, where Lord Mansfield upheld the parish's refusal. There seem

to have been no studies done on white servants but intermittent references in parish records suggest a proportion, especially under the age of majority, were not paid. There is no indication of Charlotte's age.
39. The *Proceedings* of the Old Bailey give several examples.
40. GL, Ms 5294, 28 March 1773.
41. SoG, unpublished transcript, KE/R 115–22, Registers of East Greenwich: Charlotte Loeza, bap. 12 October 1718; George, bap. 11 September 1720 (his parents are given as Michael and Mary, presumably a clerical error) and Sarah, bap. 11 September 1725.
42. Venn J., *Registers of St Michael Cambridge* (Cambridge, 1891).
43. Stout, H.B., *Registers of St James, Whitehaven* (1964), 13 September 1807, 10 December 1818, 13 June 1813, 2 March 1817.
44. HS 76, *Registers of St Katherine by the Tower*.
45. I have Huguenot ancestors and note that their first-generation French origin was recorded in some registers. Second and subsequent generations were not recorded as being any different from the indigenous population.
46. SoG, unpublished transcript, HA/R 79. Riach, H.F., Registers of Lymington Hants (1990), 16 September 1787.
47. GL, Ms 3572/2, Registers of St Mary Aldermanbury, 14 December 1771.
48. GL, Ms 4108, Registers of St Andrew Undershaft, 14 July 1798.
49. Gronniosaw, *Narrative*, p. 35.
50. I am grateful to Dr Robert Morkot for the reference to James French and to Andrew Morgan for Isaaq Glode. Mr Morgan said that Glode was later naturalised.

Part III
Living and working in the wider community

Chapter 6

Assimilation or integration?

Statistical analysis provides information rather than meaning. To say that the average Black inhabitant of Britain during the period of the British slave trade was, at the point of baptism, a young man from the New World, Africa or the Indian subcontinent can be deduced from other sources. Such statistics capture only a moment in what might have been a long and eventful life. This section, therefore, raises perhaps the most interesting aspect of the history of Black people in England during the period of the British slave trade: what were their lives like day by day? As the Mansfield Judgment concluded, they were legally free, even if this was not popularly understood. There is, however, always a gap between what the law dictates and what people do. Although during the long eighteenth century the law discriminated less against Black people than against those immigrants born outside British territories and Roman Catholics, private and semi-private organisations, such as the Corporation of London, could and did discriminate against specific groups, and Black people were among them. The edicts of Elizabeth I issued in 1596 and 1601, expelling Black people from England, have been much quoted by historians who regard them as evidence of racial discrimination, but there may be a more complex agenda. In addition to the general xenophobia and protectionism of the time (the end of the war against Spain and other economic conditions brought widespread unemployment), there was another motive. Miranda Kaufmann, for example, concluded that these edicts were not the result of racial prejudice but driven by a desire to profit from the ransoming of English prisoners in Spain and Portugal.[1]

Beyond the letter of the law, it is not clear how Black people integrated or assimilated into wider British society. Integration, living within a society while retaining the cultural practices of the homeland, is the United States model: for centuries this was a place to which people migrated in order to preserve or practise a usually religious way of life.

The Amish are perhaps the example that springs most readily to mind. The size of North America made it possible for groups to create separate townships. Black people there did suffer legal discrimination, even after slavery was abolished, and developed a parallel society. Education was segregated, and within living memory it was possible to live in an almost entirely Black world, as, for example, Henry Louis Gates has described in his autobiography.[2] The cultural dominance of the United States today means that the integration model is now regarded as the ideal, but in the past the practice in Britain was different. The British Isles are geographically much smaller and more densely settled. Though immigrants settled (and still settle) in distinct areas, these were within established towns and cities. The proximity to the indigenous British and the necessity of dealing with them on a daily basis meant that assimilation became the British model. The first generation or two of all immigrant groups tended (and still tend) to marry and remain within their communities, but thereafter they increasingly married outside, and their cultural practices and beliefs became those of the majority. In Britain Jews were, until the twentieth century, the exception to this. Their different cultural and religious practices bound them together, unlike Christian immigrant groups. In the eighteenth and nineteenth centuries the larger minorities, like the Huguenots and the Germans, had schools, charities, hospitals and the like to keep them united, support them and ensure the continuation of remnants of their cultural identity, although eventually they were assimilated.

Before the late nineteenth century there were always a few individual non-Christian immigrants from the Middle East, India, China and other places who arrived in cities and towns, mainly ports, but never in sufficient numbers to create the kind of social infrastructure that grows up around dedicated places of worship and through segregated education. During the period of the British slave trade there were never enough Black people in any one place in Britain to form a distinct community. Over the long eighteenth century people of African origin were largely drawn into the established church and nonconformist denominations. The imbalance between the number of men and women also meant for half the Black men a white partner was the inevitable choice, and their wives' network of family and friends would draw them into mainstream society. Other factors may be that they came from a diverse range of linguistic, religious and cultural backgrounds and that they were concentrated in the kind of occupations that did not allow them to interact only with other Blacks, should they choose to do so. Although there were some Black shopkeepers, no Black doctor, for example, has yet been found, nor have any references to religious or spiritual ministers, like the practitioners of *obeah* found in the Caribbean. Assimilation therefore became the norm. There are, however, occasional examples of Black people banding together for social and political reasons. Philip Thicknesse said that there were clubs to support men out of place.[3] As a hostile witness, Thicknesse needs to be treated with caution, although on the surface there is no need to disbelieve him. There were informal clubs to help unemployed members.[4] The existence of such a club, as Thicknesse claimed, suggests that there was a large number of independent Black workers earning enough money to make contributions. An exclusive organisation, however, would surely have been mentioned by other people, not least by Olaudah Equiano, whose dealings with both white and Black political activists would have brought him into contact with it. Ignatius Sancho had a wide acquaintance among the fashionable and, through his previous employers, knowledge of the aristocracy. Both sections of society had Black servants, but he mentions no club. Nor does Ukawsaw Gronniosaw, who had periods of unemployment, seem to have joined or even heard of one. There was probably a club, or perhaps more than one, to which many Black people belonged, but it was not confined to Blacks. The Sons of Africa was a group of Black men who signed five letters to the press between 1787 and 1788 and might be regarded as a political organisation.[5] Ottobah Cugoano and Olaudah Equiano were among them and they are the only two about whom anything else is known, although Joseph Almaze, who signed the first letter, is probably the Joseph Allamaze who, with his wife Hariot and two children, signed an agreement to go to Sierra Leone in 1786.[6] It is impossible to know whether this was a formal political organisation or a small, ad hoc lobbying group. There are no other contemporary references to the Sons of Africa, nor has evidence of meetings or other activities beyond the letters yet been found.

The *General Evening Post* reported in 1773 that two Blacks committed to the Bridewell for begging were visited by over three hundred Black people, who also gave money to support them. Shyllon commented: 'The magnitude of arranging for upward of 300 blacks to visit their brothers, and the administrative complexity of collecting monies for their maintenance would seem to reveal how well developed was the social and communal life of the blacks.'[7] This would be true in twentieth-century America, but eighteenth-century London was very different. In addition, there are some problems in accepting the newspaper's account. At this period the editor was usually the sole writer of the four closely printed pages of the standard county newspaper of the time, which generally appeared twice a week – although there were daily papers in London from 1702. The reporting of Parliamentary proceedings was a mainstay, so in London there was usually also someone who took down what happened there. To fill the rest of the space, the editor copied from other papers and relied on correspondents, literally letter writers, for additional items of local and regional news. His main original contribution was the writing of leaders and probably the coverage of Quarter Sessions, Assizes and inquests, which formed the bulk of county news until the growth of more local newspapers towards the end of the nineteenth century. Who counted these visitors to the gaol? A busy editor was unlikely to be able to spare enough time to do so. How many people came more than once and therefore may have been double counted? The figure of three hundred seems a sensationalist exaggeration, like the estimate of the number of Black people in the country made by other newspapers: no other publication seems to have mentioned this remarkable occurrence. Money did not need to be collected by an intermediary: it could simply be handed over in the gaol. The same problem about numbers arises in the reports of Black people's reaction to the Mansfield Judgment. In 1772 the *Morning Chronicle* reported that 'several' were in court to hear the delivery of the judgment.[8] The *Middlesex Journal* said there were 'a great number' in court for this momentous event.[9] How many is 'several' and how many 'a great number'? This imprecision suggests that the editors relied on amateur reporters. A few days after the judgment, as reported by the *London Packet*, some two hundred gathered in an unnamed Westminster public house to celebrate it.[10] Again, who counted them and how? A modern parallel can be drawn with the figure that a lobbying organisation gives for the number attending a demonstration and that made by the police in attendance. When dealing with such estimates, especially in the past, it is important to retain a professional scepticism.

There were undoubtedly social events attended only by Black people: John Baker mentions his servant Jack Beef going to a 'Ball of Blacks' and in 1764 the *London Chronicle* reported a dance to which white people were not admitted.[11] Evidence of informal social centres comes from another source: in 1787 Joseph Curry, accused of theft, was pursued into a public house in East Smithfield where there were some forty black people, presumably hoping to hide himself among them.[12] Whether this was a regular meeting place or just an indication of the number of Black people in East Smithfield, where lodging houses for Black and lascar mariners abounded, is not stated. Nor is there any indication of how many white people may also have been present there: whether it was a place used exclusively by Black people is not clear. These, however, are all solitary references. None of the writers of travel books, either from overseas or native born, who described London seems to have mentioned sites of regular or permanent gatherings or any long-standing Black organisations. Had such places or societies existed, they would surely have been of interest to tourists.

Racial prejudice

The subject of how Europeans and later Americans saw and still see Black people is a subject of endless examination among academics. Many simply look at the stark opposites: black and white. There is less literature on the subject of how those of mixed race, or biraciality or interraciality, or what is now called dual heritage, were perceived. In addition, it is accepted that the term 'race' is not helpful, as it is so often confused with ethnicity. Jews, for example, are not a race but a religious/cultural group. It has also been observed that perceptions change over time in response to a number of factors.[13] However, I do not propose to re-examine these explorations and theories in detail, for two reasons. The first is that the subject has been extensively covered and the focus of this book is Black people's experiences in England and how they were treated in practice, and discussing racial prejudice in detail means changing the focus to white people's beliefs. The second is that it is unsurprising that white Europeans should find black Africans inferior. As Debra J. Dickerson wrote, 'what is racism but a fascination with oneself?' She quoted an anthropologist, Earl Shorris: 'Ethnocentrism was not . . . a European invention.' He went on to point out that many Native Indian peoples' names, like Apache, are derived from their neighbours' words for 'enemy' or the like.[14] Working in the Cameroons in Africa, Nigel Barley observed, 'Every tribe had someone to despise. For the Dowayos the Koma filled this very necessary function.'[15] Many peoples' names for themselves simply mean '*the* people', as if everyone else is not fully human. The Chinese word for their country translates as 'the Middle Kingdom', i.e. the place between heaven and earth, as if they were somehow on a more elevated plane than all the other occupants of the world. The logical extension of this self-esteem is that evil is universally regarded as the opposite of oneself: in Europe the devil was represented as black. In Africa evil spirits are white. In China and Japan devils have red hair. A tour of the prejudices of the world's inhabitants soon turns into a depressing and repetitive list. All immigrant groups in virtually every society initially encounter prejudice and discrimination. What is heartening is how often such prejudices are overturned by contact with real people, as opposed to the theoretical stereotype. Peter Fraser is among those who noted how trading with Africans brought a different perception of them 'after the original extravagant descriptions. One trades with humans not monsters or mythical creatures'.[16]

'Racism' and 'racial prejudice' are shorthand terms for a range of unfavourable responses to people from different ethnic communities. As E. Ellis Cashmore put it:

> Up to the late 1960s most dictionaries and textbooks defined [racism] as a doctrine, dogma, ideology or set of beliefs. The core element in this doctrine was that 'race' determined culture, and from this were derived claims to racial superiority.[17]

Thus, two potential sources of prejudice, race and culture, were (and still are) linked together. None of the writers on Black history seems to distinguish between prejudice based on race and prejudice based on cultural factors. There is, of course, an overlap between the two where the difference between races is immediately obvious. Fryer, for example, quotes Charles Lamb as confessing that 'I should not like to associate with them – to share my meals and my goodnights with them – because they are Black.' Fryer says 'Lamb was no racist,' without adducing any evidence for his opinion.[18] This seems, however, as pure a definition of racism as possible, not wishing to associate with people on the grounds of their race rather than of how they behave or what they believe, which are cultural factors. Most people's prejudices are on cultural grounds or, as Fryer recognises in writing about race riots in Liverpool, Cardiff and London, because of what he calls 'bitter economic competition'.[19] He labels this racism, but it is more complicated than that. The willingness of immigrants to work for lower wages than the indigenous population was, and still is, a major cultural factor and cause of social tension. A distinction between racial and cultural prejudice is, however, something that contemporary commentators also fail to make. As has been argued, there were simply not enough Black people in one place at any one time to sustain distinct cultural practices, which reinforce racism. There is, especially in Britain, a further factor, which is class or, in pre-nineteenth century terms, rank. This is something that Gerzina seems to have been the first to recognise, but class was, and still is, a major source of prejudice in British society.[20]

Conclusions about how white people reacted to Black people have largely been drawn from on a small number of published writings, particularly by Philip Thicknesse, Edward Long and Bryan Edwards, precursors of Victorian theories of scientific racism. The first, however, was equally vituperative about the French. The second and third were men from the West Indies, who therefore had a vested interest in the institution of slavery as a source of profit. Samuel Estwick, another writer on the subject, was 'by both birth and fortune, connected with one of the Islands in America' and is also quoted by Shyllon, for example, who deduces that these three, along with Gilbert Francklyn, James Tobin and several anonymous writers of letters to the newspapers, are proof that 'racism has been a way of life ever since the first blacks arrived in Britain'.[21] This is an oversimplification. A further factor is that Black people were not always regarded in the same way during the 150 years of long eighteenth century. The association between colour, race and slavery developed in Britain over the period of the slave trade, as Roxann Wheeler has explored in *The Complexion of Race*.[22] She dates the beginnings of such an association to the 1770s and finds that before that date prejudice was on the grounds of class or religion. In the early days of colonisation there seems to have been little differentiation between white indentured servants and Black slaves on plantations but, as Black slaves became the main source of manual labour, the association of race and slavery became fixed and synonymous.[23] As the abolitionist movement in Britain grew, Black people were represented as poor victims, in contrast to how they appeared earlier in the eighteenth century: 'The negro became a sentimental trope: he was usually shown as helpless, abased, solely reliant on the Christian goodwill of the European to rescue him from his miserable plight.'[24] The popularity of Josiah Wedgwood's iconic plaque of 1787 depicting a kneeling Black slave, subservient and in chains, both encapsulated this view and gave it widespread currency. In addition, Rousseau's concept of the noble savage and Harriet Beecher Stowe's novel *Uncle Tom's Cabin* (1852) contributed to the nineteenth-century view of Black people as unsophisticated, persecuted victims. This is the standard method of gaining public sympathy when launching charitable or political campaigns, whichever group is the object. Making people feel guilty about their comparatively good fortune and virtuous about relieving the sufferings of others is still effective, but it requires victim figures, who are consequently perceived as inferior in some way because they are disadvantaged.

It is also a mistake to assume that racist writers had universal approbation. Thicknesse, for example, was heartily loathed by some, if not many, of his contemporaries. A group of them paid the caricaturist James Gillray to produce *Lieut Gover' Gall-stone inspired by Alecto; – or the Birth of Minerva*, a complicated (and therefore expensive) print which was 'the culmination of a concentrated and sustained attack; anonymous verses were published and an insulting card was sent out on the publication of the print'. Nor was Gillray the only producer of such insulting caricatures. William Dent, 'a crude but effective and productive caricaturist', also produced one, entitled *The Cutter Up or the Monster at Full Length*. This likened Thicknesse to a man in London whose activities, cutting women and their clothes with a knife, was at the time a source of public panic.[25] Dent's was not the only print to make such a spoof accusation.[26] Although these attacks on Thicknesse were not made because of his racist views, they are evidence that he was by no means representative of public opinion. Shyllon observed that two of the anonymous writers to the *Gazetteer* during the period of the Somerset case were probably the same person.[27] This suggests that there were not enough people who felt strongly enough about the issue to write. The then-standard practice of writing anonymous letters to newspapers was a godsend to editors, who themselves wrote letters to prolong or spice up a correspondence. The newspaper editors may have felt the need to ensure that such a topical subject remained at the forefront of public consciousness, even though not enough readers felt strongly enough to write. Fryer looked beyond the diatribes of Long and Thicknesse against Black people, which previous writers had simply reproduced, and used their writings to examine the roots of racism in 'ignorance, fear, and the need to find a plausible explanation for perplexing physical and cultural differences'.[28] He also looked at Long and Thicknesse's individual characters and observed that Long had political, sexual and social anxieties and that Thicknesse was 'a quarrelsome eccentric'.[29] I would argue that those who shared the views of the plantocratic writers in the eighteenth century were a small and unrepresentative group but highly vocal. Because this same handful of racist writers from the pro-slavery lobby is repeatedly quoted at length by historians, it gives the impression that their views were more widely held than they actually were. Historians looking at Black people in isolation also believe that there was widespread prejudice, because they are using a limited number of partisan sources and not looking for parallel situations in wider society to determine what was unique to Black people and what was experienced by other minority groups. Those, like Dorothy George, who were looking at eighteenth-century society as a whole, came to the conclusion that there was no widespread prejudice.[30]

Shyllon also quoted writers who noted the number of mixed-race children in the eighteenth century. These writers used their presence to condemn miscegenation.[31] These children are surely additional evidence that there was no widespread discrimination outside a very small number of vocal and literate cranks. A perpetual problem for historians is to distinguish between what a small, highly vocal minority wrote and what the silent majority did without leaving a written, and therefore easily researched, record.[32] Evidence given in the case that followed the death in 1793 of a lascar, John Dullen, put out from a lodging house into the street to die when he was ill, is a rare example of contemporary attitudes to Black people among the poor. The evidence given by Ann Dollar shows that there were at least two opinions. She claimed that William Hooper, with whom she lived in Jeggett's lodging house, said Dullen was 'a black b----r, and that he had served him so and so, and that he ought not to have that countenance shewn him, because they were such bad people, where the black people came from'. Asked why he said that, Dollar answered: 'Because Mr Driver [another lodger in the same room as Dullen, Hooper and Dollar] often swore to him.' She seems to have been a more tolerant woman, because she added, 'I said to him, I must leave the room if you swear to him so, let him be a black or what he will'. She was 'a common woman of the town', so it can hardly have been the swearing to which she objected: it was the racism that annoyed her.[33] As this neatly encapsulates, there were at least two views on Black people at this level of society as well.

Stereotypes

There are a handful of twentieth-century riots and racist demonstrations, although these took place against a background of economic problems, but not even eighteenth-century abolitionists could find examples of atrocities in Britain against individuals on the basis of their colour. They were assimilated with little trouble, but this is not to say that they did not experience occasional discrimination and prejudice in everyday dealings, as other minority groups also did. Such prejudice is usually the result of stereotyping. The memorial inscription to Nestor, the servant of James Ramsey, an abolitionist, says 'His neat dress, his chaste sober life, his inoffensive manners subdued the prejudice his colour raised.'[34] It was perhaps less his colour than his slave origin (he came from St Kitts) that was a potential source of prejudice: again, class rather than race complicates the discussion.

In 1767 a newspaper reported an incident:

> Yesterday [11 January] a Moor was grossly insulted by some fellows on the canal in St James's Park who kept them at bay until some persons of more sense and humanity came to his rescue.[35]

That this incident was reported is an indication of its rarity: news consists of the unusual. If it were an everyday event, familiar to the newspaper's readers, it would not be worth covering. Nor did the reporter or the bystanders endorse such behaviour. Other scattered and fragmentary references to Black people in newspapers usually simply report an event in which a Black person was involved, with colour or race included as a newsworthy feature (since Black people were comparatively rare) without editorial comment, like an incident in London in 1751:

> Thursday [3 October] there appeared a remarkable Trial of Manhood in St James Park between two Cripples, who had but one leg between them: one of them, a Black . . . by the Assistance of the Bystanders got rid of his two tottering wooden Supporters and manfully fought on his Stumps. The Contest was obstinate and bloody, and lasted near a Quarter of an Hour; . . . at length victory declared itself in favour of the African.[36]

The reporter simply described what must have been a truly bizarre event, but he did not characterise the African as more prone to violence, impervious to pain or savage than his opponent, as might be expected were he stereotyped in a racialised way.

Coverage of criminal trials of Black people in London and elsewhere in the country never carries any suggestion that they were less law abiding than other sections of the population. Ann Duck, tried several times for theft in 1743 and 1744, was one of the Black Boy Alley Crew, a notorious gang based in Clerkenwell. It might be expected that much would have been made of her colour, given the name of the gang, but even the newspaper that reported her death sentence did not mention it.[37] Black people are also absent from publications on other, specialist areas of life, like pornography or insanity. Julie Peakman has written about the development of pornography in eighteenth-century England but none of the works she looked at included Black people.[38] With the mental illness of King George III, insanity became a topic of intense interest (although it had been written about earlier) and numerous theories about its causes and treatment were published.[39] None of these specifically characterised Black people as either more or less prone to mental illness. Newspapers, however, occasionally carried amusing anecdotes, and some mocked the supposed stupidity of Black people:

Assimilation or integration?   169

> On Monday last Peter Cooper, a negro, was married to a young woman at the Neptune Inn in this town [Hull]. When the ring was wanted, it was discovered that poor Mungo had omitted bringing one with him ... [the bride produced one of her own] ... this difficulty removed, the ceremony was concluded and pleasure appeared in the eyes of Molly and her dingy dear when a demand of the customary fees dispelled for a moment their happiness ... the surrounding spectators with great cheerfulness paid the fees and relieved the lovely pair from all their present embarrassments.[40]

Peter Cooper cannot have been the only man ever to have forgotten to bring a wedding ring or enough money to cover fees: it was his colour that the newspaper used to make this risible. Such anecdotes can, however, be matched by similar items on British people, notably the poor and uneducated, but also about other minority groups. In his extracts of newspaper items covering a single year, 1784, Duncan Sprott selected four anecdotes about the peculiarities of foreigners which appeared in the press: one was about the Irish, another about Jews, and two on that perennial source of dislike, the French. The stories about the French have a subtext about the reprehensibility of Roman Catholicism.[41] There were almost certainly more: these are just the ones that Sprott thought worthy of inclusion. He also reproduced several stories involving Black people, but none of these made an issue of their colour or race.[42] The small number of Black people in Britain meant that the indigenous population did not meet enough to detect any common characteristics.

The Irish, who formed a substantial sector of the population, were stereotyped. As a witness in a case at the Old Bailey in 1732 remarked, 'But he's an Irishman, God bless him; I consider his Country, and know he will swear any thing.'[43] As well as being seen as inveterate liars, the Irish were also the butt of jokes similar to those current today, depending on not exactly stupidity but not quite working out the implications of what is being said, as this joke from a chapbook shows:

> A very harmless Irishman was eating an apple pie with some quinces in it. Aarh now, dear honey, said he, if so few of these quinces give it such a flavour, how would an apple pye [sic] taste made all of quinces.

The preceding joke in the same chapbook is about the Welsh,

> A Welshman, bragging of his family, said that his father's effigy was set up in Westminster Abbey; being asked whereabouts, he said, In the same monument with Squire Thynne, for he was his coachman.[44]

The Welsh were then regarded as boastful and, as the nursery rhyme 'Taffy was a Welshman, Taffy was a thief' suggests, larcenous. The subtext is that both the Irish and the Welsh were regarded as less intellectually sophisticated than the indigenous population.

Other minority groups did not attract stereotyping. There were some forty thousand Huguenots in London in the eighteenth century,[45] far more than Black people, but this was still not enough for the creation of a stereotype. Although many people were hostile to the Huguenots, their criticisms were the standard accusations made against all foreigners, i.e. that they wear strange clothes, eat disgusting food and take the jobs of the indigenous population by working for less money. It was only in the middle of the nineteenth century, long after the Huguenots were largely assimilated, that the picture of them as the epitome of the Protestant work ethic was created. Some nationalities, notably the French and Italians, also provoked, and still provoke, sexual anxiety in men, who fear their women will be seduced by their superior amatory abilities. Although this particular myth does not seem to have been believed about Black men in the eighteenth century, it was certainly a fear in the twentieth century.[46]

Long and other plantation owners may have called Black people lazy, savage and prone to rebellion, but this picture of estate workers is an extreme version of how many people in England regarded their indigenous servants: lazy, uncouth and prone to disobey or leave on a whim. In 1758 the *London Chronicle* published a letter from 'P.L.C.' which started 'The most general complaint I know about this metropolis is the badness of servants, the female part especially.' The writer went on to say, 'she quits at a moment's notice.'[47] Even during the trials of those arrested during the Gordon Riots in 1780 there are no editorial comments of this nature in newspaper coverage about the Black people involved in the disturbances, even though at least two of them, Benjamin Bowsey and John Glover, had been in service.[48] The stereotype of the faithful Black servant was not created until the nineteenth century. Although many memorials testifying to individual Black servants' virtues were erected by grateful masters, white servants' merits were similarly recorded.

Private documents, like letters and diaries, written by other members of the communities in which they settled, contain passing allusions, occasionally denigratory, like a reference to Brian Mackey. He was born in the West Indies to a white man and a Black woman, who was presumably a slave. After studying at Oxford University he became minister of Coates in Gloucestershire. It is the diary of William Holland, incumbent of Over Stowey in Somerset, that reveals the full details of his parentage, which are absent from the official records that chart his career. On 25 January 1805 Holland wrote:

> I met today young Mackay [sic] who is come to see his sick father. This young man is his son by a Negro Woman and has had from the father an excellent education and is in Orders and has two Livings and is in good circumstances. Pity that he should suffer his father to suffer distress in his later days, but he is so far from assisting him that in all his visits he is drawing money from him and plundering him and I fear that poor Mrs Mackay will be left without a shilling – I am not very partial to West Indians, especially young Negro Half blood people.[49]

Even Granville Sharp noted, 'I am far from having any particular esteem for the Negroes; but I think myself obliged to consider them *as Men*.'[50] Similar references, however, can be found to other immigrants, particularly the French, or sections of the population, especially the poor. The majority of the Black population, like the indigenous population, were poor, and attitudes towards them, increasingly in the nineteenth century, conflated poverty with race – in Britain, the Caribbean and Africa.[51] To balance this, occasional expressions of delighted surprise surface. In 1808 in Moretonhampstead, Devon,

> Married with licence Peter the Black, servant to General Rochambeau, to Susanna Parker. The bells rang merrily all day. From the novelty of this wedding being the first negro ever married in Moreton, a great number assembled in the churchyard, and paraded down the street with them.[52]

The writer did not think it necessary to explain exactly why he was so pleased to have a Black person in the community: he assumed that it was self-evident, so it must have been a widespread belief. This may be connected to the association of blackness with good fortune: black cats are still regarded by some as lucky and chimney sweeps were invited to weddings to bring luck into the 1960s.[53] The converse seems not to have been believed. Although by the eighteenth century a widespread belief in witchcraft had largely disappeared, occasional examples of its survival crop up. As previously noted, in many rural parishes there might be a sole Black inhabitant over hundreds of years (as there was in Moretonhampstead), yet no references to any association between such a person and what might, very appositely, be called 'black magic' have been found, even though the devil was conventionally represented as a black man and appears thus in many supposed witches' confessions.

Only a handful, notably Olaudah Equiano, Ignatius Sancho, Ukawsaw Gronniosaw and Mary Prince, wrote of their daily life and experiences.

Equiano and Gronniosaw seem to have recorded no incidents of prejudice based on their colour, although their inexperience of Britain was exploited. Phyllis Wheatley, the poet, was brought to England from Boston, Massachusetts, as a slave in mid 1773 and was applauded by many.[54] Ignatius Sancho and his family were insulted when they visited Vauxhall Gardens, but this was probably not motivated solely by his colour: Londoners often treated foreigners with contempt, as Pierre Jean Grosley and others observed. Grosley, who published an account of his impressions of England in 1765, was particularly aware of how violently xenophobic the English were and recounted several examples of foreigners being insulted and even struck. Although Mary Prince was ill treated by her master and his family, plantation owners who brought her to London from Antigua in 1828, in England she met practical help from white women who were servants like herself. When she was unable through ill-health to do laundry work, English washerwomen did it for her. The wife of a shoeblack took her to the Moravian missionaries, who protected her and enabled her to procure her freedom.[55] This looks like class solidarity or fellow feeling among women, overriding any racial prejudice. As will be explored in Chapter 9, class played a great part in how Black people were assimilated into wider society.

Notes

1. Kaufman, M., '"the speedy transportation of Blackamoores", Caspar Van Senden's search for Africans and profit in Elizabethan England', BASA *Newsletter* 45, April 2006, pp. 10–14. Also, Kaufman, M., 'Casper Van Senden, Sir Thomas Shetley and the "Blackamoor" Project' on <www.Blackwell-synergy.com/doi/10.1111/j/1468–2281.207.00416x>.
2. Gates, H.L., *Coloured People* (1995).
3. Dover, *Hell in the Sunshine* (1943), quoted in Shyllon, *Black People*, p. 80.
4. They were legally recognised by an Act of Parliament in 1793 (although some organisations may predate this by up to seventy-five years) and in the nineteenth century they developed into Friendly Societies. Logan, R. *An Introduction to Friendly Society Records* (2000), p. 5.
5. The first letter, the only one to mention the Sons of Africa, was signed by twelve men: Ottobah Cugoano, Jasper Goree, John Stuart, Gustavaus Vassa, George Robert Mandeville, James Bailey, William Stevens, Thomas Oxford, Joseph Almaze, John Adams, Broughwa Gegansmel and George Wallace. The other four were signed by the same six: Thomas Cooper, Gustavus Vassa, Ottobah Cugoano Steward (Cugoano was given the name John Steward or Stewart), George Robert Mandeville, John Christopher and Thomas Jones.

Equiano always appears in records as Gustavus Vassa and the only place his African name is mentioned is in his autobiography.
6. TNA, T1/638/248. Neither he nor his family appear on the lists of those who embarked on three ships to Sierra Leone in 1787 and what happened to the family after is not yet known.
7. *General Evening Post*, 27 August 1773, quoted in Shyllon, *Black People*, p. 81.
8. *Morning Chronicle*, 22 June 1772, p. 2.
9. *Middlesex Journal*, 20–23 June 1772, p. 3.
10. *London Packet*, 26–29 June 1772, p. 3.
11. Baker, *Diary*, p. 201; *London Chronicle*, 17 February 1764, quoted in Shyllon, *Black People*, p. 80.
12. *Proceedings* 1785-6, no. 559. From this it can be inferred that Curry himself was Black, although this is not mentioned in the trial transcript.
13. In *'Race', Racism and Psychology: Towards a Reflexive History* (1997) Graham Richards examines how one profession, psychology, has perceived the issues surrounding 'races' from the middle of the nineteenth century to the end of the twentieth. Although he does not specifically look at these factors in detail, passing references make it apparent that intellectual fashions in other disciplines, like politics and sociology, influenced the theories of psychologists.
14. Dickerson, D.J., *The End of Blackness* (NY, 2004), pp. 55–6.
15. Barley, *The Innocent Anthropologist*, p. 161. In a later work dealing with Indonesia, where he found the same phenomenon, Barley observed, 'That everyone hates the people "next door" is about as close as you get to a universal in anthropology.' Barley, N., *Not a Hazardous Sport* (1988), p. 63. I have frequently quoted Barley rather than other anthropologists because one of his aims in writing his books was to show what lay behind published studies, how experiences are tidied up for publication. It may not be a coincidence that Dickerson has a background in journalism. Like anthropologists, journalists soon learn this universal truth through meeting people, as opposed to reading texts.
16. Fraser, P.D., 'The Status of Africans in England', in Vigne & Littleton (eds), *From Strangers to Citizens*, p. 257.
17. Cashmore, E.E. *Dictionary of Race and Ethnic Relations* (2nd edn, 1988), p. 247.
18. Fryer, *Staying Power*, p. 188.
19. *Ibid.*, p. 312.
20. Gerzina, *Black England*, p. 27. Such distinctions are not unique. Hindus also discriminated (and still do) on the basis of the caste, or echelon in society into which a person is born.
21. Shyllon, *Black People*, p. 105.
22. Wheeler, R. *The Complexion of Race* (Philadelphia, PA, 2000).
23. Kolchin, P., *American Slavery 1619-1877* (Canada, 1993), pp. 16–7.

24. Sandhu, S., 'Ignatius Sancho: An African Man of Letters', in King et al., *Ignatius Sancho*, p. 48.
25. Godfrey, R. *James Gillray: the Art of Caricature* (2001), pp. 84–5.
26. Bondeson, J. *The London Monster* (Philadelphia, PA, 2001), pp. 59, 63 and 66.
27. Shyllon, *Black Slaves*, pp. 140–5. In covering the letters to the press at the time of the Somerset case Shyllon says: 'One of the most curious aspects of the Somerset case was the complete disregard of one of the traditional clichés of British justice – the non-discussion in the press of a matter that is *sub-judice*' (p. 141). Under the laws on *sub-judice*, it is the publication of factual information that might prejudice a current case that is forbidden, not comment upon it or issues that it raises.
28. Fryer, *Staying Power*, p. 133,
29. *Ibid.*, p. 70.
30. George, *London Life*, p. 137.
31. Shyllon, *Black Slaves*, pp. 151–2 and 162–3.
32. Roxann Wheeler, for example, uses published works. Although these come from a wide range of sources – literary (like Daniel Defoe), factual reference works and philosophical (like David Hume) – they are the product of a small elite, the eighteenth-century equivalent of what are today called the 'chattering classes'. I do not argue with her conclusion but I would argue that the views of such people take time to filter down to the majority and still never become universal.
33. *Proceedings* 1793–4, I, no. 45.
34. BASA *Newsletter* 37, September 2003, p. 27, reported by Sheila Crowson. Nestor was buried in Teston, Kent, on 14 December 1787.
35. *Lloyds Evening Post*, 9–12 January 1767, p. 59.
36. *London Daily Advertiser*, 5 October 1751, p. 2.
37. *London Evening Post*, 18–20 October 1744, p. 4.
38. *Mighty Lewd Books: the Development of Pornography in Eighteenth Century England* (Basingstoke, 2003) and *Lascivious Bodies: a Sexual History of the Eighteenth Century* (2004).
39. Ingram, A., *Patterns of Madness in the Eighteenth Century: a Reader* (Liverpool, 1998) is a useful introduction.
40. *Hull Advertiser*, 28 July 1798, p. 3c. *The Greenock Advertiser* carried an anecdote about a similarly unintelligent black man named Peter Cooper which was reproduced in *The Times* of 7 July 1827, p. 3. It is possible that 'Peter Cooper' was a generic name, like Jim Crow, for Black people.
41. Sprott, *1784*, pp. 18, 99, 224 and 281.
42. *Ibid.*, pp. 141, 143, 208 and 242. Other items mention people who were possibly Black, pp. 69, 92, 84 and 232.
43. *Proceedings* 1731–2, V, no. 13.
44. 'Joe Miller's Jests' (1882) in Ashton, J., *Chap-Books of the Eighteenth Century* (repr., nd [?1980s]), p. 290.

45. Gwynn, R.D., *Huguenot Heritage: the History and Contribution of the Huguenots in Britain* (1985), p. 144. There were other communities in towns and cities in the south of England.
46. Shyllon, *Black People*, pp. 106–10. Most of the writers he quoted in support of his argument were, however, American.
47. *London Chronicle*, 1758, p. 116.
48. Sherwood, M. 'Blacks in the Gordon Riots', pp. 24–7.
49. Ayres, J. (ed.), *Paupers and Pig Killers: The Diary of William Holland a Somerset Parson 1799–1818* (Stroud, 1984), p. 106. At this time, West Indian meant all people from the West Indies, not just Black people. On 30 November 1799, Holland noted, 'Met Mr Mackay and his inevitable companion Mr Everett Poole . . . Oh, brave – an Old Buck of Sixty and a young buck not thirty. Hum – .' This presumably refers to Mr Mackey senior and the suggestion of an improper relationship may account for Holland's remark that he does not like West Indians in general. It should be added that, on the evidence of the rest of his diary, he liked or approved of very few people. Because of his general sourness, I had not read the entire book (bought many years ago), so I am grateful to an anonymous member of the Hertfordshire Family History Society for drawing my attention to this entry.
50. Sharp, G., *Letter Book*, p. 159, quoted in Gerzina, *Black England*, p. 178.
51. The wealth of the upper classes in India largely protected them from such disdain, as David Cannadine explores in *Orientalism* (2001).
52. Treleaven, S., *A Moretonhampstead Diary* on <www.moretonhampstead.org.uk>. General Rochambeau was a French officer sent on parole from Wincanton, Somerset, during the Napoleonic Wars. In the parish register Peter's surname is given as Courpon (though his colour is not mentioned). The couple had at least three children, one of whom, John Peter, bought a house in Moretonhampstead in 1870. MacKeith, L., *Local Black History: a Beginning in Devon* (2003), pp. 28–30.
53. Paul Boateng, MP, recalled that his father, who came to England from Ghana, was frequently touched 'for luck' by white Londoners in the 1950s. 'The Great British Black Invasion' (Twenty-Twenty Vision) broadcast on Channel 4 on 5 August 2006.
54. She was freed on her return to Boston later that summer.
55. Prince, M., *The History of Mary Prince* (1831, rev. edn, Michigan, 1997), pp. 87–8.

Chapter 7

Names and identities

All societies have what are called 'rites of passage', ceremonies to mark significant events in a person's life which make them part of a community or society. The three universal ones are birth, marriage and death, although how they are celebrated varies according to the local culture. Black people in Britain came from a number of ethnic backgrounds and would have had different rites of passage and ways of marking them: circumcision and menarche still seem today to be particularly significant for many non-Muslim African peoples, because they signify the point at which an individual becomes capable of producing children.[1] Although from the twentieth century onwards there are professional, anthropological descriptions of such ceremonies in Africa, it is now impossible to reconstruct what happened in the eighteenth century, both because they were not previously recorded in writing and because they may have changed over the centuries, not least in response to European influence. Twin sacrifice, for example, sometimes with the social exclusion of the mother, was practised in some African societies until Christian missionaries put an end to it. Those practices which Europeans could tolerate, however, were not radically altered.

The first rite of passage, birth, is usually accompanied by a naming ceremony. In the Americas and the Caribbean most Black slaves were assigned names by their owners without any ritual.[2] In England it is far less clear how Black people came to have the names by which they were known. Many, however, were baptised in a religious service, which had significance for the community. Different Christian sects have varying practices and beliefs around baptism. In the majority of denominations this takes place shortly after birth, although some, like the Baptists, practise adult baptism and others, like the Sandemanians, did not practise baptism at all. I shall concentrate on the practices of the Church of England, since this was both the established church and the one to which the majority of people conformed. It is also where the majority of Black people on the database enter the official records.

Children baptised as infants into the Anglican church are later expected to confirm the promises made on their behalf at confirmation or first communion, which takes place at an age when they are considered capable of understanding the vows they make. They can at this point add names with a particular significance to those originally chosen for them. The Book of Common Prayer stipulates that a licence to baptise an adult should be obtained from the bishop. Those baptised into the Church of England as adults should be immediately confirmed: this may be linked to the obtaining of a licence, since it is a bishop who carries out the confirmation service. Whether this was done on a systematic basis for adult Blacks, who would not have been christened as infants, is not known. There are occasional references to the receipt of authorisation, such as the baptism of George 'an African bap[tised] by order of the Bishop of Chester', which took place in Altrincham, Cheshire in 1806.[3] It does not, however, seem to have been a regular practice, since very few licences have survived and it is rare to find any note to this effect in registers.

Historians have noted that Black people in Roman Catholic countries were baptised immediately, while in Protestant British colonies plantation owners actively prevented missionaries from proselytising among their slaves. This is seen both as evidence that the plantocracy wished to prevent their slaves from learning arguments that would lead to even more dissatisfaction with their position and foment rebellion, and as evidence of the Roman Catholic church's greater acceptance of Black people's humanity. This is, however, to misunderstand one of the fundamental differences between Protestantism and Roman Catholicism. This difference reveals theological complexities. The Roman Catholic church has a magisterium, a body of official teachings. Membership of the church came by baptism followed by acceptance of these doctrines and the practice of confession, penance and communion.[4] Protestants, however, have never had a centrally imposed theological authority: it is the personal and individual acceptance of faith in Christ that brings membership of the church, and it requires knowledge of what is involved before acceptance and baptism.[5]

In Britain, the Anglican church required (and still does) that those baptised as adults understood what they were doing and positively wanted to take the step. This usually meant a period of instruction, although there are examples of Black people christened without preparation because they were likely to die, like Edward Peter Scipio a 'Negro

Boy', baptised in 1724 'in extreme danger of Death'.[6] The unbaptised were often refused burial in consecrated ground and it was popularly believed that such individuals would not be accepted into heaven. Even if there is no specific reference to the imminence of death, it can be surmised that some Black people were baptised so that they would have 'sure and certain hope', as the Book of Common Prayer has it, 'of the Resurrection to eternal life'. William Murray, for example, is one of many for whom the interim between baptism and burial was brief. He was baptised in Battle, Sussex on 1 May 1768 and buried twelve days later on 13 May.[7]

The obituary of the rector of Wapping, the Reverend Herbert Mayo, shows how seriously some took their role in bringing Black people to Christ and ensuring that they understood the step they were taking:

> nor did he at any time baptize them without much previous preparation; that the inward and spiritual grace might accompany the outward and visible form of baptism.[8]

Occasional notes in parish registers show that elsewhere ministers were equally determined that the Black people they baptised were truly convinced of the truth of their church's teachings. In October 1664 Richard Indem was 'catechized and Baptized' in Little Stanmore, Middlesex.[9] The clerk of Wytham, Oxfordshire noted that Peregrine Hector, an 8-year-old boy from Bengal, was baptised in 1700 'after having been instructed by [his mistress's] order in as much as he was at that time capable of understanding the Christian religion'.[10] In Harmondsworth, Middlesex in 1761 Charles Comba, 'a Black aged 28 years born on the coast of Guinea', was baptised 'after having been competently instructed in the Church Catechism'.[11] Adults were considered capable of understanding the significance of the step they were taking because they had to give informed consent. Ralph Truncket was 'willingly' baptised in Southwark in 1668.[12] Charles Comba, mentioned above, was baptised 'at his own earnest request'.

Nor was baptism into the Anglican church solely a spiritual matter. After the Reformation, ministers were part of local government, which meant that their role, especially in rural areas, was as much about maintaining social cohesion as imposing doctrine, as the diaries of parsons like James Woodforde demonstrate. His entries show equal concern with carrying out his duties in church, giving support to his flock both spiritually and practically, and maintaining a social round. In towns, however, matters were different. As Christopher Hill put it:

The gentry – with parsons in tow – re-established their pre-eminence in the countryside, except in rural industrial areas like the West Riding; but in towns dissent had come to stay. Those who set the tone in villages tended to be unsympathetic to new ideas generally and all too often to regard education for the lower classes as politically dangerous.[13]

Both adults and children were supposed to be baptised in the presence of a congregation: private baptisms at home were sometimes called half-baptisms and were expected to be repeated in church. The Anglican parish church was at the centre of everyday life, not only because the majority of parishioners belonged to it but also because it was the source of local civil government, so to become part of it through baptism was an important step in the assimilation of Black people into British society. The differences between town and country raise questions about possible differences in the treatment of Black people in these two environments, which must await further investigation. All that can be said at the moment is that the baptism of adult Black people marked their acceptance into the local community, especially in rural areas. The Protestant requirement to make a positive assent to baptism meant that Black people made a choice to join English society. Whether this would be in the established Anglican church or in one of the dissenting sects was another point of individual choice.

Some of the problems of defining a community also surface when the issue of 'identity' is raised. As Kobena Mercer wrote:

> Just now everybody wants to talk about 'identity'. As a keyword in contemporary politics it has taken on so many different connotations that people are not even talking about the same thing. One thing at least is clear – identity only becomes an issue when it is in crisis, when something assumed to be fixed, coherent and stable is displaced by the experience of doubt and uncertainty. From this angle, the eagerness to talk about identity is symptomatic of the postmodern predicament of contemporary politics.[14]

It is difficult to know how eighteenth-century Black people perceived themselves, as there are so few autobiographies. Mercer sees this concern with identity as a postmodern phenomenon. It would be a mistake, therefore, to imagine that people in the past shared twentieth- and twenty-first-century concerns about or definitions of 'identity'. Certainly both Ignatius Sancho and Olaudah Equiano were very aware of being African, but how they understood this is not clear. It would be wrong to impose on them our present-day definitions. In any case, Sancho, who was born at sea and orphaned before he was two, never knew any other society but the English one in which he was raised. Although Equiano says that he left Africa as a child, it is possible he was born and spent his formative years in North America.

When individuals take another name it is usually to signal that they have changed, or intend to change, their life. Some non-Muslim African tribes bestow new names on boys at puberty, when they have undergone initiation ceremonies to mark their entry into the adult world. Women might similarly change their names when they had children. The position of children and baptism is discussed below, but Black adults in Britain were not simply being deprived of their old identity in a passive way but were actively changing or adapting it to take on a new one. To claim that all Black people lost their 'identity' when baptised with Western names is simplistic and reduces them to passive victims. Black people gained an identity in their new society by taking on a new name, one that did not mark them out as different from their neighbours, in the way that many Jews in Britain and America changed their names on arrival or, in the case of Germans in Britain in the First World War, to avoid prejudice and to emphasise where their loyalties lay.[15] Some Black people, like a few of the Sons of Africa, used both their African and their British names.

Until the second half of the twentieth century those entering the religious life, particularly Roman Catholics, took the name of a saint whose virtues they hoped to emulate. Many of those who convert to Islam today take a Muslim name, like the American boxer Cassius Clay, who became Muhammed Ali. In the past, when women were considered to have no identity outside marriage, they almost invariably took their husbands' surnames on marriage and became subsumed into their men's identities, being known as Mrs John Smith, or whatever.[16] Most still do. These actions mark the leaving behind of an earlier phase in their lives to begin a new and different one. For Black people in Britain, receiving a Christian name was such a rite of passage. As well as the belief that baptism conferred freedom, genuine conversion from their previous beliefs, or signalling their desire to join British society, there was a fourth reason for taking this momentous step. Some may have been baptised as a prerequisite to marriage. In 1774 the minister of St Marylebone in London refused to marry Henry Greenwich, 'a Black Man' and Mary Fisher because he was not baptised.[17] John Juba was christened and married by licence on the same day at Lowestoft, Suffolk in 1737.[18]

Some masters may have put pressure on their servants to take instruction, especially if they themselves had a strong faith. Susanne Redonnel, for example, was baptised at the French Huguenot Church of Le Carré and Berwick Street and there is a detailed description of what brought her there (I have preserved the original spelling):

> Aujourdhuy 9 Oct 1715, a été batizé par Mr Lombard, une fille née en Afrique, esclave dans la Jamaique, élevée presque sans aucun sentiment de religion jusqu'à l'âge de vingt cinq ans ou environ. Mais la Providence de Dieu l'ayant fait tomber entre les mains de M[r] et de Mad[elle] Redonnel, Protestants, français refugiez cy devant dans la Jamaique et presentiment à Londres, ils ont eu tant de soin de l'instruire dans la Religion chrétienne qu'elle a voulu en faire profession et en prendre les saintes livrées dans le batême, auquel elle a été presenté par Mr Redonnel qui lui a serui de parrain et par Mad[elles] Redonnel et Peschain qui ont été ses marraines et qui luy ont donné le nom de Susanne.[19]
>
> [Today 9th October 1715 was baptised by Mr Lombard, a young woman born in Africa, a slave in Jamaica, brought up with almost no religious feeling to the age of twenty-five or thereabouts. God's Providence having made her fall into the hands of Mr and Miss Redonnel, Protestants, previously refugees in Jamaica and currently in London, they took so much care to have her instructed in the Christian religion that she wanted to make profession of it and to take the blessed books in the baptism ceremony, to which she was presented by Mr Redonnel, who served as her godfather and by Misses Redonnel and Peschain who were her godmothers and who gave her the name Susanne.]

There is no indication in the entry of how Susanne came to be in the Redonnel household nor of how old she was when she left Africa, but no doubt the Redonnels were horrified by her lack of religious upbringing. It would take a lot of commitment to any previous religion on the part of a slave to withstand the atmosphere in a devout household of refugees who had endured much for their faith. The emphasis on her slave status in Jamaica suggests that she was regarded as free in London. Perhaps Susanne genuinely believed that the faith her employers espoused had a lot to commend it, but there is no doubt that her life in their household would be considerably easier, were she to become a member of their church. This would, of course, apply to other Black servants, as it was customary for a household to pray together every day.

Although this entry makes it clear that Susanne's name was given by her godmothers, we do not know who chose the majority of Black people's names. Most were probably given by their masters, but some must have been selected by the person being baptised. In the Anglican ceremony of baptism of both infants and adults, it is the godparents or sponsors who tell the priest the name of the person to be christened. The Book of

Common Prayer states that the priest names the child 'after them', which suggests either that the individual takes the name of one of the godparents or that they bestow the name. It may be assumed that in the past godparents, or sponsors as they were called in the case of adult baptism, were told the parents' or individual's wishes in advance, as they are at present. Until the twentieth century, however, it was common to give children the name of a godparent, literally to name them after them. Thomas Carter, 'a Black from Guinea aged about 18 years', was baptised in the City of London in 1742. His sponsors were Edward Carter, Thomas Hughes and Martha Smith. It is possible that Edward Carter was the master and Thomas Hughes a friend of the family, or vice versa.[20] The names of very few sponsors were given in parish registers, but at least 27.77 per cent of Black men were given one or more of the names of their sponsors. For women the figure is apparently 26.08 per cent, but it must be emphasised that the numbers involved are very small: so far, fewer than 1 per cent of baptismal entries have been found to give the full names of sponsors. In some cases only the surnames or titles, not the forenames, of sponsors were given, so the true percentages may be higher.

Christian names

In today's largely secular society it is difficult to empathise with, or even understand fully, what it was like to live in a society where Christianity was all-pervasive. By the time Black people started to arrive in Britain in great numbers the Puritan fashion for giving children names of Christian virtues like Charity, Love or Repentance had largely passed, but there are a few examples of these among the Black population. Mary Prudence received her double helping of Christian name and Christian virtue in 1707.[21] George Goodchild, 'a Negro youth supposed to be 14 years old', was christened in 1736.[22] This may have been a reflection of his obedient nature or a hope that he would prove so. It may also have been a translation of his original African name or the name of a sponsor, as Goodchild is a British surname.

Some names do seem to have been selected for their religious connotations, like that of Polycarp Kent, 'a negro servant to Mr John Wicker', who was christened in Kent in 1716/7.[23] St Polycarp's feast day is 26 January and his namesake was baptised on 20 January. The date of the ceremony, combined with the rarity of the name, suggests that it had significance for either the servant or the master. St Polycarp was an important saint in the early church because he had known St John and other people who knew Jesus Christ personally. He was martyred following his betrayal by a servant, burned and then stabbed because he refused to curse the God he had followed for eighty-six years.[24] Peregrine Hector (mentioned above) is another whose name seems to have had particular religious importance. It is derived from the Latin for 'pilgrim'. Another name with apparently significant connotations is Bartholomew. A few Bartholomews, like the son of Thomas Ruford '(a Black and a Drummer)' and his wife Catherine,[25] were baptised on or around 24 August, the saint's day of this apostle, who is traditionally supposed to have spread the Gospel in India. This tentative link (he is also connected to other places) may suggest that those so named were from the East Indies rather than of African origin, but this is conjecture. The apostle Thomas is linked more firmly to India, where the Christians of Kerala still call themselves 'St Thomas Christians'.[26] Certainly there seems to be a large number of Black people of Indian origin being given the name Thomas but, as origins are often not recorded in baptismal entries, this cannot be conclusive.

The names of other saints – Joseph, Mary, Anne, Elizabeth, Matthew, Mark, Luke, John – may also have been chosen for religious reasons by the Black people who took their names or by their masters but, since they were also common names among the white population, the import is lost today. Mary, which was the most popular name for women for most of the nineteenth century and in the top ten from the Middle Ages onwards,[27] was the most popular name for Black women. As the name of the mother of God, it may have had particular significance. In 1781 in East Barnet in Hertfordshire,

> Pamela a Negro servant belonging to Major General Prevost of Green Hill Grove in the Parish of Chipping Barnet was Baptised in this Church by the name of Mary. The sponsors were The Lady of Gen. Prevost, Miss Juliana Yonge of East Barnet as proxy for Miss Mary Burton of Upper Brook Street Grosvenor Square and The Rev William Tait.[28]

Not only the name, but the date chosen was momentous: the christening, the only one that day, took place on Christmas Day, so the name is particularly apposite.

Generic names

There were a few names given only to Black men which must have been their masters' choices. Mingo or Mungo became a generic name for a Black servant. Other generic names were Sambo and Pompey. Thomas Sambo, 'Mr Hayward's Black boy', and Pompey Shadwell, 'a Negro Infant of Six years of age', were baptised in the City of London in 1710 and 1716/7 respectively.[29] It was largely the aristocracy who gave these names, the kind given to a pet, to their servants and they are much less common than standard names. I know of no study of the names given to pets in the eighteenth century, but the family of Elizabeth Ham had a dog called Caesar.[30] Of those on the database, just under 4 per cent were given this kind of name or a classical name, as either a forename or a surname. In the case of women only two (Mary Negro and Maria Sambo) had such names.[31]

Only men were given what might be called stereotypical names and these were not the most common. The name Caesar, both a first and surname, seems to have been confined to Black men. Although it appears high on the list of surnames for Black men (see Table 10) only twenty-six were given this first name. Other classical names given to Black men include Cato and Scipio, the latter presumably a reference to Scipio Africanus, the Roman senator, but are found as forenames in the white population as well. There were fewer of these stereotypical names for women but Dido (Queen of Carthage in North Africa, and the subject of an opera by Henry Purcell) is occasionally found. Dido Elizabeth Belle, the great-niece of Lord Mansfield, is the best-known example, but there are others, like Elizabeth Dido, 'A Moore formerly called Dido', baptised in 1688 in the City of London.[32]

It has been claimed that these names mocked their recipients: that some amusement was derived from the contrast between the men's slave status and the grandiose names by which they were called. Folarin Shyllon wrote:

> The black . . . was often made to bear an absurdly pompous classical name, the exalted associations of which contrasted sharply with his lowly estate as a chattel or plaything . . . Why such classical names should have been bestowed upon these poor black lads is hard to say, unless the practice arose from a cruel inclination to mock at them by contrasting their grand appellations with their abject fortunes.[33]

Given the importance of servants in everyday life and the intimate ways in which they served their masters, this would seem to be a mistake on the masters' part. The opportunities for a mocked and humiliated servant to make disagreeable the lives of the members of the family he or she served were numerous. In the West Indies there were cases of masters being poisoned by servants. Use of a name intended ironically may possibly have happened in a few cases in Britain, but this is perhaps to misunderstand the situation based on looking only at Black people, rather than at the wider population as well. Classical names were in vogue in the eighteenth century, although they are found from the Renaissance onwards. The Master of the Rolls from 1614 to 1636 was a Sir Julius Caesar, and another Julius Caesar was a physician in Rochester in the early eighteenth century. Julius Caesar Ibbetson was a painter based in Ambleside, in the Lake District.[34] Dorothy Wordsworth mentions his son in her journal, but she finds nothing worthy of comment in his name.[35] Sir Caesar Child was a member of a family prominent in the East India Company. Military men were particularly fond of Caesar and Hercules for their own children, as parish registers in garrison towns attest. The forename Scipio seems to have had a local popularity in Devon, to judge by both the International Genealogical Index and documents in the local record offices there.[36] Even lower down the social scale people gave their children such names. Claudius Caesar Turner was buried from the workhouse in Chiswick, London in 1829.[37] Based on his name, I presumed he was Black until I found an account of a trial at the Old Bailey in which he was involved as a witness. There is no mention there that he was other than white.[38] The abolitionist James Ramsey's servant was named Nestor, presumably after one of the Greek leaders at Troy, who was famed for his wisdom. An abolitionist would surely not have a Black servant with a name that mocked him. The officiating minister, who must have been white, at Pompey Shadwell's baptism was one Ptolemy James, but a classical Egyptian name was rare and it is unlikely that James's parents intended to mock their infant. Scipio may also have had naval connotations: it was the name of a ship in the Royal Navy. To call a ship by a name regarded as derisory would be unthinkable now and even more so in the eighteenth century, when the navy played such a large part in the expansion of British influence throughout the world and was therefore held in high esteem. As well as being the name of one of the triumvirate who ruled Rome with Julius Caesar, Pompey is the nickname given by Royal Navy sailors to Portsmouth and, as the home port to which many hoped to return safely, must have carried affectionate connotations.

Heroic and whimsical names

Olaudah Equiano was baptised Gustavus Vassa,[39] the name of the man who was elected King of Sweden in 1523 after leading a rebellion against Danish rule over his country and who established Lutheranism as the state religion. This might be seen as an ironic usage, intended to mock, since Vassa freed his people from what they saw as slavery, but Equiano himself does not interpret it this way: he used the name throughout his life and it is only in his autobiography that the name we prefer to use today appears. Someone so sensitive to his slave status would surely have been aware of any ironic or power-based intention. To suggest that Equiano was ignorant of his master's 'irony' seems patronising, suggesting that he was unable to comprehend the concept. Gustavus Vassa must have had some significance for Equiano's master, but whether he admired his military skill or respected his religious beliefs is not known. Equiano's enthusiastic conversion to Christianity may suggest the latter. His later fight to overthrow slavery also has parallels with the Swedish king's struggle against the foreign rulers of his country. Was his master being prescient, or did Equiano live up to his name? Nor, apparently, did the wider population see these names as ironic. It was an age which revered heroes. The foundlings left at Thomas Coram's hospital were rebaptised and given the names both of heroes and of the noble and socially conscientious people who gave financial support. Among the first foundlings taken in were two Francis Drakes, Walter Raleigh, Andrew Marvel, Emma Plantagenet, Elizabeth Tudor, William Hogarth, Augustus Caesar and Isaac Newton.[40] Coram and the directors did not intend to mock or humiliate the children they rescued: they genuinely wanted them to begin a new life with a name to live up to. Other parallels can be found in the white population. In the City of London in 1776 a child named Raphael Titian Corregio Bartolozzi Coleman was buried. These names cannot have been given in an ironic spirit: would a father ridicule his infant's inability to paint? This father was so keen to commemorate his admiration of these artists that he gave another child, buried in 1780, the same names.[41] The conclusion must be that he hoped his son would grow up to emulate the painters. This is not a unique example.

There are always parents who think it witty to give their infant an amusing name. One of the commanding admirals at the Battle of Copenhagen in 1801 was called Hyde Parker. Perhaps his parents were commemorating a place that was important to them. Such examples in the white population, like Olive Branch, the daughter of John and Olive Hutchinson, baptised in Putney in 1717,[42] or Charlotte Brown Blankett, daughter of William and Elizabeth Blankett, baptised in 1773 in the parish of St Katherine by the Tower in London,[43] can be multiplied by many hundreds. These humorous names were surely not meant to mock their parents' offspring but had some private significance. Such names were also given to Black people. Ignatius Sancho, for example, was actually baptised Charles Ignatius (the names of kings and saints).

The aristocratic ladies whom he served as a pageboy in his childhood thought he resembled Sancho, a servant in Cervantes' popular novel *Don Quixote*.

It is more likely that those Black men given generic, classical or whimsical names by their masters were seen as pets: not perhaps fully human but still regarded with affection and having a place in their households. Unlike field-hands, Black domestic servants brought from the American and Caribbean colonies had a privileged position and had been selected and carefully trained for this role. It may also be significant that these whimsical names seem to have been bestowed mainly by the upper classes. Conscious of their rank, they were making it clear that their servants were not on an equal footing but still had a place in their lives. The lack of stereotypical names for Black women suggests that they were not regarded as pets. Unlike Black men, they were not used as highly visible status symbols: they were there to work, just like other servants, and the use of commonplace names for them perhaps reflects this. Women, whether white or Black, had even less power than men in society and were therefore open to more ridicule, so this reinforces the argument that giving a stereotypical name to a Black man was not intended to belittle him. It is also possible that these generic names were used in the same way as Taffy became a nickname for Welshmen and Mac or Jimmy for Scotsmen. There were, in the twentieth century at least, a number of English surnames linked to standard nicknames, like 'Chalky' White or 'Nobby' Clark. There is no equivalent for women. Stereotypical names were more likely a reflection of mental laziness on the part of masters, rather than an intention to mock.

Standard names

For Black people, much more common were names indistinguishable from the general population, the names that parents give to their children. Tables 8, 9 and 10 give the most popular first names for men and women and surnames for both sexes. The most popular names in the white population are given for comparison. Naturally, between 1660 and 1812 fashions brought minor changes of position to the names in the top ten. I have not broken down the names given to Black people according to date because there were relatively few, so the figures would be less statistically significant.

The three most popular names for white men (John, William and Thomas) were also the three most popular for Black men throughout the entire long eighteenth century. John is by far the front runner, being

Table 8 Most popular names of white and Black men, seventeenth to nineteenth centuries (percentages)

	General population[a]		Black men 1660–1812
	c.1610	c.1825	
John	21.0	13.5	John
William	11.4	16.3	William
Thomas	11.4	8.6	Thomas
Richard	5.2	[not in top 10]	George
Samuel	5.0	[not in top 10]	Charles
Henry	4.8	7.6	Joseph
Edward	4.5	3.5	Peter
James	3.5	8.6	Richard
Joseph	2.6	3.7	Henry/Harry
Robert	2.4	3.1	James
George	[not in top 10]	9.4	Robert
Charles	[not in top 10]	5.8	Samuel

Note: [a] From Douglas Galbi's tables on the ten most popular names for men in London between 1120 and 1994 on <www.galbithink.org/names>, p. 12.

found almost twice as frequently as William, the next most popular. George was not much used in Britain until period of the Hanoverian kings. Its frequency among Black men probably reflects the fact that the majority came to Britain while one of the kings named George was on the throne. Some of the Harrys may be more properly spelled Hari, a name used in India, and may indicate that these men were of Indian origin. The only name popular for Black men which does not appear in the list of favourite forenames for white men is Peter. The first of Christ's apostles, and originally called Simon, Peter was the rock (*petros*, the Greek translation of the Aramaic *cephas*, the name Christ gave this disciple) on whom the Church was built and this may be a further indication that religious significance played an important part in the naming of many Black people.

Women's forenames were, and still are, more susceptible to fashion. The popularity among Black women of Susan/Susannah, Maria and Charlotte probably reflects the fashion of the mid-late eighteenth century, as George does for men. The eighteenth century also saw the invention of a number of women's names. Sarah Clarinda, 'a Negro child', was baptised in Bath in 1779, combining a standard Biblical name with a fanciful novelty.[44] Melinda Phillips, 'a Black about 17 years old', was baptised in Westminster

Table 9 Most popular names of white and Black women, seventeenth to nineteenth centuries (percentages)

	General population[a]			Black women 1660–1812
	c.1640	c.1730	c.1825	
Elizabeth	16.6	15.3	12.9	Mary
Ann/e	16.4	18.1	11.6	Elizabeth
Jane	13.1	11.2	13.5	Ann/e
Margaret	12.8	10.6	9.4	Sarah
Mary	9.9	16.7	20.3	Susanna/h
Isabella	5.9	4.8	6.2	[not in top 10]
Ellen	3.6	2.9	3.3	[not in top 10]
Alice	3.6	[not in top 10]	[not in top 10]	[not in top 10]
Dorothy	2.9	2.6	[not in top 10]	[not in top 10]
Frances	1.9	[not in top 10]	[not in top 10]	Jane
Hannah	[not in top 10]	3.0	3.6	K/Catherine
Sarah	[not in top 10]	2.1	5.8	=Margaret
				=Maria
Catherine	[not in top 10]	[not in top 10]	1.6	Charlotte

Note: [a] From Douglas Galbi's tables on the ten most popular female names in Northern England c.1350–c.1994 on <www.galbithink.org/names> p. 14. The north of England had close links to Scotland, so names like Margaret, Isabella and Ellen would be commoner there. There seems to be no comparable study of female names in London.

in 1787.[45] But these fanciful names are also found in the white population. They never, however, became popular enough to displace the standard names in the top ten for either Black or white women.

Surnames

In Britain, surnames have no religious significance: they are a means of distinguishing one individual from another according to family ties. It is the first, or Christian names, that are significant and given at baptism. Surnames are not bestowed at the font, which is probably why only the literally Christian name or names appear in many entries of the baptisms of Black people.[46] On the database 15.18 per cent of men and 22.57 per cent of women appear without a surname. However, a number were given second forenames, like Francis or Thomas, which could have been used either as Christian names or surnames, which further confuses the issue.

Table 10 Most popular surnames of white and Black people, seventeenth to nineteenth centuries

Surname	Frequency in England and Wales, 1853[a]	Frequency among Black people, 1660–1812	
		Men	Women
Smith	1	Williams	Williams
Jones	2	Brown	=Smith
			=Johnson
Williams	3	Smith	
Taylor	4	Johns(t)on	=Jones
			=Lewis
			=Young
Davies/Davis	5	Thomas	
Brown	6	=Jones	
		=Caesar	
Thomas	7		Harris
Evans	8	Moore/More	=Blake
			=Hamilton
			=Jackson
Roberts/Robertson	9	=Roberts	
		=James	
Johnson	10		

Note: [a] Cottle, B. *The Penguin Dictionary of Surnames* (2nd edn, 1978). Cottle states (p. 24–5) that the data on popularity of names in 1853 is from government sources, although he does not cite the name of any publication. It is likely to have been the 1851 Census.

It is possible that these individuals used other surnames which were not recorded in the registers. Until the nineteenth century, the law recognised a married couple as one person – the husband.[47] In many seventeenth-century burial registers, women appear only as 'the wife of X' or 'Widow X'. The primacy of men as the heads of households extended to their apprentices and servants, Black or white, and some early burial records do not record their names either. In 1692 'Mr Powers Black' was interred in the vault of St Peter le Poer in the City of London.[48]

There were only twelve Black men who took the symbolic name Freeman, plus one Free and one Freeland. However, Freeman is also a standard British name, so it is difficult to know whether these individuals chose to commemorate their freedom and independence or were named after a sponsor. The names of the masters of only four of these men with symbolic names are mentioned, but none of them was called Freeman, and no sponsors are given for any of them.

The preponderance of patronymics for the white population is partly due to their frequency in the population at large, but must be heavily weighted by the Welsh element, especially Jones, Davies and Evans. The Welsh did not use fixed surnames until the beginning of the eighteenth century and most were patronymic.[49] The lack of Black people called Evans, a specifically Welsh name, may reflect the comparatively few Welsh people who had connections with the Caribbean or North America. Williams was widespread in both England and Wales, which may account for its high placing in the list for both white and Black people. Although it was third in the general population, it was the most common surname for both Black men and women. William was the second most common forename for men in the general population. The most common forename for both Black and white men was John. John Williams may therefore be the most common name for Black men, because these individuals were given the forenames of both of their male godparents or sponsors. Black women may have been given the surname Williams to honour a male sponsor whose forename was William.

The close correlation between the popularity of surnames in both the general and the Black population does suggest linkage. Names are bound up with identity: it is how one individual is distinguished from another, and to give another person one's name is a significant step: it is a permanent and public declaration of a connection which lasts a lifetime and suggests that masters and sponsors took their responsibilities seriously. Thomas Craufurd, 'a Black aged ab^t 15 years, serv^t to Alexander Craufurd esq^{re}', was baptised in Richmond, Surrey, in 1774.[50] As noted above, giving Black people the same name as their masters may be more common than it appears: the masters' names were usually omitted and only a few parishes recorded sponsors or godparents. Where they are given, the Black person often seems to have been called after one or more of them. Some historians have seen this practice as a sign of ownership, but it may be an indication that the master regarded the servant as part of the family, although in a patriarchal society it is difficult to separate ownership from family ties. In at least one case a family connection was made explicit. In 1752 in Westminster, London, Joseph Harvey, 'a Black of Mr Hamiltons Family', was baptised.[51] Describing someone Black as a family member is, so far, rare: only one other example, also in Westminster, has been found.[52] Joseph Harvey may have been the mixed-race son of a family member, brought to England from the colonies for his education, but, as Hamilton is a Scottish name, Joseph may have been regarded as a member of the clan, the extended family. Although a clan is defined as a group related by a common ancestor, in Scotland it came to include anyone giving allegiance to a chief. Alternatively, it may have been a survival of the practice of regarding all the members of a household as part of the family, because it seems to have occurred with white servants as well. On 14 February 1660/1 Samuel Pepys and Sir William Penn went to Woolwich. Pepys's serving boy, Wayneman Birch, accompanied them and 'hath all this day been called young Pepys, as Sir W. Pen's boy young Pen'.[53] In Pepys's annual assessments of his life, he often mentions the servants and calls them part of his family. On 31 December 1664 he wrote:

> My family is my wife, in good health, and happy with her; her woman Mercer, a pretty, modest, quiet maid; her chambermaid Bess; her cook maid Jane, the little girl Susan, and my boy which I have had about half a year ... and a pretty and loving quiet family I have as any man in England.[54]

In 1711 Joseph Steele, in an essay on that perennial topic of servants' behaviour, wrote:

> the general corruption of Manners in Servants is owing to the Conduct of Masters. The aspect of everyone in the Family carries so much Satisfaction, that it appears he [i.e. the servant] knows the happy Lot which has befallen him in being a Member of it.[55]

This lack of distinction between household and family seems to have continued well into the eighteenth century. As late as 1784, when reporting the death of Dr Johnson, the *Public Advertiser* mentioned that he 'supported in his family an indigent old lady who was stone blind'.[56] Anna Williams was no relation to Johnson, but she lived under the same roof and was treated like a relative. Johnson also made his Black servant, Francis Barber, his main heir, as if he were a son. Johnson's lack of blood relations probably led him to create his own 'family', but the newspaper made no distinction between family and household, without further comment. Additional evidence that at least some Black servants were regarded as part of the family comes from the fact that a number were baptised on the same day, and presumably at the same time, as a child of their master, like Joseph, 'a black of riper years, serv^t to Govr Forbes Esq', christened in Richmond, Surrey on the same day in 1779 as Richard Gordon, the son of Gordon Forbes Esq and Margaret, his wife.[57] In Chatham in Kent, George St George, 'a Negro boy belonging to George Cherry', was baptised on 7 March 1763, the same day as his son John Hector.[58] As well as those entries where it is obvious that a servant and child were baptised on the same day because the master's name is given, there are many others where a link may be conjectured. On 13 February 1697/8, for example, Joseph Williams, 'A Black', and Ann, daughter of Arthur and Ann Zouch, were both baptised. The two entries in the register of St Dunstan in the West in the City of London were annotated 'in Chancery Lane', but the others around that period were usually recorded as having taken place 'at the Font'.[59] It seems as if the couple's child was privately baptised at home and their servant was christened at the same time. Linking the baptism of a child, welcoming it into the congregation and the wider Christian society, with that of a servant must have had some significance. Masters would have been aware that, unlike the majority of their white servants, Black people had no family ties in Britain, and the more responsible of them realised it was their duty to provide a substitute. George Cherry gave his 'boy' his own personal name, as fathers habitually did to their sons. The right to control the lives of family and household members was balanced by responsibilities towards them and by baptising child and servant at the same time such familial links and responsibilities were made public. Other baptisms of Black servants seem to have taken place on dates important to their masters' families. Lady Emma Hamilton, Lord Nelson's mistress, had a Black servant who was baptised on 26 April 1802 in Merton, Surrey. The date was significant: it was Lady Hamilton's birthday.[60] The woman was given the name Fatima Emma Charlotte Nelson Hamilton, publicly linking her to both the Nelson and Hamilton families. Whether other Black people were also baptised on days that commemorated some special date or event in the lives of the families they served must await further research.

African names

A few Black people retained African names as forenames, and more kept them as surnames, thus acknowledging their dual identity as both Christian and African. In West Africa children may be called after the day of the week on which they were born, so it is easy to identify those who kept their original African name as surname to which was added what was literally a Christian name. Kofi for those born on Friday occurs in a number of the Akan-speaking West African peoples, the Agni of Ivory Coast and the Gen of Togo. This was written down by parish clerks as Cuffey or Coffee. William Cuffay, the grandson of a slave in St Kitts and a prominent member of the Chartist movement, retained this reminder of his ethnic heritage, as did seven others on the database. Another day-of-the-week name from this part of Africa is Kwesi and variants (Kwasi, Kossi, Kouassi), meaning Monday, Saturday or Sunday in different languages. John Quashey was baptised in Bath in 1745/6[61] and Rosanna Quossey in London in 1730.[62] In 1756, Agnes McBracka, 'a Negro woman, a servant to Jacob Allen Esq of Jamaica', was baptised in Bath. In the Bishop's Transcripts, a list of all the ceremonies carried out in a church which was sent annually to the bishop of the diocese, the name appears as 'Brack'. 'Buckra' or 'backra' was a West African word meaning 'he who rules' and was used by slaves to denote whites. The fact that a woman, and a Black woman at that, was called by this name suggests someone of authority or commanding character.[63] Juba was another name often given to Black people, either as a first or a surname. This name is conjectured to derive from a popular play, *Cato, a Tragedy* (1713) by Joseph Addison, in which there is a Black character called Juba, but it may have been a real African name. It was also given to women. For example, Elizabeth Jewber, 'a blackmore', appears in London in 1716.[64] Even where it is not explicitly stated that the surname is the original name, some can be presumed to be so, as in the case of Elizabeth Quedia, 'A Moore formerly called by ye Name of Quedia', who was baptised in 1659.[65] Nathaniel Narrangue, Edward Malimbo and John Ancoo also seem to have retained African names.[66] Katherine Auker is well known to historians because in 1690 she went to court to be released from her master, Robert Rich of Barbados.[67] Katherin Aufra, 'A Blackmore Mayd of Lady Littletons', was baptised in 1665.[68] They are unlikely to be the same person, so the similarity suggests that Auker or Aufra was an African name.

The meanings of most of these names are now lost, between the passage of time and the limitations of English clerks in trying to write down what they thought they had heard (at this time, of course, most Africans had no written language[69] and the British population was also largely illiterate, so clerks were used to approximating spellings). This may account for some of the odder names, like Jack Beef, the servant of John Baker, magistrate and lawyer in London and Solicitor-General of St Kitts in the West Indies. Tom Pop was baptised in the City of London in 1749.[70] Whether John Heart (baptised in Bath in 1734/5)[71] and Thomas Chest (baptised and buried in Covent Garden in 1737)[72] got their names from the clerk's attempt to reproduce an African name or from some physical peculiarity cannot be known, although the two possible explanations are not necessarily incompatible. Many British surnames are derived from personal attributes, like Cruikshank ('crooked legs'), Russell ('red hair'),

Puddephat ('bulgy barrel', for a man with a large belly)[73] and this may be a universal characteristic of personal names. A man named John Chest (apparently white) was transported to Virginia in 1738,[74] which shows that this kind of name was also found in the general population. By the time Black people came to be baptised they would have spoken enough English to understand what they were doing. Those born in Africa would therefore have been able to explain what their original name meant, so some of the names they received are possibly English translations. It may be coincidence that the two previously mentioned Black women surnamed Auker or Aufra were both christened Katherine, meaning 'pure', or that may be the meaning of their original African name. In many cultures that value female chastity, calling girls after this virtue occurs. Giving children a name intended to ensure good luck is also virtually universal. Olaudah Equiano says that his first name meant 'fortunate', and the surname Fortune was given to some Black people, like Susannah Fortune, 'an adult Negro aged about 32', christened in Kent in 1757[75] and Ziphares Fortune, 'an Indian boy, a native of Barbadoes about 10 years of age', who was 'admitted a member of the Protestant Church of England' in 1700.[76] Were these translations of their original names?

Place names

The names Blackmore and Moore are fairly common British surnames borne by people presumably descended from those living on or near moorland. In Hampshire there is a place called Blackmoor and in Essex a parish named Blackmore. In Yorkshire there is the parish of Hemsley Blackmoor.[77] Some of the Blackmores may originally have been Blackmere (= black pool). Imtiaz Habib, though he recognises that Blackmore and Blackman are English surnames, seems to believe that all those of these names were of African origin, even when there is no indication of this in the original documents. He even includes a goldsmith in the City of London named Blackmore in his list of references to Black people in archives. Given the City's strict stance against aliens and the children of aliens at the time covered by his work (1500–1677) and until much later, this is virtually impossible.[78] Blackamore and variants seem to have been much rarer. There are a few examples, like Charles Blackamore, baptised in the City of London in 1690. His ethnic origin, a 'Moore', was specified.[79] Other examples, however, may have been instances of epenthesis, the insertion of an additional sound, which is not uncommon in English (and no doubt other languages), and may refer to white people. The Essex parish of Blackmore was written Blackemore in an entry in the marriage register of St Margaret Moses in the City of London in 1632/3.[80] In pre-twentieth-century documents 'Henry' is often written as 'Henery', even in signatures, which must indicate how their owners pronounced the name. Present-day examples include the words 'athelete' and 'grievious' for 'athlete' and 'grievous'. This practice adds to the difficulty of identifying Black people in records. The word 'blackamoor', referring specifically to Black people, would originally have been Black Moor: perhaps the form using epenthesis was adopted to distinguish it from white people surnamed Blackmore and variants. The name Moore was also sometimes given to Black people and was probably a reference to their race, but in some cases may have been the name of a sponsor.

Specific place names form a significant proportion of the surnames taken by Black people. Jasper Goree, one of the Sons of Africa, was called after an island off the African coast where slaves were held before being sold to traders.[81] Others were called after the English places where presumably they or their masters lived, like Robert Sandwich, John Cranbrook and Thomas Shoreham, who were given the names of towns and villages in Kent.[82] Peter Truro was christened in that Cornish town[83] and there are numerous other examples of this kind. As well as town and village names, Black people were often given the name of the parish in which they lived, particularly in London, like Charles and Andrew Limehouse, baptised in 1802 and 1810 respectively,[84] and Hannah Foster 'and [sic] Indian' christened in St Vedast Foster Lane in 1664.[85] These names suggest that these individuals were not attached to a family, who would have provided sponsors willing to give their names or suggested a surname with some particular significance. The alternative is that the parish was accepting responsibility for them, as it did for foundlings, who were also regularly given the names of the parish or the streets in which they were discovered. These infants crop up regularly in baptismal registers and examples are too numerous to cite, but any parish register in any large city will provide ample evidence. Daniel Coventry, baptised in London in 1783, is most likely named after a street in Westminster, but it is a long way from the church where he was baptised. Alternatively he may have had an African name that sounded like the Midlands town or his master (not named in the baptismal entry) may have been one of the Coventry family or have come from the town.[86] Coventry is, however, in an area with no obvious connections to the slave trade. Could Daniel have arrived in England or been a sailor on a ship called the *Coventry*? Charles Active and John Active were probably named after a Royal Navy ship of the time.[87]

Baptisms of children

In the case of children, of course, the situation was different. They had far less control over their names and it is notable that a larger proportion of the names given to children by their masters tended to be of the classical or whimsical kind, like Gustavus Vassa, Pompey Shadwell or Ignatius Sancho. Some were apparently regarded as pets. A 'For Sale' advertisement for a 6-year-old Black girl in 1699 described her as 'very comely and witty, and has an abundance of very taking little actions'.[88] Sometimes the boundary between pet and child substitute was blurred. As a child, Julius Soubise was brought from St Kitts by a captain in the Royal Navy. The childless Duchess of Queensberry found him enchanting, and he became her pageboy. The Duchess dressed him elegantly (and therefore expensively), took him everywhere with her and generally indulged him to an extent that her contemporaries found excessive. Excessive, that is, for a servant, but such treatment of sons was not unknown. Soubise was taught horsemanship and fencing, the elegant accomplishments of a young aristocrat. He also had private apartments, a mistress, and hosted dinners at fashionable inns, all bankrolled by the Duchess. She found his behaviour problematic but she did not summarily dispose of him, again suggesting that he filled the role of son rather than pet.[89]

In this context, it is worth considering the silver collars which some Black servants wore, although they could also be discussed under the heading of slavery and ownership. Although Shyllon said 'collars and padlocks were deemed a necessary part of the livery of black chattels'[90] and Fryer said Black servants 'were customarily obliged to wear metal collars riveted around their necks', only some runaway notices mention them.[91] They are seen in a few paintings and on the bust of a favourite servant of William III at Hampton Court. However, the majority of runaway notices and paintings of Black servants do not include them. This is probably a further piece of evidence that Black people in the early days of their presence in England were regarded at the same level as their masters' pets, especially as the collars seem to have been worn mainly by the young. At this time, of course, Black people were a less familiar sight than they later became, valued for their exoticism. Although an often-quoted advertisement which appeared in 1756 mentioned 'silver padlocks for Blacks or Dogs collars', the last reference to someone actually wearing one seems to have been in 1728.[92] In a case at the Old Bailey in 1716/7, a servant out on an errand was enticed into a drinking house and had his collar bitten off by the women who robbed him there.[93] This suggests that the collars may not have been particularly substantial, decorative rather than symbolic of slavery, although they did mark possession.

It must be concluded that the naming of Black people was a more complex and variable issue than is suggested by simplistic claims that they were given names that both took away their identity and mocked their lack of control over their own lives. The Protestant insistence on understanding the beliefs to which an adult had to subscribe before undergoing baptism means that it cannot be assumed that the names selected were invariably the choice of a master. In the service of adult baptism there are adequate opportunities for the catechumen to reject the proposals to which he or she and the sponsors must assent. Masters or sponsors who gave their names created a link to the Black individual. Those who took places names similarly established ties to the location. Their names gave them a new identity in their new society. The next rite of passage would be marriage and the founding of a family.

Notes

1. Barley, *The Innocent Anthropologist* and *A Plague of Caterpillars* described ceremonies among a present-day tribe, the Dowayo, in the Cameroons. Although superficial aspects of their lives (like tape recorders and modern music) have been changed by industrialised countries, their fundamental beliefs showed little or no sign of twentieth-century influences.
2. Burnard, T.G., 'Slave Naming Patterns: Onomastics and the Taxonomy of Race in Eighteenth Century Jamaica', *Journal of Interdisciplinary History* 31 (3) Winter 2001, pp. 325–46.
3. BASA *Newsletter* 38, January 2004, p. 23.
4. The Roman Catholic church now requires adult converts to undertake a period of instruction.
5. Although I was aware of this difference, my understanding of it was illuminated and clarified by a lecture about the Reformation given by Professor Keith Ward at Gresham College on 7 February 2006. See <www.gresham.ac.uk>.
6. Campbell, M.V., *Registers of St Andrew Clifton, Bristol* (Bristol, 1989), 17 April 1724. He was buried on 12 May 1730, when he was noted to be 'servant of Edw. Jones'.
7. Sussex RO, transcript, Registers of Battle. He was a 'Negro servant to the Honorable General Murray'.
8. *The Orthodox Churchman's Magazine*, 11 January 1802, p. 30, quoted in Banton, M., *The Coloured Quarter* (1955).
9. LMA, Registers of Little Stanmore, Middlesex. No exact day is given.
10. BASA *Newsletter* 41, p. 15. Peregrine's mistress was Anne, Countess of Abingdon.

11. LMA, Registers of Harmondsworth, Middlesex, 7 July 1761.
12. LMA, Register of St Saviour Southwark, 11 October 1688.
13. Hill, C., *Reformation to Industrial Revolution* (rev. edn, 1969), pp. 195–6. Hill then quotes a Tory who objected to permitting dissenters to teach writing as they could teach reading as well. This, incidentally, shows that it was not solely in the Caribbean that there were objections to educating the lower orders because it would make them dissatisfied with their lot.
14. Mercer, K., 'Welcome to the Jungle: Identity and Diversity in Postmodern Politics', in Rutherford, J. (ed.), *Identity: Community, Culture, Difference* (NY, 1990), p. 43.
15. The Royal Family was perhaps the most prominent example of the latter, changing from the House of Saxe-Coburg and Gotha to the House of Windsor.
16. On the title page of the 1930 edition of *London Life in the Eighteenth Century*, M. Dorothy George is noted in parenthesis to be Mrs Eric George. Only on widowhood would women recover their first name in formal address, becoming Mrs Jane Smith, or whatever. Before the rise of feminism in the 1970s, when the practice largely ceased, this was a way of knowing whether the husband was deceased and the woman now had a separate legal identity.
17. HS 48, 4 October 1774.
18. Crisp, F.A., *Registers of Lowestoft* (privately publ. 1904), 17 November 1737. It is unlikely that there was time to instruct Juba fully, but his bride's pregnancy was undoubtedly a major consideration for the parish authorities.
19. *Registers of the Church of Le Carré and Berwick Street*, Huguenot Society Quarto Series Vol. XXV (1921), p. 13. Three years later, on 28 December 1718, a Susanne Redonnel was married to Jean Giraldel (alias Constantin) in the same church (p. 32). This is most likely to be the black Susanne (although her colour is not actually mentioned in the baptism entry) but it could, possibly, have been her godmother, if she was called Susanne after her. It would, however, have been confusing to have two Susanne Redonnels in the same household, especially if one were the mistress and the other the Black servant. I am grateful to Randolph Vigne of the Huguenot Society for drawing this entry to my attention.
20. GL, Ms 924, Register of Holy Trinity Minories, 4 March 1742.
21. GL, Ms 3572/1, Registers of St Mary Aldermanbury, 21 April 1707.
22. *Ibid.*, 23 July 1736.
23. SoG, unpublished transcript, KE/R 159-160, Registers of St Margaret, Rochester, 20 January 1716/7.
24. Attwater, D., *A Dictionary of Saints* (1965), p. 290. Did the master mean this as a model for a servant to follow or was it the servant who chose the name to signify his fidelity to his new god?
25. Herefordshire RO, MX 164, Registers of Hereford St Peter, 29 August 1729.
26. Attwater, *Dictionary of Saints*, pp. 58 and 324.

27. Galbi, D., <www.galbithink.org/names>, p. 14.
28. SoG, unpublished transcript, HT/R 72. Graham, C.P. et al, Registers of East Barnet, Hertfordshire (1994).
29. GL, Ms 6764/2, Registers of St Ann & St Agnes, 29 October 1710; GL, Ms 6831/3, Registers of St Helens Bishopsgate, 23 January 1716/7.
30. Ham, E., *Elizabeth Ham by Herself 1783–1820*, ed. Gillett, E. (1945), p. 21.
31. Registers of Exeter St Stephen, 16 February 1688/9; Registers of Earls Colne, Essex, 4 May 1766.
32. GL, Ms 9238, Registers of Holy Trinity Minories, 25 June 1688.
33. Shyllon, *Black People*, pp. 15–16.
34. *Concise Dictionary of National Biography*, Vol. II (Oxford, 1992).
35. Wordsworth, D. *The Grasmere Journals*, ed. Woof, P. (Oxford, 1991), p. 3, mentions Elizabeth Simpson who married the son of Julius Caesar Ibbetson. The notes (p. 147) record that DW called her foolish to marry a man half her age, but did not comment on the foolishness of her father-in-law's name.
36. See the Access to Archives website <www.nationalarchives.gov.uk/a2a>.
37. SoG, unpublished transcript, MXR/112, Registers of Chiswick.
38. *Proceedings* 1785–6, II, no. 176.
39. CWA, Register of St Margaret Westminster, 9 February 1759,
40. LMA, A/FH/A09/002/001, nos. 37 and 379, 54, 90, 85, 86, 195, 205 and 384.
41. GL, Ms 8886/1, Registers of St Faith under St Pauls, 20 October 1776 and 1780.
42. LMA, Registers of Putney, 11 May 1717.
43. GL, Ms 9668, 22 September 1773.
44. HS 27, *Registers of the Abbey Church of SS Peter & Paul, Bath*, 5 April 1779.
45. CWA, Registers of St James, Piccadilly, 20 January 1787.
46. The format used by many clerks to record the names of all infants in baptism registers is John, son of John and Mary Smith.
47. Until the last part of the nineteenth century, married women could not own anything: on marriage, everything they had became their husband's property unless protected by a trust, administered by men. It was only in the latter half of the twentieth century that the tax laws were changed to give women a status separate from their husbands.
48. GL, Ms 4093/1, 21 November 1692. Burying a servant in what was presumably the family vault seems to suggest that he had a valued position in the family.
49. Cottle, *Dictionary of Surnames*, p. 13.
50. Surrey History Centre, unpublished transcript, The Registers of Richmond, Surrey, 24 August 1774.
51. CWA, Registers of St George Hanover Square, 4 December 1752.
52. CWA, Registers of St George Hanover Square, 26 March 1752, Frederick Cudjue 'of L[or]d Hallifax's Family aged 12 y[ears]'. Another boy, William Agree, was baptised on the same day and described in the same way.

Although the lads' colour/ethnic origins are not given, Cudjue is a known African name.

53. Pepys, S., *The Diary of Samuel Pepys*, ed. Latham, R. & Matthews, W. (1983), Vol. 1, p. 250.
54. *Ibid.*, Vol. 5, p. 225. Lawrence Stone attributes the decline of this practice to the growth of what he calls 'affective individualism' throughout the first part of the eighteenth century. Stone, L., *The Family, Sex and Marriage in England 1500–1800* (rev. edn, 1979), pp. 149ff.
55. Steele, J., *Spectator* 107, 3 July 1711.
56. *Public Advertiser*, 20 December 1784
57. Surrey History Centre, unpublished transcript, The Registers of Richmond, Surrey, 21 August 1779.
58. BASA *Newsletter* 35, January 2002, reported by Mike Ray. The classical name Hector for his own son shows that they were in vogue among the general population.
59. GL, Ms 10,348.
60. Gérin, W., *Horatia Nelson* (Oxford, 1970), p. 49.
61. HS 27, *The Registers of the Abbey Church of SS. Peter & Paul, Bath*, 23 March 1745/6.
62. LMA, Registers of St George the Martyr, Bloomsbury, 14 October 1730.
63. HS 27, *Registers of Bath*, 27 April 1756.
64. GL, Ms 6667/7, Registers of St Andrew, Holborn, 5 December 1716.
65. GL, Ms 9238, Registers of Holy Trinity Minories, 25 September 1659.
66. GL, Ms 4312, Registers of St Swithin London Stone, 25 February 1726/7; SoG, unpublished transcript, GL/R 103, Registers of Childwall, Lancashire,15 January 1741; Campbell, M.V., *Registers of St Andrew Clifton, Bristol* (Bristol, 1989), 14 December 1744.
67. Hardy, W., *Middlesex County Records* (1905), quoted in Shyllon, *Black People*, p. 80.
68. HS 33, *Registers of St Paul's Church, Covent Garden*, 28 May 1665.
69. Arabic script was used to record a few African languages spoken by Muslim peoples in West Africa and some others had methods of keeping written records, but this was a tiny proportion of the total number of languages on the continent.
70. HS New Series 1, *Registers of Temple Church, London*, 2 October 1749.
71. HS 27, *Registers of the Abbey Church of SS Peter & Paul, Bath*, 18 March 1734/5.
72. HS 33, *Registers of St Paul's Church, Covent Garden*, 13 and 16 May 1737.
73. Cottle, *Dictionary of Surnames*.
74. Coldham, P.W., *The King's Passengers to Maryland and Virginia* (Baltimore, MD, 1997), p. 78.
75. SoG, unpublished transcript, KE/R 159–160, Registers of St Margaret, Rochester, 15 January 1757.

76. SoG, Mfm 1732, Registers of North Mimms, Hertfordshire, 31 July 1700. The name Ziphares is rare: it was, like Juba, the name of a noble African in a play, but did not acquire the same popularity.
77. One of my correspondents sent several references to marriages of people 'of Hemsley Blackamoor' and also a woman included in a pawnbroker's records similarly annotated. I was puzzled by what appeared to be such a number of Black people in this particular place until I discussed this with a local historian, who told me that was the full name of this parish.
78. Habib also assumes that women called Barbary, then the most commonly found English form of the name Barbara, were of African origin. He has no corroboration for these and other assumptions beyond 'an intuitive consideration of their black content, and a method of analysis that can only be *sui generis*'. Habib, I., *Black Lives in the English Archives 1500-1677: Imprints of the Invisible* (Aldershot, 2008), pp. 46-7 and *passim*.
79. GL, Ms 9238, Registers of Holy Trinity, Minories, 23 November 1690.
80. GL, Ms 3480, Registers of St Margaret Moses, 31 January 1632/3.
81. He gave this as an alternative to Jorgesmal Broughwar, presumably his original name, in a letter published in *The Diary or Woodfall's Register*, 25 April 1789.
82. SoG, unpublished transcript, KE/R 159-160, Registers of St Margaret, Rochester, and 20 November 1795; and Registers of Shoreham, Kent, 14 January 1770. There was, however, a plantation in Jamaica called Cranbrook.
83. Gay, S.E. et al, *Truro, St Mary, Christenings, Marriages and Burials 1597-1837* (1940), 3 October 1777.
84. LMA, Registers of Limehouse, 23 July 1802 and 27 June 1810.
85. HS 29, *The Registers of St Vedast, Foster Lane 1558-1836*, 11 July 1664.
86. GL, Ms 6541/1, Registers of St Bride Fleet Street, 28 September 1783.
87. Surrey RO, Registers of Shalford, bap. 4 September 1785; Essex RO, Registers of West Ham, bap. 2 October 1778.
88. *The Post Man and the Historical Account* [newspaper] 22-29 June 1699, quoted in Waller, M., *1700* (2000) p. 280.
89. Angelo, H., *Reminiscences* (1834) summarised in Shyllon, *Black People*, pp. 41-3. The Duchess asked Ignatius Sancho to give him advice and act as a mentor to him but this failed. Soubise attempted to rape, or perhaps did rape, a servant girl, who refused to be bought off but was firm in her intention of bringing a case against him, so the Duchess arranged for him to go to India, where, with her backing, he set up a school to teach his riding skills and break in horses for the government. He died in a riding accident there.
90. Shyllon, *Black Slaves*, p. 9.
91. Fryer, *Staying Power*, pp. 22-3.
92. *Daily Journal*, 28 September 1728, quoted in Shyllon, *Black Slaves*, p. 9.
93. *Proceedings* 1716-7, 13 January 1716/7.

Chapter 8

Marriage and family

Marriage between Black men and white women seems to have been common but, as was noted in Chapter 5, it is rare for colour or ethnicity to be recorded in marriage registers and so it is impossible to tell from them alone how many Black people married. It is usually necessary to cross-reference several sources to deduce colour. The father of Ann Duck, for example, was known to be Black, and her mother white, because this was mentioned both in the transcript of her trial for theft and in the account she gave to the Ordinary of Newgate before her execution, when she said she was born in Little White's Alley in London. John Duck married Ann Brough in St Clement Danes, Westminster in 1717, three weeks after their daughter, Ann, was baptised in Cheam, Surrey.[1] There is no indication of John Duck's colour in either of these records but confirmation of it and the link to Surrey are established by a bastardy examination. While visiting London from Nonesuch Park in Cheam, John Duck, then a servant, had fathered a child by another woman in 1716 and his colour is mentioned in this document.[2] The Ducks went on to have at least two other children, baptised in London in the parish of St Dunstan in the West, where Little White's Alley was situated and where Ann must have assumed that she, too, was born.[3] Had Ann not become a criminal and had her father not had an illegitimate child, there would have been no way to identify their colour: none of the other records mentions this. How many other law-abiding and/or pre-maritally chaste Black people married and raised families in England must remain an open question.

It is impossible to tell whether any, like Henry Greenwich, previously mentioned, were refused a marriage ceremony because they were not baptised. A few people, like William Precious in Westminster, were baptised after marriage, so it may have been down to individual ministers to decide whether or not to marry unbaptised Black people.[4] Members of nonconformist denominations which did not practise baptism seem to have had no trouble getting married in the Anglican church, which was the only way of contracting a legal marriage after the 1753 Act, from which only Jews and Quakers were exempt. No record of opposition to a Black person's marriage on the grounds of race or colour has yet been found in either official or private documents, although it is possible that the Marylebone minister was using Henry Greenwich's lack of baptism to cloak a racist reason. Some couples were married by banns, called on three successive Sundays before the marriage ceremony, allowing ample time for objections to be raised. Others preserved their privacy by obtaining a licence, and one such case shows how common mixed marriages were, especially in London. In 1766 Joseph Alexander, a Black man, swore an affidavit to obtain a licence to marry Charlotte Nesbit and said that she was over 21. In fact she was 16, and Alexander was tried for perjury. The entry of the marriage in the register says nothing of Alexander's colour. The Rev. Mr Skinner of St James Piccadilly, who married the couple, could not identify the groom because, he said, 'there are so many couples married, I cannot recollect that'. Although he may have been trying to protect them, it is more likely that the marriage of a Black man and a white woman was comparatively common and therefore not memorable. There were, after all, many Black people in Westminster at this period. The case only came to court because Charlotte's father, a stonemason, had hired Joseph Alexander to give his daughter French lessons 'to compleat her', hoping to increase her marriage prospects. As the account of the trial in 1767 shows, Nesbit was incandescent with rage, not because of Alexander's colour but because he had planned to choose his daughter's husband and Alexander was only a servant.[5]

It is often stated that the Sanchos (Ignatius and Ann) and the Hylases (John and Mary) are the only two documented Black couples in eighteenth-century England,[6] but there is also a much-quoted item published in the *St James Evening Post* in 1726 describing the baptism in St Giles in the Fields of a baby whose parents and godparents were all Black. A search of the register reveals that there is no baptism around this date giving details of either colour or ethnic origin.[7] Nor are any of the children noted as being illegitimate. The parents must have been married. However remarkable the newspaper reporter thought the event, the parish clerk saw it as normal and regarded the couple and their child as settled in the parish. There are, however, a number of marriages where both parties are stated to be Black, so it might be more accurate to say the Sanchos and the Hylases are the only well-known Black couples of the eighteenth century. The earliest marriage found so far seems to be that of Robert Catharick and Mary Ember 'two blacks' in 1687 in Putney, Surrey,[8] although in Seaford in Sussex four years previously there is an entry 'was richard ena havelle gome maried to blaks'.[9] Two Black couples are noted in the records of the Chapel and Rules of the Fleet Prison: the marriage of John Ando 'Black man Bat[chelo]r' and Joanah Chester 'Black woman Sp[inste]r' took place on 15 March 1706, and that of John More 'Woolwich Mariner' and Catherine Abbey 'Stepney' '2 Negroes' on 23 December 1716.[10] A settlement examination in Westminster in 1710 mentions Elizabeth Praro and her husband Peter, both described as 'a Niger'.[11] In St Giles Cripplegate in the City of London, John Chapell and Mary Shirby, 'both Blacks', were married by licence on 17 November 1723.[12] In Monkton, Pembrokeshire, on 30 March 1785 Richard Rivers and Charlotte Charles, 'African Negroes Both of [this] Parish were married in this Church by Banns'.[13] William Weymouth 'a negro' and Maria Blackall 'w[idow] a Black woman' were married in St Gluvias, Cornwall on 28 June 1801.[14]

Besides these seven, other entries relating to the baptisms of children state that both parents were Black. John and Rosanna Blunt, 'Blackamoors', had two sons, both named John, baptised in 14 August 1690 and 1692 in Bury St Edmunds, Suffolk.[15] Mary, daughter of Thomas and Sarah Russell, 'two blacks', was baptised in Putney, Surrey in 1714[16] and James, son of Samuel and Susan Blake, was baptised in 1716 in St Clement Danes, Westminster.[17] Henley Blizard, son of Jeremiah and Phillis, who were both 'Negroes', was baptised in Kensington in 1777.[18] The colour of William and Lucy Phipps, previously mentioned, can only be deduced from entries in the parish registers relating to their children.[19]

During and following the American War of Independence, British Loyalists returning to Britain brought their servants with them. A number seem to have settled around Kensington and the parish register there records the baptisms of several Black people, among them three couples. The Pinkney family (Essex 'a Negro', Lucy 'a Negro' and Essex, son of Essex and Lucy) were all christened on 28 May 1777. The Allen family (Geoffrey 'a Black', Sarah 'a Black' and Jared of Geoffrey and Sarah 'a Black') were baptised a month later, on 14 June 1777.[20] In neighbouring Chelsea, Robert Cottle, 'a negro', and Kitty Cottle, 'a Negro, his wife', were both baptised in 1786.[21] In addition, there were the parents of Grace, 'A Blakmore daughter of Peter May and Mary his wife', who was baptised in the City of London in 1668/9.[22] At this time parish clerks seem to be quite specific about identifying the colour of individual parents if one is Black and the other white. As Grace was Black, both of her parents must have been, or she would have been described as 'mulatto' or 'tawney'.[23] Other possible Black couples can be found by cross-referencing entries. The parish registers of Topsham in Devon contain two burial entries of what appears to be a Black couple. In 1805 John Williams, 'a Negro', was buried. Two years later, in 1807, Mary Williams 'Wid[ow] a negro woman' was buried. The marriage register records that on 20 May 1787 John Williams, labourer, married Mary, alias Flora, Willey.[24] Ann Berry, 'a Negro and a Negro's wife', was buried in the parish of Minster in Sheppey, Kent in 1788.[25] In Greenwich on 15 May 1783, Charles and Mary Jones were both baptised. They are described respectively as 'a Negro said to be born in March 1758' and 'a Negro, whose surname by marriage is Jones, said to be born in 1759'.[26]

Family reconstruction

The descendants of a few Black men, like Edward Juba of Leicester, John Cranbrook of Clapham and Joseph Emidy, the Cornish musician, can be tracked to the present day. Using census returns, others can be tracked for up to four generations, although reconstructing their families depends primarily on the distinctiveness of their names, as colour/ethnic origin is not mentioned after the first generation, and not always then. Daughters, of course, took their husbands' surnames on marriage and the majority of them inconveniently married men with common names. Tracing families from the past to the present is extremely difficult unless the name is in some way unusual or unique. The usual method is to trace backwards from the known to the unknown, but very few people in Britain combine an interest in family history with awareness that they may have Black ancestry. Genealogists, particularly those researching comparatively common names, also rely on references to siblings and other relatives in parish records and legal documents like wills, to sort out branches of the same family or people with the same name who may or may not be related. Those working on poor people who did not possess property or enough chattels to make leaving a will worthwhile face greater difficulties. Large towns and cities make this task harder, because a family could change parishes by moving only a few streets. Within the Square Mile of the City of London, for example, there were 110 parishes in 1660. Although some were not rebuilt following the Great Fire of London in 1666, it is virtually impossible to trace a poor family with even a comparatively uncommon name, like Chater.[27] These problems are experienced to a greater extent by researchers trying to reconstruct the families of Black people. They were alone in Britain, with no parents or other relatives here and the majority had common names. Very few were prosperous enough to leave wills, which did not in any case include colour or race. It has therefore only been possible to reconstruct families which have names which are either rare or particular to Black people, especially those in rural areas, but it must be presumed that their experiences are representative of many others.

It is far more difficult to find Black brides of white men. Lord Mansfield's great-niece Dido Elizabeth Belle married a man with the rare name of Davinier and her descendants have been traced to the 1970s.[28] However, there is no indication in the marriage register of St George Hanover Square of her colour: this is known only because of her great-uncle's prominence. Lower down the social scale, this information is harder to recover. As explored in Chapter 5, illegitimate children either took the settlement status of their mothers or became the responsibility of the parish where they were born, so Black women's colour or ethnic origin largely appears in entries relating to illegitimate children. This gives the impression that Black women were sexually used and discarded. Some undoubtedly were. Others attained the respectable status of legal wives but have disappeared because, on marriage, women took their husbands' status and so their colour or ethnicity were rarely noted in official records. There are only a handful of examples where the bride's colour/racial origin is given. The earliest found so far seems to have been in 1649 in Leicester, where Thomas Garrett of Mountstrill married 'Black Bess Mr Mountney's mayde', although it is not certain that she was Black.[29] A few decades later, the marriage register of Redbourne, Hertfordshire records the marriage of 'A white man and a blackamore woman'.[30] In the register of marriages performed in Bedford, Bedfordshire in 1745 Robert Newton and 'Salma the Black' appear.[31] In Earl's Colne, Essex, Maria 'a Negro, the wife of Warren Hull [or possibly Hall] was buried'.[32] The captain of the *Belisarius*, one of the three ships that took Black people to Sierra Leone in 1787, recorded the colour of all those on board, among whom were eighteen Black women married to white men (there were also sixteen white women married to Black men).[33] This suggests that it was not uncommon for Black women to marry white men. Other examples are more difficult to recover. In St John Wapping, a chapel within the parish of Stepney, in 1706 Ann Grigg was baptised on the same day as her daughters Elizabeth, Phoebe and Anne. The entry in the register is ambiguous. It reads 'Ann wife of Thomas Grigg a black a native of ye Island of barbadoes 30 years old'. It is not clear from this whether Ann or Thomas was the Black born in Barbados. It is Ann's age at baptism that suggests she was Black. The entry for her daughter Anne reads 'Anne daughter of Thomas Grigg mar[iner] & Ann uxor [Latin = wife] in parrat alley'.[34] As the couple were married and resident in the parish, as the address indicates, Ann's colour and place of birth are irrelevant. This is another indication that she was the Black partner in the marriage: had Thomas been Black, this would probably have been noted in the entry.

Given the fact that most ages at baptism are estimates or are simply not recorded, it is not easy to ascertain age at marriage. Both John Cranbrook and William Cuba married young, by the standards of the period. Cranbrook was about 21 and Cuba was under the age of majority, then 21. In the general population men were usually around 27 at marriage, women about 25.[35] This late age is explained partly by the length of time apprenticeship lasted – to the age of 21 or 24 – plus a few years in which to accumulate savings on which to set up a household. Women also expected to save from their own, lower wages, which were usually earned in service. I have noticed that servants and farm labourers, as Cuba may have been, often seem to have been slightly younger on marriage than this average age. This may be because servants and farm labourers were already working and earning money while their apprenticed contemporaries did not yet have an income. In African societies early marriage is common, and appears to have been so in the past. Whether this cultural practice survived in England remains to be discovered when more families are reconstructed.

Black men seem to have had no problems in attracting a white mate.[36] There are a number of possible explanations for this. The first is lack of alternatives. As there were about three times more Black men than women in England outside the ports, there were simply fewer Black women around. This would have been especially true in rural areas, where the Black servant of a member of the local gentry would have had little choice but white women. In the 1960s and 1970s, when Walvin and Shyllon were writing, the issue of interracial marriage began to be a political topic. James Walvin wrote: 'The consequences of this sexual imbalance were profound and far reaching... A majority of Black males would find it impossible to form permanent relations with a woman of their own colour and inevitably many settled down with local white women of the class the Blacks were closest to – the poor whites.'[37] Shyllon said that 'Alliances and marriages between Africans and Englishwomen were not unusual: in fact, given the very small number of Black women, they were inevitable.'[38] Many activists maintained that Black people should take Black partners for various reasons, such as racial solidarity or to prevent the dilution of African ancestry. Saying that eighteenth-century Black men could not find a Black partner suggests that their choices would have been primarily political, but there cannot be many people who marry for ideological reasons: love, financial security, desire for children and common interests are the factors that figure most prominently in people's choices of a spouse, both in the past and now. Ukawsaw Gronniosaw's motives in marrying seem to have been a combination of his wife's affection for him and their shared religion. He lived in London, where there must have been a number of Black women from among whom to choose a mate. As his friends pointed out, in order to cast doubts on the purity of the woman who showed him affection, he was an apparently good catch for a poor widow but they saw nothing unacceptable in her colour, it was her poverty that bothered them. They tried to arrange a better marriage with a white Dutchwoman, but Gronniosaw would not fall in with their attempts to arrange a logically more suitable match.[39]

The theory that many Black men could not find someone of their own ethnic background to marry also reduces women to the role of passive recipients of a marriage proposal, with no choice in the matter. Why did white women choose to marry Black men when they had other alternatives? Their motives are also unlikely to have been political. It is perhaps significant that this question has not been explored by male historians, who seem complacently to assume that any woman would be so flattered by a proposal that she would leap at the chance to marry, no matter from whom it came, but most women were, and are, much more shrewd than that. Before the early nineteenth century fiction was mainly written by men and in their works women generally wait to be courted, but cases in the church courts throw some light on the aims of real women and how they went about achieving them. Abigail Harris, with the apparent connivance of her mother, acquired five suitors before settling on Jack Lingard, who combined higher social status and greater wealth than she possessed with a willingness to marry her.[40] Nor were women always more eager to marry than men. Lawrence Stone describes the case of Mary Stenson. Initially she seemed eager to marry and was courted by two men, but after inheriting a legacy from her grandfather, which gave her a degree of personal autonomy, her interest in them waned.[41] This and other instances detailed by Stone, show that many women were clear-eyed about the financial standing and prospects of potential husbands. Doctor Johnson noted that his Black servant, Francis Barber, had been followed to London 'for love' by a Lincolnshire haymaker. This is not to detract from Barber's charms, which were observed by others, but the possibility remains that the Lincolnshire lass wanted a more interesting and prosperous life than rural haymaking could provide.

There is a further possible issue in the women's choice of marriage partner. This is the attraction of the new and exotic. Being courted by and married by someone out of the ordinary might give a woman status among her friends, especially in a rural area where Black people were a rarity. Yet another consideration, linked to this, is what might be called the holiday-romance factor. The lack of a common language and culture between a man and woman allows both parties to read into the other what they want to believe. Unfortunately very few people, Black or white, from the lower social classes have recorded their reasons for marriage so these possibilities must remain speculative.

Little is yet known about the social status of women who in the past married Black men. The supposition (as the quotation from James Walvin above shows) has been that they were poor, but there is no proof of this yet. The majority of Black men seem to have begun their working lives as servants. Men who worked for a high-status family and had an important position in the household gained standing from this connection, as the hierarchy below stairs was as carefully preserved as that above. Women of the lower classes would therefore be improving their position by marriage, as well as gaining security. Those who were also servants would be marrying on more or less equal terms. Most people, then as now, marry someone from their own class or, as the eighteenth century would have had it, rank in life. Olaudah Equiano, for example, married a daughter of a member of the provincial middle class. Equiano may have started life as a slave, but by his efforts was one of the few Black people to reach a position where he had influential connections. He was appointed by the government to an important post in the Sierra Leone project, had the regard of Granville Sharp, the son of an archdeacon, and, as the list of subscribers to his autobiography shows, had the patronage of the rich and powerful. He had also proved himself to be a capable breadwinner. He could have had his pick of Black women, but there must have been few who shared his level of education and experience of the world. Although politically engaged and active, he chose someone white who presumably had similar tastes and interests to his own and was from the class into which he had risen. Vincent Carretta believes that Equiano thought that his inclusion of the news of his marriage to a white woman 'would appal racist readers like James Tobin', but Equiano does not mention his wife's colour. Instead he calls her 'Miss Cullen'.[42] To me, the use of the honorific suggests that it was her social status that he was emphasising. Of course, this would also appal racists, who were as aware of their social superiority as of their superior colour. In America, Black people were never accorded an honorific but, as newspaper reports and other sources show, Black people here were called 'Mr' or 'Miss' if their social status warranted it.

A further matter when considering marriage is the acquisition of a second family, the in-laws. On marriage, Black men acquired a family, something they lacked in England. Family and friends were important sources of support in eighteenth-century English society. Ignatius Sancho's letters frequently mention his wife's family. The white wives of Black men, however, did not have to form a whole new set of relationships, a process often fraught with difficulties, especially when women were regarded as inferior and their personal ties were expected to take second place in their priorities to the interests of their husbands' families. It was not until after the First World War that women first began to gain independence because they could earn enough money to support themselves. Before then, families played an important part in the making of marriages, as the Harris case mentioned above (and many others) shows. The two families' interests might be in conflict. Marriage to a Black man, therefore, might be seen as a benefit to both sides: the man gained a source of extended emotional and practical support and the woman did not have to contend with the potentially conflicting demands of two sets of relations.

The special circumstances of the mixed-race children of plantation owners in the West Indies are considered in Chapter 9. Identifying the children born in England to Black parents is problematic. As was noted earlier, some parishes seem not to have recorded the colour of children born after their parents had gained settlement. Fewer than 150 children can be identified as Black or of mixed race in baptismal registers, either so described directly or, more frequently, by reference to the colour/ethnic origin of one of their parents. Many others, like the children of Ignatius and Anne Sancho, are known through family reconstruction or can be conjectured, like Ann, the daughter of William Marshall and Mary Camell, who was baptised in 1794 in Lambeth, nine months after the baptism of Mary Camell 'a Black'.[43] The majority of those in parish registers have Black fathers, unless the mother is unmarried. In most cases, where the child is the product of a married couple, the wife appears to be white but this is because her colour or ethnic origin were irrelevant under the poor laws, and so not included.

Although in the colonies children inherited their parents' slave status, no mention of this possibility has been found in English records, where there are no court cases about the status of any black servant's child.[44] Although some may have voluntarily followed their parents into service, a number did not. Reconstructing the families of a large number of Black people should produce information on the social and geographical mobility of their children and subsequent descendants, but so far relatively little work has been done. What follows is therefore anecdotal and can only suggest further avenues for exploration when looking at the perception and status of Black people and their descendants in Britain in the eighteenth and nineteenth centuries.

Among the well-known Black people in eighteenth-century England, Ignatius Sancho's son William became a publisher. He published the fourth and fifth editions of his father's letters, and other works, including Voltaire's La Henriade.[45] Whether William married and had children is as yet unknown, although it seems unlikely: he lived in London and the records there have been thoroughly searched. All Sancho's daughters seem to have died unmarried. Dido Elizabeth Belle's son Charles became a captain in the East India Company's army, and later a lieutenant colonel in the Indian Army.[46]

Prosperity leaves a paper trail. More is known about George John Scipio Africanus and his family than about most others, because he was successful and had a distinctive name (Illustration 8). Had he been called John Williams there would be nothing to connect the baptism of a Black child aged around 3 in Wolverhampton in 1766 with the arrival of a brass-founder in Nottingham in 1784. It might also be difficult to connect the brass-founder who married Esther Shaw in 1788 with the man who set up an agency for domestic servants soon after. Although George had several children by Esther, only one of them, a daughter, survived to marry. On the evidence of George's will, it was not a happy marriage and the first granddaughter seems to have been disabled in some way. Thus only the younger, born after George's death and called Esther Africanus to commemorate both her maternal grandparents, married.[47] Her husband, Charles Turnbull, was a businessman, like her grandfather. They moved to London, where he came from. At the time of the 1891 Census the family was living in Surbiton and Turnbull was employing his sons Arthur and Frederick in the family business, importing timber. The couple also had a daughter, Margaret, who was probably married by then as she was not living at home, or she may have died young.[48]

Edward Juba was the son of a Black servant of a family in Earl Shilton, Leicestershire, baptised in 1757. He was later apprenticed as a needle maker in Leicester and became a freeman on the successful completion

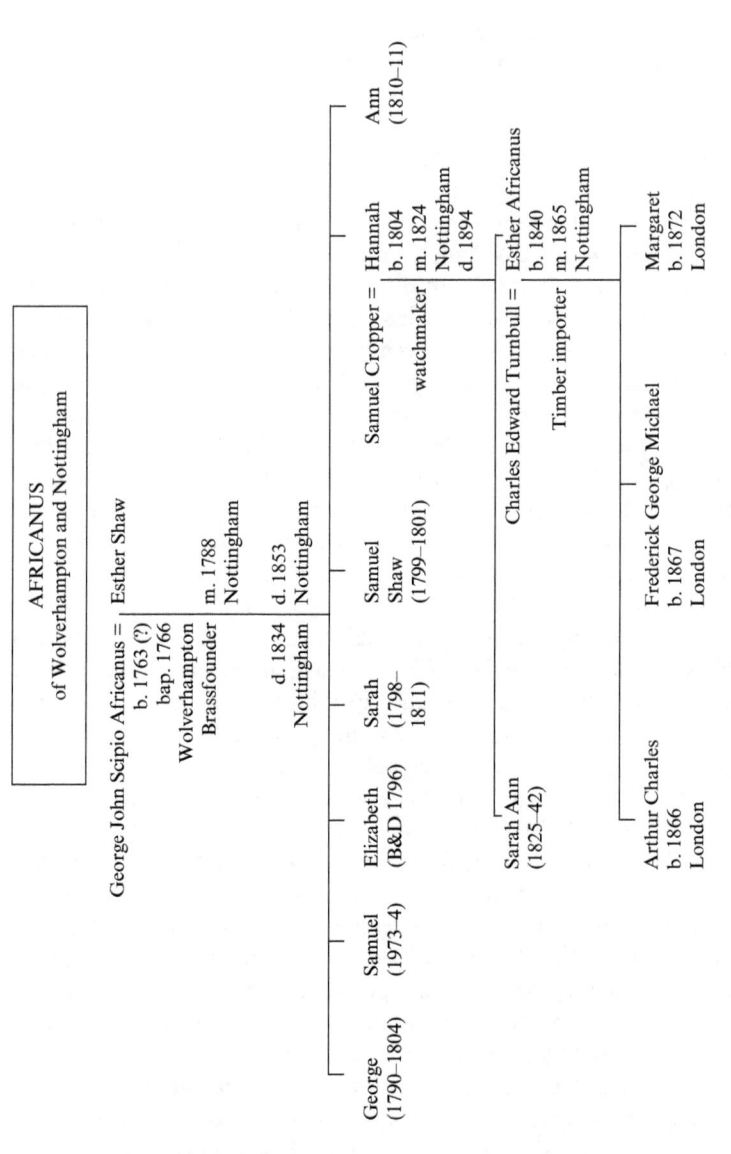

```
                          AFRICANUS
                  of Wolverhampton and Nottingham

            George John Scipio Africanus = Esther Shaw
                    b. 1763 (?)
                    bap. 1766
                    Wolverhampton       m. 1788
                    Brassfounder        Nottingham

                                d. 1834    d. 1853
                                Nottingham Nottingham
```

George	Samuel	Elizabeth	Sarah	Samuel	Hannah	Ann
(1790–1804)	(1973–4)	(B&D 1796)	(1798–1811)	Shaw (1799–1801)	b. 1804 m. 1824 Nottingham d. 1894	(1810–11)

Samuel Cropper = Hannah
watchmaker

Charles Edward Turnbull = Esther Africanus
Timber importer   b. 1840
                           m. 1865
                           Nottingham

Sarah Ann (1825–42)

Arthur Charles   Frederick George Michael   Margaret
b. 1866   b. 1867   b. 1872
London   London   London

8. Family tree of George John Scipio Africanus

of his term. One of his sons became a baker, then a framework knitter and finally a brewer. As Leicester is one of the places where the freedom of the city is inherited by the eldest son, one of today's freemen owes his position to this Black ancestor. There are numerous other descendants, some still in Leicestershire, others elsewhere, who are identifiable by the unusual name.

John Cranbrook, the Clapham greengrocer, seems to have had at least ten children (Illustration 9). His daughters, Elizabeth, Hannah and Rebecca, changed their names on marriage. Descendants of the last, who married a man named William Gregory, are traceable to the present day because they include family historians. Among the occupations in this family tree are hairdresser, cab driver, merchant's apprentice, commercial traveller, clergymen, and descendants live in England and Australia. It is not yet known what occupation John Cranbrook's youngest son, James, followed but his eldest son, another James, became a nonconformist minister, first an Independent, then a Unitarian and finally a Congregationalist. The birthplaces of James the younger's children (Suffolk, Ireland, Staffordshire) show that he had a mobile career as a minister. In 1851 he was in Stratford-upon-Avon, Warwickshire,[49] later moving to Liscard in Cheshire, and to Liverpool, finally serving as pastor of Albany Street Congregational Church in Edinburgh. Some of his sermons and works on theological matters were published. One of his sons was called William Wallace and another John Hampden, suggesting his politics were radical. In Edinburgh the unorthodoxy of his sermons and his invitation to Thomas Huxley to address his congregation in 1868 caused conflict with the Congregational authorities and he left. He gathered a small flock around him, but died in 1869.[50] James sent his eldest son, a third James, to Trinity College Dublin (at this time only Anglicans could attend Oxford or Cambridge) but, as is the way in many families, his son proved more conventional than his father and he became an Anglican minister, first in Donnington, Herefordshire, and later in Burnley, Lancashire. He too published theological works. He married the daughter of an Army officer.[51] Another of James's sons, Algernon, was apprenticed to a merchant and seems to have moved to Ireland, where there may be more descendants. What became of his daughters is not yet known.

Peter George Florida was baptised in 1769 in the parish of Radnage, Buckinghamshire, where he was described as 'a negro child about eight years of age.'[52] He married Phillis Newell in 1781 and the couple had at least four children: George, Charles Anthony, Jane Maria and Ann (Illustration 10).[53] They may have had another daughter, Elizabeth.[54] Peter George was

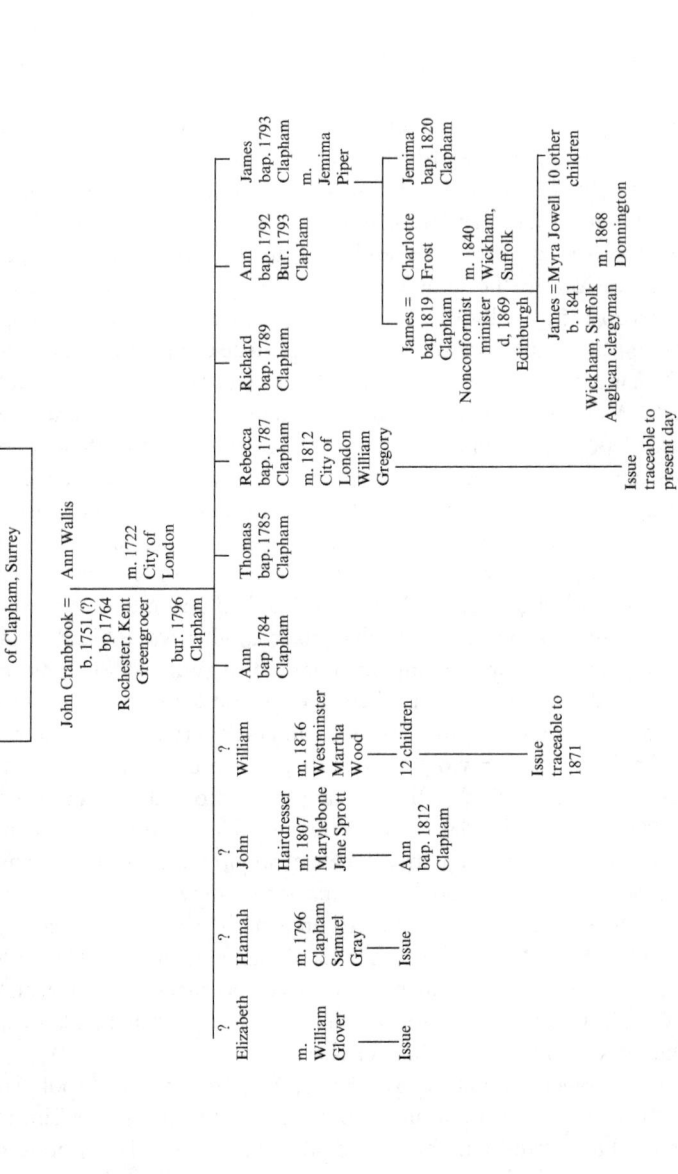

```
                            CRANBROOK
                          of Clapham, Surrey

                    John Cranbrook = Ann Wallis
                       b. 1751 (?)    m. 1722
                       bp 1764       City of
                    Rochester, Kent   London
                       Greengrocer
                       bur. 1796
                        Clapham
```

?	?	?	?					
Elizabeth	Hannah	John	William	Ann bap. 1784 Clapham	Thomas bap. 1785 Clapham	Rebecca bap. 1787 Clapham	Richard bap. 1789 Clapham	Ann bap. 1792 Bur. 1793 Clapham	James bap. 1793 Clapham

m. William Glover

Hannah m. 1796 Clapham Samuel Gray

John Hairdresser m. 1807 Marylebone Jane Sprott

William m. 1816 Westminster Martha Wood

Rebecca m. 1812 City of London William Gregory

James m. Jemima Piper

— Issue

— Issue

— Ann bap. 1812 Clapham

— 12 children

Issue traceable to 1871

Issue traceable to present day

James = Charlotte Frost
bap 1819   m. 1840
Clapham   Wickham,
Nonconformist Suffolk
minister
d. 1869
Edinburgh

Jemima bap. 1820 Clapham

James = Myra Jowell   10 other
b. 1841   children
Wickham, Suffolk
Anglican clergyman
m. 1868
Donnington

9. Family tree of John Cranbrook

described as 'poor' in 1790, so he was presumably not a servant, although it is not known what occupation he then followed, and he was buried on 22 July 1793, when he would have been about 32. His widow remarried five years later.[55] The eldest son, George, may have gone into the army. A witness at Peter George's wedding was the daughter of James Patterson, an army captain who presumably helped the lad, or may have taken him into his household on the early death of his father. George Florida moved to Monmouth (Patterson was in the Welsh Regiment), where he married and had at least seven children. Whether George actually served in the Army is not yet known. At the end of his life he was living in Newport, Monmouthshire in the household of a son-in-law who was a market gardener in 1851 but by 1861 had become a butcher.[56] George's occupation in both censuses is given as market gardener. One of George's sons, Richard, was also a gardener. George left numerous descendants in Wales and the Marcher counties. Because so many of his descendants were named George after him, it is difficult to sort out the separate branches of his family. Some became nonconformists, and the church records relating to them are less accessible than Anglican records.[57] One branch seems to have had a mechanical aptitude, becoming engine fitters and later working on railway engines for the Great Western Railway. By 1891 one of George's descendants, James Florida, had become a train examiner, a highly skilled and responsible job.[58] Another was a blacksmith.[59] One became a sea captain, and apparently died young.[60] Some did not have such skilled jobs: among them are general labourers and factory workers. The women mainly went into domestic service in middle-class households before marrying, but one became a milliner and others, the daughters of a factory operative making boots, worked as boot fitters.[61] Ann, Peter George Florida's daughter, remained in Buckinghamshire and became a lace-maker. She married a farm labourer, John Fletcher, which indicates either marriage on equal terms or even downward social mobility, but she did have an illegitimate son, Charles, before her marriage, which must have damaged her chances of marrying upwards.[62] Charles, who used the surname Fletcher, became a cabinet maker, which required apprenticeship. He moved to Devon but had only daughters, so any further descendants require further research.[63]

Another Black servant in rural Britain was Henry Northbrook, later Norbrook. His colour was a subject of interest to the minister of Tunstall, Suffolk, who recorded it in the entry of his daughter's baptism, wondering how long it would take to disappear among his descendants. Whatever his descendants looked like, their colour faded from official records. Among

FLORIDA
of Radnage, Buckinghamshire

1. Peter George Florida = Phillis Newell*   = 2. Thomas Ives
   b. 1761 (?)
   bap. 1769
   Radnage
            m. 1781   m. 1798
            Radnage   Radnage

   bur. 1793
   Radnage

Children of Peter George Florida and Phillis Newell:

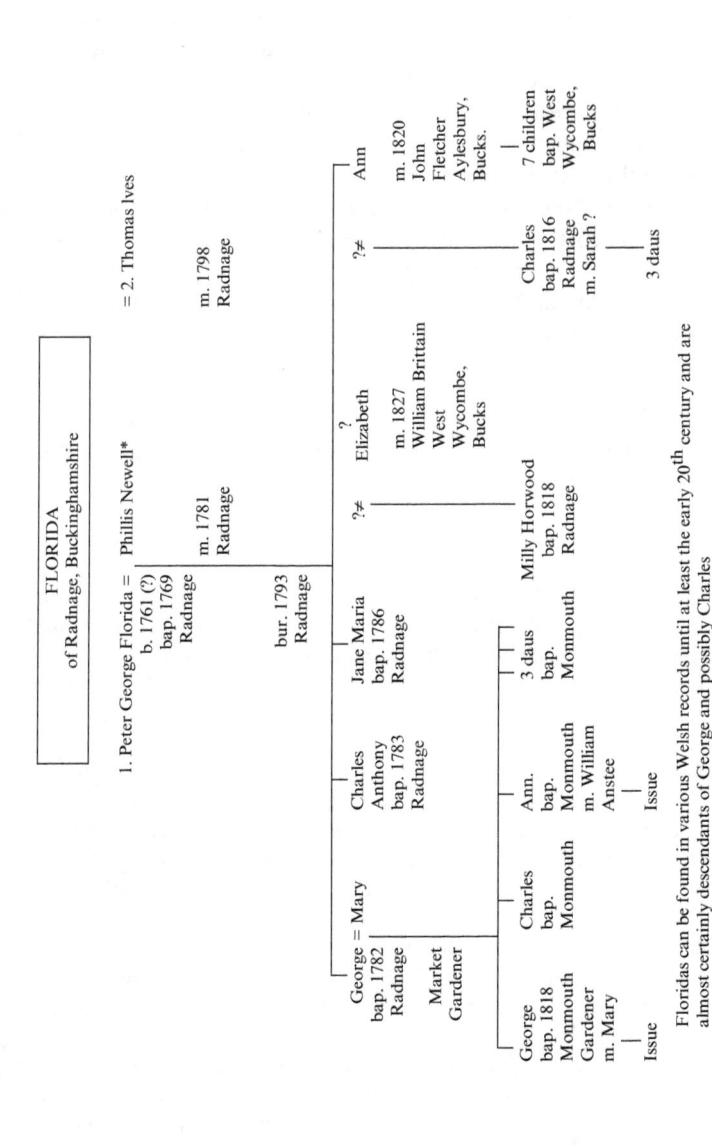

- **George** bap. 1782 Radnage, Market Gardener = Mary
- **Charles Anthony** bap. 1783 Radnage
- **Jane Maria** bap. 1786 Radnage
- **?** ≠ **Elizabeth** m. 1827 William Brittain, West Wycombe, Bucks
- **?** ≠ **Ann** m. 1820 John Fletcher, Aylesbury, Bucks. 7 children bap. West Wycombe, Bucks

Children of George and Mary:
- George bap. 1818 Monmouth, Gardener, m. Mary — Issue
- Charles bap. Monmouth
- Ann bap. Monmouth, m. William Anstee — Issue
- 3 daus bap. Monmouth

Children of Elizabeth:
- Milly Horwood bap. 1818 Radnage

Children of Ann:
- Charles bap. 1816 Radnage, m. Sarah?
- 3 daus

Floridas can be found in various Welsh records until at least the early 20th century and are almost certainly descendants of George and possibly Charles

*Her name seems to have been wrongly given as Elizabeth in the marriage entry

10. Family tree of Peter George Florida

those Henry Norbrook left in Suffolk (others may have moved out of the county) were a servant and a harness-maker.[64] Like the blacksmith in Peter George Florida's family, this was a skilled job which offered steady employment at a time when horses were the standard form of transport as well as being used in agricultural work.

This preliminary reconstruction of a few family trees reveals nothing unusual. The children of Black servants were not limited to service as an occupation, although some did follow their parents into the job. As in the white population, some of their descendants remained on the same social level as their parents, others completed apprenticeships and/or moved into the skilled artisan class or professional classes, and some slid down the social scale. Not all Black people remained in service, and the next chapter looks at their working lives.

Notes

1. Surrey RO, Registers of Cheam, Surrey, 22 July 1717; CWA, Registers of St Clement Danes, 12 August 1717.
2. CWA, E2574, p. 242.
3. GL, Ms 10,351, Registers of St Dunstan in the West, 24 August 1724 and 27 November 1729.
4. CWA, Registers of St James Westminster, bap. 12 November 1777, mar. Ann Estill 24 February 1775. The couple's first child, Ann, was bap. on 30 June 1776, almost nineteenth months before her father was baptised.
5. *Proceedings* 1766–7, II, no.128. The case was respited and there is no further mention of it in the *Proceedings*, so it seems likely that Mr Nesbit was persuaded to accept the situation.
6. Sancho, ed. Carretta, *Letters*, p. 250, n14.
7. I was unable to find a copy of this newspaper in any of the major British repositories. I consulted the original registers, which were then at the church of St Giles in the Fields in London (a filmed copy has since been deposited in LMA). Because of the ambiguity of the newspaper date, I checked February–March 1725/6 and 1726/7.
8. LMA, Registers of Putney, 19 May 1687.
9. SoG, unpublished transcript, Sx R/127, 15 February 1683/4. The anonymous transcriber noted that many entries at this time were 'so corrupt as to be meaningless'.
10. Herber, M., *Clandestine Marriage in the Chapel and Rules of the Fleet Prison 1680–1754*, Vol. 2 (1999), p. 41 and Vol. 3 (2001), p. 35. They were almost certainly not prisoners – this place was the most notorious in England for clandestine and irregular marriages because it was an area outside the ecclesiastical jurisdiction of the Bishop of London.

Marriage and family

11. CWA, F5004, p. 231, quoted in CWA, *Sources for Black and Asian History*.
12. GL, Ms 6419/15. I am grateful to Paul Hitchings for this reference.
13. I am grateful to Richard Rose for this reference, which he found while researching his book *Pembroke People* (2000). He thinks they were probably servants of the Owen family of Orielton. He found no records of baptisms for any children of the marriage.
14. Taylor & Phillimore, *Cornwall Parish Registers: Marriages, Vol. XIII*.
15. SoG, unpublished transcript, SF/R 239, Register of St Mary Bury St Edmunds, 14 August 1690 and 18 January 1691/2.
16. LMA, Registers of Putney, 27 June 1714. Thomas Russell was buried on 7 April 1745 and Sarah Russell on 14 December 1753, although their colour was not recorded in the burial register.
17. CWA, Registers of St Clement Danes, 10 June 1716. On 12 June 1716 Thomas Blake, son of a 'blackamoor' was buried. He is probably another child of the Blakes.
18. SoG, unpublished transcript, MX/R 129-135, Hill, J.P., Registers of St Mary Abbotts, Kensington (1979),18 May 1777.
19. CWA, Registers of St Clement Danes, Antony, bur. 21 April 1704 and William, bap. 27 November 1715.
20. SoG, unpublished transcript, MX/R 129-135. Hill, Registers of St Mary Abbotts, 18 May 1777.
21. LMA, Registers of St Luke Chelsea, 5 July 1786. The witnesses were John Cottle and Grace Cottle of Crown Court No. 4 Westminster, presumably their masters.
22. GL, Ms 4107/2, 2 February 1668/9.
23. This is one of the rare instances where the child's colour is described, rather than that of her parents. Peter May and Mary Sepher were married in St James Duke's Place in 1684 and they were probably her parents, although their colour is not recorded in the register there. This was a church that conducted irregular marriages. GL, MS 7894/1, 17 October 1684.
24. Devon & Cornwall Record Society, *Registers of Topsham, Devon* (1938).
25. BASA *Newsletter* 38, January 2004, p. 24, sent by Maureen Robertson.
26. SoG, unpublished transcript, KE/R 115-122, Registers of East Greenwich (1976).
27. There are at least five separate Chater families in London and Westminster in the mid-eighteenth century, in addition to a branch originating in Newcastle-upon-Tyne and then living in Stepney. Two, because they were rich enough to leave wills, are distinguishable. The other three, being poorer but not so poor as to come to the attention of the authorities, are not.
28. Minney, S., 'The Search for Dido', *History Today* 55 (10) October 2005, pp. 2-3. Her research was incorporated into a booklet produced by Kenwood House, the Mansfields' home, in 2007.
29. Hartropp, H. (transcriber), *The Registers of St Mary Leicester in the County of*

Leicestershire (1909), 12 July 1649. Habib gives references for others, like Susan Ethuop in 1600/1 in Hemel Hempstead, Hertfordshire, but he used the IGI, which records only dates, and is making the supposition that this is Ethiop.
30. Neither the names of the parties nor the exact date are recorded. I am grateful to Dr Jill Barber of Hertfordshire RO for this reference.
31. Bedfordshire Parish Record Society, Vol. 58C, *Registers of Bedford St Pauls*, 23 December 1745.
32. SoG, microfiche ES/REG/94100, 4 May 1766. Glenda Thornton was the first to draw my attention to this entry. Maria presumably died in childbirth, since her daughter Ann was buried on 1 September 1766.
33. TNA, T 1/643. The captains of the other two ships did not record these details.
34. LMA, Registers of St John at Wapping, 8 July 1707.
35. Laslett, *The World We Have Lost Further Explored*, p. 83.
36. This seems to be true today: from the 1991 Census it was found that 50 per cent of black men had a white partner. Only 25 per cent of black women had a white partner.
37. Walvin, *Black and White*, p. 52.
38. Shyllon, *Black People*, p. 103.
39. Gronniosaw, *Narrative*, pp. 35–8. His heart ruled his head and his faith in her was justified. Later, his Betty demonstrated her practical contribution to the partnership when she worked to support their family because he could not do so through illness: she did not abandon him for a better prospect when he fell on hard times.
40. Stone, *Uncertain Unions: Marriage in England 1660–1753* (Oxford, 1992), pp. 48–67. Other case studies here cast interesting light on courtship, particularly the role of women.
41. *Ibid.*, pp. 41–3.
42. Equiano, ed. Carretta, *Interesting Narrative*, pp. xxiii and 235. The fact that her Christian name is not given indicates that she was the eldest, or only, daughter, another significant point in a society where primogeniture was important. Carretta is American, and in America race is paramount. Being British, I see class as more significant.
43. LMA, Registers of Lambeth, 30 October 1793; 11 July 1794. It may be a coincidence that Mary Camell was baptised nine months before the birth of her daughter, but did her baptism mark the beginning of her relationship with William Marshall?
44. There was legal slavery for poor white people, whose children might also be enslaved, in Scotland until 1799.
45. Sandhu, S., 'Ignatius Sancho'.
46. TNA, HO107/1468, f. 791, p. 93 and RG9/14, f. 156, p. 22. The East India Company was dissolved in 1858, between these two censuses, and its army taken over by the government. Charles Davinier's son, also Charles, became a clerk in the War Office.

47. In October 1997 an exhibition about his life was mounted in Brewhouse Yard Museum in Nottingham, using information gathered by Nottingham Family History Society members and other local historians, on which I have drawn.
48. TNA, RG13/667, f. p. 50.
49. TNA, HO107/2074, p. 45
50. Lake, J.W., *Discourses in Memoriam of the Rev. James Cranbrook* (1869); *Scotsman*, 2 March 1868; Huxley, T., 'On the physical basis of life (A Lay Sermon delivered in Edinburgh, on Sunday, the 8th of November, 1868, at the request of the late Rev. James Cranbrook; subsequently published in the Fortnightly Review)', in *Lay Sermons, Addresses and Reviews* (1870).
51. Gloucester RO, Registers of Donnington, 21 January 1868.
52. The rector of this parish was Charles William Tonyn, late of the 6th Regiment of Dragoons, whose daughter Juliana was married to Francis Levett of the Province of East Florida, which probably accounts for Peter George's surname and indicates his origin. I am grateful to Brian Jackson for this information.
53. Buckinghamshire RO, Registers of Radnage, Buckinghamshire, 22 October 1769. Her name seems to have been wrongly entered as Elizabeth. Their children were baptised on 5 May 1782; 2 November 1783; 21 May 1786 and 26 January 1794 respectively.
54. An Elizabeth Florida had an illegitimate daughter, Milly Horwood, baptised in Radnage on 15 January 1818, and in West Wycombe on 16 May 1827 married William Brittain. Buckinghamshire RO, Registers of Radnage and Registers of West Wycombe.
55. Buckinghamshire RO, Registers of Radnage, 8 October 1798.
56. TNA, HO107/2451, f. 22, p. 21 and RG9/4016, f. 27, p. 5.
57. On 6 January 1833, two children of William Anstee and Ann (nee Florida) were baptised in the Tabernacle Independent or Congregational church in Monmouth (IGI).
58. TNA, RG12/4361 f. 45, p. 38.
59. TNA, RG11/5239, f. 20, p. 34 and RG12/4369, f. 34, p. 2.
60. TNA, RG10/5340, f. 19, p. 32. Tabitha Florida, aged 29, is given as a sea captain's wife and head of the household. Ten years later, in 1881, she was a widow keeping a lodging house. RG11/5261, f. 77, p. 26.
61. TNA, RG12/4375, f. 43, p. 28; RG12/1980, f. 156, p. 30 and RG13/2375, f. 134, p. 23.
62. Buckinghamshire RO, Registers of Radnage, bap. 21 April 1816; Registers of Aylesbury, mar. 21 August 1820.
63. TNA, RG9/1440, f. 20, p. 34 and RG11/2195, f. 95, p. 7. He used the surname Fletcher. One of his daughters married a man named St John.
64. TNA, HO107/ 1503, f. p. 48 and HO107/1800, f. p. 34.

Chapter 9

Working lives

From earlier historians' work – and the work of those who have followed them – a stereotyped picture of a Black person in eighteenth-century England has emerged. It is usually that of a servant in the shadows of an aristocratic family or of a fashion accessory, a pageboy or small girl servant (Illustration 11). As David Dabydeen wrote, 'What emerges from English painting is a sense of the solitude of Blacks in the alien environment of the aristocratic household';[1] but this is to confuse their artistic and social presences. They seem to be isolated in portraits of them with their masters because white servants are less often depicted: white servants were the norm and did not attest to the master's wealth and/or overseas connections. Their appearance is sometimes unsettling, because their skin tones were not reproduced with the same skill and fidelity as their white masters', due to a technical factor. By the eighteenth century painters had had hundreds of years to perfect their techniques for depicting the flesh tones of white people, but far less experience of black skin. The art historian Reyhahn King's analysis of the colours used to paint Black people contrasted Hogarth's use of 'violet pigments, which result in a greyish skin tone' with the browns used by Gainsborough in his portrait of Ignatius Sancho. This suggests that there is a technical explanation for what she has described as the 'vanishing effect so often suffered by the faces of Black servants in the shadows of 18th-century portraits of their masters'.[2] This specialist knowledge may show that the effect of isolation and appearing 'alien' which Dabydeen noted was less to do with Black servants' social status than the artists' technical limitations. An aristocratic household at the end of the seventeenth century might contain over a hundred servants,[3] so Black servants were in company below stairs. A few paintings and prints show them in close contact with their fellow servants.[4]

Rich merchants, like the Whatman family of Turkey Court in Kent, employed a host of people, some permanently, others temporarily, to

11. Elizabeth Keppel by Sir Joshua Reynolds, 1761.

carry out the numerous chores on which the smooth running of the house, the land and the inhabitants' lives depended.[5] In the seventeenth and eighteenth centuries the majority of visible servants were male, and having a Black servant was a status symbol because of their novelty value. The pageboy who accompanied the lady of the house wherever she went was one such. Another was the footman who carried messages for his employers and, when they were travelling, oversaw arrangements and went ahead to book accommodation. These were probably the positions that most Black male servants in large households initially occupied. When older, they might be promoted to valet or butler. The first had the care of his master's clothes and personal accoutrements and the second of the household's domestic property, like plate and chinaware, as well as the food that both the family and the servants ate. Others might deal with the family's horses and carriages, such as the grooms and coachmen who would be seen when the family travelled.

Women servants, apart from ladies' maids, mainly worked out of sight, so Black women servants had less kudos. It is more difficult to discover what positions they held. As a personal maid, women preferred someone who could be a social companion. J. Jean Hecht says that in an upper-class household this position would often be filled by a member of the respectable classes who had fallen on hard times: a poor relation, the widow of a clergyman, the daughter of a professional man, or the like.[6] These must have been rare in the Caribbean, so women returning from estates there may have brought Black maids with them. However, there seems to have been a less often-observed fashion for Black maids in England. In 1739 a Yorkshire woman mentioned having a new maid who was 'a perfect Mallotto [sic], 'tis so much à la mode'.[7] Black women in general, however, seem to have been more likely to be used for household work behind the scenes. A 1761 advertisement for a Negro girl mentioned that she 'works well at her needle, washes well, does household work'.[8] By contrast, advertisements for Black boys concentrate on their appearance and tractable natures, although some do mention their domestic abilities, like waiting at table, a visible position through which guests would be made aware of their masters' wealth.

Black servants had sources of income from their work, whether or not they received wages. At the level at which the majority were employed, among the aristocracy and the better-off, it was customary for a large part of any servant's income to come from vails, or tips, given by guests, as also in the case of servants in inns. Servants were also entitled to perquisites, or perks. Their masters and mistresses would give valets and maids old clothes which could be sold in the substantial second-hand clothes market. Cooks sold off dripping and other remains of food preparation; housemaids collected and sold wax candle stubs (cheaper, tallow candles were used by the household staff). Coachmen sold worn wheels and other equipment. Those with responsibility for purchasing household goods could command a commission from tradesmen. This applied to both white and Black servants and it was accepted that these practices supplied part of their income.[9]

Pictures of Black servants to the aristocracy are easily accessed, but they record only a moment in what may have been an eventful and mobile life. Many Black people started off their lives in Britain as servants, but it must be remembered that so did most of the white population, at least until the end of the First World War in 1918. At the beginning of the period of the slave trade many were found in the households of the aristocracy and of wealthy merchants either based in Britain or connected in some way to the West Indies or the Indian subcontinent. From around the middle of the eighteenth century they are found lower down the social scale, when even lower middle-class families had a servant or two and a Black person might be among them, although this practice is also found earlier. At the time that Samuel Pepys began his main diary in 1659 he was a junior clerk living in a small house. He employed one servant. By 1669 there were five, one of whom, Doll the cook, was Black.[10] Another diarist, John Baker, a magistrate from the Caribbean, noted his servants' doings, among them recording errands and tasks carried out by his Black servant, Jack Beef. Pepys' and Baker's diaries are unusual in mentioning servants so often. For most people, however, servants were so much part of everyday life that they were not thought worthy of mention in diaries or letters unless they caused problems.

There is another consideration – the word 'servant' itself. Today it means almost exclusively a domestic servant, someone doing household tasks, but in the eighteenth century it had a much wider meaning: employee is probably the closest equivalent. It cannot, therefore, be assumed that every Black person described as a 'servant' was involved exclusively in domestic work. Even in the early days, it is clear that many were not tied to one master, but independent and free to arrange their own working lives. When this independence began to be widespread cannot yet be reliably conjectured, but in some cases it was early in the eighteenth century. In 1717 John Duck, for example, was the servant of a member of the minor gentry living in rural Surrey. He married and moved to Westminster, where he became a teacher of sword fighting to gentlemen in the Inns of Court.[11] About this time William Smith was also in service. By 1722 he had left and was running a sutler's booth (a kind of fast-food stall) in Hyde Park.[12] The Old Bailey *Proceedings* contain a number of examples of servants who testified in court that they were 'out of place', i.e. between hirings, like John Vernon[13] and William Henry.[14] John Moreton came to London from High Wycombe, Buckinghamshire 'to see after a place'.[15] There was also Thomas Wheeler, who burgled the premises of Mr Norris, a druggist for whom he had once worked as a servant. Wheeler, 'a loose Liver' according to Norris, seems not to have run away from his master's service but how they parted is not explained.[16] Others seem to have done the job temporarily, like Thomas Coffee, who testified he was 'not in a proper service'. He was originally a sailor but by 1786 was working as a servant until he could return to the West Indies. He said that he lived in Oxford but always lodged with a Mrs Green in Hounslow, Middlesex.[17] Another Black servant who gave evidence at the Old Bailey was working for a ships' chandler in Limehouse. This was not the kind of household that would have been able to employ a Black servant for status, or even purely for domestic purposes. It must be presumed that Edward Thompson was an assistant in the warehouse.[18] John Commins was a gardener. He did not give his master's name, as most servants of whatever colour did, but simply said that he 'had been working in the neighbourhood of Whitechapel' when he was robbed, so he was probably self-employed.[19] No one found this mobility odd: none of these men was questioned about it, which suggests that it was a normal circumstance.

Master–servant relationships

In the seventeenth century the (male) head of the household was seen as representing God, a belief that continued into the eighteenth century. This was justified by scripture, especially St Paul's instructions: 'Wives, submit yourselves unto your own husbands as unto the Lord. For the husband is the head of the church and he is the saviour of the body. Therefore as the Church is subject to Christ, so let the wives be to their own husbands in everything.'[20] Women were also told: 'thy desire shall be to thy husband and he shall rule over thee'.[21] But with this right came the man's responsibility to care for and educate the members of his household. Most masters seem to have felt accountable for their Black servants' spiritual welfare. Not only did servants attend church with them, they also took part in family prayers at home, a practice which reinforced the bonds between members of the family and their household. Pepys' diary reveals how intimately servants were involved in their masters' everyday lives. Servants were expected to carry out the most menial of tasks. Stories are found of women unable to dress and undress themselves unaided because help was needed, for example, to cope with lacing and unlacing stays. Such close intimacy inevitably led to strong emotional ties with servants. Being unable to prepare food or to dress without help must have created an almost childlike state of dependence, especially on the part of women. A number of guides for young women to instruct them in correct behaviour were produced in the eighteenth century. They included advice on the treatment of servants. *Advice of a Mother to her Daughter* by the Marchioness de Lambert was first published in England in 1727, although it was probably written earlier. She emphasised at some length the need to treat servants humanely, but added, 'A mean familiarity with them is ever to be avoided . . .'. Later British writers gave similar advice. Dr Gregory of Edinburgh dwelt on the need for caution in selecting intimate friends and added, 'Beware of making confidants of your servants.' Lady Pennington, as well as some practical advice on supervising a household, observed that 'the habit which very many ladies have contracted of talking to and consulting with their women' had spoiled servants. She added the need to treat domestics with such good nature that they will serve from affection, rather than fear.[22] None of these works specifically mentions Black servants; presumably they were not regarded as needing any special treatment, nor were precautions against their absconding considered important.

As well as a sense of responsibility towards their servants, some masters seem to have developed a warmer regard for them, although the conduct books warned against this. In 1761 Thomas Percival, Lord Kenyon, wrote to a lawyer about his Black servant, Juba:

> These dismal thoughts [Percival's wife was ill] naturally put one in mind of preparing for all events, and, as you are a lawyer, I beg you will put me into a proper way to settle an annuity on Juba, my Black boy; as he is an alien, there must be some care taken in it, and I fancy you have cases of that kind occur sometimes in London; whether it is possible to do it, I own it is to me a doubt, without trusting some friends absolutely, and I would choose to avoid that if I could, and I know no one more capable in directing me than yourself. Surely, somebody besides me have had a *friendship* for an alien; and if so, where would they apply for advice but to the Temple?[23] (My italics)

Some white servants remained in service all their lives.[24] A wider study of Black servants remains to be done for comparison, but there is evidence of a number for whom service was also a lifetime career. In 1770 Robert Wadeson said that he had been in England for about twenty-six years and was a gentleman's servant. It is not stated whether he had always worked for the same master.[25] Tobias Pleasant testified that he had been in service with Mr Lane of Hillingdon, Middlesex for thirty-two years.[26] Pamela, the Black servant of the Prevost family, spent her last years at the home of one of the children to whom she had probably been a nanny or nursemaid.[27] Another servant who remained with the same family for life was James Price, who worked for Maurice Nelson, Horatio Nelson's brother. In 1801, after his brother's death, Admiral Nelson wrote to Emma Hamilton from the Baltic, 'there is an old Black servant James Price . . . as good a man as ever lived, he shall be taken care of and have a corner in my house as long as he lives'.[28] A number of memorials in churches and churchyards scattered over the country commemorate Black servants who died in their masters' service. They testify to the affection and esteem in which many Black servants were held. One, on a gravestone in the churchyard of Ashton-under-Lyne, Lancashire reads:

>Here was interred the Body of
>Augustin Leonard
>A Black Man
>A Native of the Island of
>Martinique, who died in this
>Town April 2nd, 1793, aged 42
>He was a faithful servant
>And affectionate Husband
>And sincere friend
>And Beautiful companion[29]

Another is on the wall of Werrington church, near Launceston, Cornwall, where a tablet was erected around 1700 by Lady Morice (grandmother of Humphry Morice, the MP and dealer in slaves). It reads:

>Deposited Here
>Are the Remains of Philip Scipio
>Servant to the Duke of Wharton
>Afterwards to Sir William Morice
>an African
>whose Quality might have done Honour
>To any Nation or Climate

> And Give us to See
> That Virtue is Confined
> To no Country or Complexion
> Here Weep
> Uncorrupted Fidelity
> And Plain Honesty[30]

The emphasis on the fidelity and commitment to their masters' service may suggest comparison with white servants, about whom there were constant complaints. Most Black people, unlike native-born servants, did not have a network of family and friends who could support them while between posts or help them to find new ones, so were perhaps more likely to remain with their masters.

It is not only memorial inscriptions to Black servants that testify to their masters' regard and trust. John Ystumllyn became the estate manager of Ynysgain Fawr after his master, Ellis Wynne of Ystumllyn in Carnarvonshire, Wales, sacked him when he married. This was an important post, responsible for the management of the estate on which the family's livelihood mainly depended.[31] Some Black servants, like Daniel Jones, betrayed that trust by theft.[32] Others, however, were proud of their responsible positions. In 1745, Philip Launder, a Black man, was tried at the Old Bailey for stealing a silver spoon from the house of Mr Kirby, where he had been having a meal with one of Mr Kirby's servants, who was also Black. This servant (unnamed) said 'it is a very hard thing if a man asks a person to eat a bit of victuals, that he must steal a silver spoon. I had a great deal of anger about it, for I have all my master's plate under my care.'[33] Samuel Seers said that John Edinburgh, a Black man, was 'a very honest fellow: my brother recommended him to me as such and I found him so; he was trusted at my brother's with horses and things, and with me with everything I had'.[34]

Apprenticeship

A few Black people were apprenticed to a trade. John Moore became a freeman of the City of York in 1687.[35] It is possible, however, that he purchased the freedom or acquired it in some other way rather than by serving a full apprenticeship. John Prince, 'a black boy lately brought to England', is the first known apprentice. In 1715 he was apprenticed to an attorney named John Trigge in Newnham on Severn, Gloucestershire, a few miles from Bristol.[36] Whether he actually learned to be an attorney or was, as parish apprentices usually were, just cheap labour is not yet

12. Bill Richmond acting as second to the Black boxer Tom Molineux by George Cruikshank, c.1820.

known. Given his name, however, he was possibly the son of an African chief sent to England to learn about the law so as to enable his father to deal better with British traders. Those who served a full apprenticeship about whom most is known are Bill Richmond (Illustration 12) and George John Scipio Africanus. The first was famous as a boxer but was originally apprenticed as a cabinet maker (after retiring from the ring he he kept a pub in London and trained boxers). The second, baptised in Wolverhampton in 1766, was apprenticed to a brass founder and later established himself in Nottingham, where he ran several businesses. His story is known because of research done by local historians in Nottingham. There were some who did not complete apprenticeships. In 1723 Samuel Johnson, the master of Anthony Emmannuell, went to court to get rid of the boy (who was Black) because he said he had run away, embezzled money and was 'incorrigible', despite a spell in a House of Correction.[37] Robert Johnson, 'negro', petitioned the Middlesex Sessions in January 1726/7 to be released from 'an inadvertent apprenticeship to Robert [blank] of Covent Garden.'[38]

These are, however, a small number. The dearth of Black apprentices may be partly due to individual prejudice, but there are other factors. One is that colour may not have been mentioned in apprenticeship records. In 1725 a Scipio Affricanus [sic], described simply as 'a poor orphan', was apprenticed to John Highfield, citizen and cordwainer of London.[39] His name indicates that he must have been Black, but how many others there were with less distinctive names is not known. By the time this Scipio Africanus completed his apprenticeship (usually seven years), he would no longer have been eligible to become a Citizen of London like his master. In 1730, a Black man called John Satia or Sapia completed his apprenticeship and became eligible for the freedom of the City with all the privileges that brought. The City jealously guarded its advantages and immediately passed an ordinance forbidding the apprenticeship of Black people. Although most histories of Black people in Britain mention this, they do not put it into context by looking at the position of all non-British people. The City had previously protected its guild and livery company members against other foreigners. From 1427, only naturalised aliens were permitted to become freemen. Under a statute of 1574, freemen were forbidden to accept the children of aliens as apprentices. This provision lasted until 1737 (after the ban on Black people was introduced), but from that date to 1855 the children of aliens had to petition the city authorities before they could become freemen. Jews had been forbidden to undertake apprenticeships from medieval times and the number of broker's licences granted to Jews in the City was limited. In 1580 there was an attempt by the authorities to have all foreigners expelled from the City, and this was followed by others. In addition to these major rulings, there were many other, lesser ordinances intended to create disadvantages for the stranger-born communities.[40] Even at Bartholomew Fair 'foreigners' had to pay double the standard fee for a stall.[41] Nor was it solely in the City of London that efforts were made to exclude or discriminate against foreigners.[42] The majority of immigrants, most notably Huguenots, arrived having already learned their skills and were able to demonstrate their abilities, in many cases superior to those of English workers. There were also many more Huguenots than Black people and they were extremely well organised. In the 1730s Huguenot refugees were still arriving and the City livery companies felt themselves beleaguered.[43] John Satia was the thin end of a wedge formed by yet another immigrant group. The livery companies might not be able to prevent him from working, but they could stop any other Black people learning a trade. Peter Fryer evaded considering the wider issue of protectionism in the City by careful wording. He wrote: 'This is the earliest known instance of an employment colour bar in this country.'[44] Strictly speaking, this is true, but it was only the latest in a long line of efforts to reserve the power and privileges of the City to native English, and later British, people. As the majority of Black people in England were based in London, this ban on City apprenticeships would have affected their chances of learning a craft. It did not, however, have any effect on those outside the Square Mile of the City. As well as those elsewhere in the country, mentioned above, Frank, 'an Indian boy', was apprenticed to Thomas Asplin, peruke maker of Lewisham, Kent in 1783.[45]

Another reason why so few Black apprentices are found may be due to the way that voluntary apprenticeships were organised (parish apprenticeships are discussed below). Children were usually apprenticed between the ages of 7 and 14 and generally completed their period of service at the age of 21. There were relatively few Black children of this age in the country. To judge by their ages at baptism, when they arrived most seem to have been older than the age at which apprenticeships were generally begun. Many children were apprenticed to their fathers or another relative. Only if it was not possible to place a child with a relative, especially if the child showed no aptitude or interest in the skill to be acquired, did parents look elsewhere. Keeping opportunities in the family removed a lot of potential placements for Black children. Although in some cases the masters of Black child servants did pay for them to learn a craft, it is possible that relatively few were interested in becoming artisans. They were used to domestic service and did not, as the children of artisans did, see what was done or become involved in the work from an early age.

The young Scipio Affricanus mentioned above was probably a parish orphan. The premium paid for his apprenticeship was only £5, which is much lower than the usual amount paid to a citizen, who could charge considerably more for taking an apprentice: £50 seems to have been the going rate at the time. One of the duties of the parochial overseers of the poor was to find apprenticeships for orphans or children whose parents could not support them. The parish paid minimal premiums. Five pounds seems to be the standard rate and this was not enough to pay for the child's keep for the full apprenticeship period, so it was rare that craftsmen welcomed a parish apprentice. It became necessary to pass a law to oblige people to take parish children as apprentices and this was usually done by ballot. Most of these children were not taught a real skill but were used as cheap labour,[46] and this may have been Affricanus's fate. Relatively few Black children seem to have become dependant on the parish, but the number who did is not easy to ascertain. It is only Affricanus's name that indicates his origin, and he is unlikely to be unique.

Life after service

Peter Earle observed that service was 'predominantly an occupation for young men'. There were elderly retainers, but he concluded most men had left service before they were 40.[47] A number of Black servants set up their own businesses, like their white fellows, and were probably given assistance by their erstwhile masters, like John Duck mentioned above. He must have been taught his skills in his master, Edward Green's, household and would have needed his master's help to set up in business, because Green was in a position to give future clients a disagreeable picture of his erstwhile servant, who had seduced at least two women. So far, Cesar Picton of Kingston-upon-Thames, Surrey, seems to be the ex-servant who made the most of his opportunities, getting a licence to trade in coal, although he was greatly helped by the legacies left him by members of the family he served. His will shows him to have possessed substantial property at his death in 1836 at the age of 81.[48] Ignatius Sancho was not, as is sometimes suggested, the first Black corner shop owner.[49] He was the first Black shopkeeper to write about his life, which is not the same thing. John Phipps, a Black man, was a victualler in Westminster during the second decade of the 1700s, some years before Sancho set up business.[50] Sancho too worked in Westminster, but there are others elsewhere in the country, like John Cranbrook, who ran a greengrocer's shop in Clapham, then in rural Surrey;[51] Affrick Hunsdon in Hertfordshire; and George John Scipio Africanus in Nottingham, mentioned above. In 1795 Connor, 'a Black man', was described as the householder of a property in Clerkenwell where an illegal, and apparently fraudulent, private lottery was held. He was not involved in the scam, nor called as a witness, but simply mentioned as the householder.[52] He was probably running some kind of business there, but what was not revealed: the authorities had no interest in him, nor in his colour, which suggests that he was not exceptional.

Ignatius Sancho was, like other respectable members of a parish, invited to take part in local government (although he excused himself on health grounds). Elsewhere, Black people did occupy parish offices. In 1676/7 John Mills became churchwarden of Wolstanton in Staffordshire. His colour is mentioned only to distinguish him from another man of the same name in the parish.[53] In 1741 the parish constable of Clerkenwell, Middlesex was a 'Negro'. When he gave evidence against a woman whom he had arrested his race was given in the *Proceedings* of the Old Bailey but the reporter missed his name, so his race was probably given to distinguish him from the other parish constables.[54] There are special circumstances why John Mills and this parish constable were identified as Black that would not have applied in other cases, so there may have been more Black men holding parish office whose colour or ethnic origin were not recorded.

Women's work is, in general, less well documented. Most were involved in their husbands' or fathers' businesses but opportunities for most unmarried women, of any colour, to earn an independent living were limited. Those from the lower classes who, like Ann Duck, could not or did not wish to spend their lives working in the family business or in domestic service had few alternatives to prostitution or crime. Some women servants turned to prostitution to support themselves between hirings, as Daniel Defoe observed in 1725,[55] and this continued into the nineteenth century. Black women, who would have lacked a family in this country to support them, must have done the same. Black Harriott is the best known of the Black women who took the prostitution route.[56] James Boswell was told that there was a brothel staffed exclusively by Black women, but it was not Harriott's. Some of her working girls are described in *Harris's List of Covent Garden Ladies*, a publication set up in 1757 by John Harrison, alias Jack Harris, which continued to be published until 1795, although only issues for nine of those years have survived in public collections.[57] The prostitutes' physical appearance, performance and specialities are described. Some Black women of the town are included, like Eliza Love, 'a downright mulatto' from the West Indies,[58] and Miss W-l-n from Jamaica who could not 'boast a complexion delicately fair'.[59] The practice of describing any dark-skinned person as 'Black' makes it difficult to determine just how many of Harris's ladies were of African or East Indian origin: others may be Mrs Edmonds, 'a fine tall and Black woman', and Poll Ch-dd-er, 'A pretty little Black girl'.[60] A few cases at the Old Bailey suggest that there were other Black prostitutes not mentioned by Harris, like Esther Allingham, acquitted of theft in 1782.[61] In 1801 a Black woman, Ann Holman, said in evidence that she was employed to bring men into a bawdy house: whether she did more than simply find customers was not stated.[62] Because there is published information about Black women who became prostitutes, it is tempting to conclude that most were sexually exploited, but in fact very few appear in official records. Their invisibility suggests that the majority lived averagely quiet, law-abiding lives.

Defending the country

The problem with researching Black soldiers and sailors prior to the nineteenth century is that records are less informative than they later became and in any case the colour or ethnic origin of the individual can often only be conjectured from a combination of birthplace and physical description.[63] These are not regularly included until the end of the eighteenth century. Registers of deserters from the Army, including a physical description, do not exist before 1811. Although there are returns of rewards paid to those who captured deserters from 1716, they do not indicate either the birthplace or the physical appearance of the deserter.[64] The presence of Black soldiers and sailors in the eighteenth and nineteenth centuries is, however, well established. John Ellis has examined the Black drummers of the 29th Regiment of Foot, which seems to have had a tradition of employing them.[65] Many others were also musicians, like Thomas Ruford, mentioned in Chapter 7; Jeremiah Salisbury, 'a Negroman and a Trumpeter in his Majesties fourth Regiment of Dragoons' baptised in Trowbridge, Wiltshire in 1782.[66] The military roles of others were not given, like Henry Moor, 'a Blackmoor, belonging to the Regiment of Collonel [sic] Evans'.[67] Although John Ellis concluded that Black soldiers and sailors in the regular forces during the nineteenth century seem not to have been promoted to the same extent that their white counterparts were,[68] the reasons need further investigation. Most promotion, especially in the army, depended on influential contacts and money, which Black men were less likely to have. At sea, although ability played a greater part, promotion was still heavily dependent on patronage. It is also likely that, because birthplace was recorded rather than ethnic origin, not all Black and mixed-race people have been found, as in many other areas of life.

A number of Black mariners appear in the *Proceedings* of the Old Bailey but it is not always clear whether they were Royal Navy sailors or merchant seamen. Some may have worked for both. A few Black autobiographers spent time at sea. Olaudah Equiano is the best known, but Britton Hammon, Boston King and John Marrant all served on board ship. Other sailors in the Royal Navy are also known to have been the slaves of white officers (as Equiano was for a time) who appropriated their pay and prizes.[69] Others seem to have been permitted to go to sea by their masters, who nevertheless retained control over them, like John Cato, 'a negro slave of HM ships Launceston and Superbe', for whom administration was granted to his master's son in 1749.[70] Cato's 'proprietor', Joseph Reade, lived in New York, which suggests that Cato was in the same anomalous situation as James Somerset and other slaves brought to England from a colony where slavery was legal. The Admiralty, however, was firmly against this practice, even before the Mansfield Judgment.[71]

One reason must have been the necessity of relying on the loyalty of all those on board. The opportunities for sabotage by disgruntled slaves who felt they had no stake in the work of the ship would have been many, and the belief among many Black people that in death they would return home to Africa was known. In the heat of battle, too, the need to have confidence in the commitment of all those on board ship must have been paramount.

Few seem to have been promoted, although, as place of birth rather than race is usually given in records, it is difficult to know the colour of all those on a ship. At some time between 1805 and 1807 Captain Rotherham of the *Bellerophon* carried out a unique survey of the 387 ordinary sailors in his crew. Thirteen were Black.[72] There is no information about his officers. One of the trainee officers on the *Bounty*, however, seems to have been of mixed race. He was Edward Young from St Kitts, a midshipman. This was an entry point for men of good family, who would expect to be promoted, and he had been taken on by Captain Bligh because of a recommendation from Sir George Young, a captain in the Royal Navy, presumably a relative.[73] On retirement from the Royal Navy (but not from merchant service) sailors were entitled to enter the Greenwich Hospital or, if they preferred, to draw a pension and live where they chose. A number of Black men availed themselves of this privilege. Black ex-soldiers also took the opportunity to enter Chelsea Hospital.[74] Other Black mariners may have become ship owners. Bolster mentions some enslaved and free Black captains of ships in North America and the Caribbean.[75] In 1760, a Sussex newspaper carried the following item:

> Portsmouth July 29 About three or four months ago, a snow was cast away at the Back of the Isle of Wight, Master's Name Bell. This unfortunate Man being, since the Loss of his Ship, driven to the last Extremity, on Monday morning last was hanging in a Cow House within two Fields of our Ramparts. On Sunday Evening, the poor Man sold a handkerchief at a Public House, near the place where he destroyed himself; part of the Money he paid for some Bread and Cheese, and Beer, which he had called for, and with the Remainder, we suppose, he bought the Rope. He was a handsome, genteel, well-made Black Man. He had on when he was cut down a Black Coat, Black Waistcoat, and Black Plush Breeches, Black Stockings and a Gold laced hat; his shirt was so dirty, that it must have been worn a Fortnight. He was seen sauntering near the place about Four o'Clock that morning, and between Five and Six was found hanging.[76]

His colour is mentioned late in the story, almost incidentally. The newspaper expresses no surprise that the master of a ship should be Black, although it is possible that the word was being used as an adjective. How many others were masters of merchant ships is not yet known, nor whether they had acquired their vessels in Britain, North America or the Caribbean.

Throughout the long eighteenth century, Britain was at war with most of the major European powers at one time or another. The chief fear of the authorities was invasion. Before the establishment of a standing army, dating from Cromwell's Protectorate, there was a requirement for all men to be trained in martial skills, and from this grew the militia. Members of the militia were selected by ballot. The records of Hertfordshire are unusually voluminous (though not complete) and include a number of people noted to be Black in the parishes' lists of those eligible to serve, like George Donay of Cashio, who appears in the Watford Militia Lists for 1782–86, and George Mitchell in the Westmill (Buntingford) Militia List between 1758 and 1801 (exact date uncertain).[77] Some did serve. In 1779 George Sydown, 'a Black Drummer in the Wiltshire Regiment of Militia', was buried at Marlborough, Wiltshire.[78] The greatest anxiety about, and danger of, invasion occurred during the French and Napoleonic Wars (1793–1815). In 1798 the government called for a posse comitatis, literally 'force of the county'. This was a list of all men between the ages of 15 and 60 who could, in the event of an invasion, be called up to fight. Owners of carts that could be used for transport and bakers to supply basic food were also recorded. The survival of these records is patchy: only the county of Buckinghamshire has a complete list. William Cuba is included in the list of servants in the parish of Beaconsfield, but his colour is not mentioned there.[79] In Hanslope, Buckinghamshire, there are three servants for whom no surname is given. They may also have been Black.[80] How many others there were with commonplace names is unknown.

The professions

Some mixed-race children of West Indian settlers were sent to Britain, presumably to evade the restrictions their parentage caused there. It is significant that only those of mixed race with a rich, white father seem to have been able to enter the professions.[81] Nathaniel Wells was perhaps the one who rose to the greatest heights, becoming deputy lieutenant of Monmouthshire. Contemporaries occasionally remarked upon his colour but, significantly, no official documents seem to have noted this: all such references come from private papers, but it was plainly no bar to achieving high office, even representing royalty in the county, as the lieutenant did.[82] William Beckford had many illegitimate children by some of his family's slaves in Jamaica, where he was born and his father was Governor of the island. He acknowledged paternity and gave the children his name (how his legitimate wife felt about this is not recorded). The eldest of these illegitimate children was Richard Beckford, who stood as a parliamentary candidate in Hindon, Wiltshire in 1774.[83] Brian Mackey, the son of William Mackey of Kingston, Jamaica, 'gentleman', was educated at Oxford University and became the parish priest of Coates in Gloucestershire after his father purchased the living for him. His origin appears only in the private diary of the parish priest of the village to which his father retired.[84] Another, better known, minister was Robert Wedderburn, the mixed-race son of a plantation owner, but he is best remembered for his involvement in radical politics and the Cato Street Conspiracy, as well as being the author of an autobiographical work, *The Horrors of Slavery*.[85] Wedderburn seems not to have been formally ordained in any mainstream denomination but was self-appointed. William Davidson (Illustration 13), the son of an Attorney General of Jamaica by a Black woman, was sent to school in Scotland and afterwards was apprenticed to an attorney in Liverpool, although he left that position, first to go to sea and then to be apprenticed to a cabinet maker. He too was involved in the Cato Street Conspiracy and was executed for his part in it.[86] Robert Laing was the son of Malcolm Laing of Kingston, Jamaica, by Elizabeth Fickle, 'a free mulatto'. Malcolm Laing was the attorney of the Perrin family, estate owners in Jamaica, and after his death his son was sent to London, where he was admitted to Lincoln's Inn and called to the Bar in 1793, although he never seems to have practised. He inherited a large sum of money but later fell into poverty when arrangements were made to educate and care for his children, one of whom was sent to Christ's Hospital and later became a teacher there.[87]

There were probably also mixed-race daughters of plantation owners who were sent to Britain for their education. Their fathers' wealth would have been an attraction to potential suitors, but so far only a fictional example, Miss Swartz of Thackeray's *Vanity Fair*, is known.[88] Marriage was the only profession suitable to their rank that would be open to them, so they would effectively disappear from public life. Katherine, daughter of James Achilles Kirkpatrick, the British Resident in Hyderabad in India, and his wife, Khair um-Nissa, was sent to England and later married Captain James Phillips of the 7th Hussars, a prestigious regiment.[89] How many daughters of men from the Caribbean by women of African origin married into the gentry or upper middle class remains to be uncovered. In

WILLIAM DAVIDSON.

Wivell Delt. *Cooper Sculp.*

13. William Davidson, engraving by Robert Cooper, 1820, from a portrait by Abraham Wivell.

the more racially prejudiced nineteenth century Robert Laing's descendants explained their colouring by claiming Spanish ancestry: there are probably other examples.

Because the occupation 'servant' is the one that is almost invariably given in baptismal registers and because of their comparatively frequent representation in paintings, the assumption has been that Black people were servants. It is true that the majority seem to have started their lives in England in this post, but from even a limited amount of research it is clear that a number (what proportion is not known) neither remained with the same master nor even remained in service all their lives. They went on to a number of trades and even, in the case of the mixed-race offspring of men from the colonies, into the professions. In the armed forces they were apparently less likely to be promoted than white people, but they nonetheless were able to avail themselves of the same benefits on retirement, like pensions or entry into sheltered accommodation like the Greenwich Hospital. Of course they were in England or Wales because of the massive slave trade: they were a very small, untypical section of it and how and why they arrived needs further investigation, but they themselves were not slaves. This is not very exciting for the historian because it is always much more interesting to write about outsiders who suffer hardship and prejudice. Nor is it useful to those with a political axe to grind. Black people are, however, just one of the many minorities who make up the rich mix of British ancestry. Like the descendants of these other minorities, Black people quickly assimilated into the general population and their very invisibility is further evidence they were neither slaves nor stigmatised outsiders during the long eighteenth century, when the British slave trade was being conducted. As previous historians have also concluded, much more work remains to be done to answer the numerous questions this work has raised: were their experiences different in rural and urban areas? What part did they play in nonconformity? What were the social backgrounds of their spouses? Who were their masters and what connections did they have with the slave trade and the colonies? Not until these are fully explored can a true understanding of Black people's history in Britain be achieved.

Notes

1. Dabydeen, *Hogarth's Blacks*, p. 21.
2. King, R. 'Ignatius Sancho and Portraits of the Black Elite', in King et al., *Ignatius Sancho*, p. 28.
3. Hecht, J.J., *The Domestic Servant Class in Eighteenth-Century England* (1956), p. 5.
4. Girouard, M., *The Country House Companion* (1987) reproduces two pictures which show Black people among the household servants of the aristocracy. The endpapers show the thirty servants of St John Boileau at Ketteringham Hall, Norfolk c.1850, among whom there are several very dark-skinned people. On p. 129 there is a reproduction of part of a painting by Gillis Van Tilborch (1670) showing the distribution of the Tichbourne Dole at Tichbourne House, Hampshire. A Black manservant appears along with many other household servants.

5. Whatman, S., *The Housekeeping Book of Susanna Whatman 1776–1800* (1956, reprinted 1991) goes into fine detail about what had to be done and when.
6. Hecht, *The Domestic Servant Class*, pp. 60–3.
7. Holmes, J., *Domestic Service in Yorkshire 1650–1780* (York, 1989) quoted in Horn, P., *Flunkeys and Scullions: Life Below Stairs in Georgian England* (Stroud, 2004) p. 87. The woman believed that she would not like her new maid and hoped that she would do something wrong so the two could part. This is odd: why choose a servant, however fashionable, if you fear you will not get on well? Was it just cold feet and fear of the unknown? Or was she in such desperate need of a maid that she took what she could get?
8. *Daily Ledger*, 31 December 1761.
9. Turner, E.S., *What the Butler Saw: Two Hundred and Fifty Years of the Servant Problem* (1962, republ. 2001), pp. 29, 128–9, 135, 160, 164–5, 176.
10. Latham & Matthews, *Diary of Samuel Pepys*, Vol. 9, p. 510.
11. CWA, E2574, p. 242. His master, Edward Green, was the tenant of twenty-nine acres in Ewell. He is mentioned in a manorial court for the Manor of Ewell and Cuddington, held on 15 October 1702 (Surrey RO, 2238/10/170, p. 165); CWA, Registers of St Clement Danes, 12 August 1717; Ordinary's *Account*, 7 November 1744, pp. 6ff.
12. *Proceedings* 7–12 September 1722, p. 5.
13. *Proceedings* 1773–4, II, no. 146.
14. *Proceedings* 1782–3, VIII, no. 640.
15. *Proceedings* 1776–7, VII, no. 609.
16. *Proceedings* 22–25 February 1727/8, p. 1. The Ordinary's *Account*, 22 March 1727 says he came from India, brought to England by a ship's captain after he was orphaned.
17. *Proceedings* 1785–6, II, no. 139. Hounslow was on the Bath Road and had coaching inns for those travelling between London and the West Country. Why he travelled this route regularly was never explained.
18. *Proceedings* 1785–6, IV, no. 325.
19. *Proceedings* 1781–2, V, no. 664.
20. Eph. 5: 22–24 (Authorised Version).
21. Gen. 4: 16 (Authorised Version).
22. *The Young Lady's Pocket Library or Parental Monitor* (1727–1790) published as *For Her Own Good: a Series of Conduct Books*, ed. Jones, V. (Bristol, 1995), pp. 183–4, 29 and 81. This is a collection of four popular conduct books, previously published separately. In *The Godwins and the Shelleys* (1989), pp. 504–11, William St Clair devoted an appendix to advice books for young women. He found that Gregory's was the one most often reprinted and that some were probably publishers' compilations of previously written works reissued anonymously.
23. Lancashire RO, DDKE/acc. 7840 HMC/1256, on <www.nationalarchive.gov.uk/a2a>.

24. Munby, A.J., *Faithful Servants, being Epitaphs and Obituaries Recording Their Names and Services* (1891) is a collection of records relating to domestic servants (the overwhelming majority of whom would have been white) whose lifetime service was appreciated by their masters.
25. *Proceedings* 1769-70, II, nos. 180-183. From the transcript of his evidence, Wadeson seems to have been particularly well spoken.
26. *Proceedings* 1780-1, I, no. 3. He died three years later, still in service. LMA. Registers of Hillingdon, 6 May 1784.
27. I am grateful to Sir Christopher Prevost, a descendant of her master, Augustin Prevost, for this information.
28. Morrison, A., *Collection of Autograph Letters, Vol. II, The Hamilton-Nelson Papers 1798-1815* (m.589), in Gérin, W., *Horatia Nelson* (Oxford, 1970) p. 47. Price had at least one son, who drowned in an accident, *ibid.*, p. 133.
29. I am grateful to Captain Robert Bonner (retd) of the Manchester Museum Committee of the King's Regiment for this delightful reference.
30. Prideaux, R.M., *Prideaux, A West Country Clan* (Chichester, 1989), p. 217. I am grateful to Mr Prideaux for drawing my attention to this epitaph.
31. Adolph, A., 'The Trial of John Ystumllyn', in *The Family and Local History Handbook* 10 (2006), pp. 140-3. He only did the job for a short while and returned to work for previous masters, the Wynne family, as a gardener. Presumably he missed his old job or did not want the responsibility. The point is that the owners of Ynysgain Fawr considered him capable of the work and to be trustworthy.
32. *Proceedings* 1783-4, III, no. 362. He was acquitted because of an 'accidental circumstance' but the evidence against him was strong.
33. *Proceedings* 1744-5, IV, no. 189. This suggests he was the butler, the senior household servant.
34. *Proceedings* 1763-4, IV, no. 22. Edinburgh was charged with horse theft from a neighbour of Thomas Seers, Samuel's brother. Though sentenced to death, he was recommended to mercy, presumably because of the glowing testimonials Seers and others gave him.
35. See website <www.nationalarchives.gov.uk/pathways/Blackhistory/early_times/settlers.htm>. I am grateful to Audrey Dewjee for drawing my attention to him.
36. Gloucestershire RO, Q/SO 4 1714-24.
37. Hanway, J., *The State of Young Chimney Sweepers' Apprentices* (1773), quoted in George, *London Life*, p. 137.
38. LMA, W.SP 1727 Jan/2. The document is too damaged to be consulted and other papers from the Sessions are missing, so it is not known what the outcome was.
39. SoG, unpublished typescript, APP, *The Apprentices of Great Britain 1710-1762*, Vol. I. This index to both apprentices and masters covers records in TNA, IR10/159.

40. Luu, L. 'Natural Born Versus Stranger-Born Subjects: Aliens and their Status in Elizabethan London', in Goose, N. & Luu, L., *Immigrants in Tudor and Early Stuart England* (Brighton, 2005), pp. 57–75.
41. GL, Ms 95, 'Pie Powder Court', preliminary material (the pages are not numbered).
42. In 1570 there were over 4,000 foreigners, mainly Flemish refugees, in Norwich and in 1574 the Mayor warned them that he would accept no more immigrants. Gwynn, R., *Huguenot Heritage: the History and Contribution of the Huguenots in Britain* (1985), p. 19. By 1620 most had been driven from there by the townspeople's hostility. Currer-Briggs, N. & Gambier, R., *Huguenot Ancestry* (1985), p. 45.
43. Gwynn, *Huguenot Heritage*, pp. 120–2, summarises the City's efforts to restrict the activities of all foreigners and details cases of refusal by various livery companies to accept Huguenots as freemen.
44. Fryer, *Staying Power*, p. 75.
45. TNA IR1/32, 16 December 1783. I am grateful to Mary Croft for this reference.
46. George, *London Life*, pp. 215–35.
47. Earle, P., *A City Full of People: Men and Women of London 1650–1750* (1994), p. 85.
48. *The Story of Caesar Picton*, undated pamphlet produced by Kingston-upon-Thames Record Office and sent to me by Marion Bone; TNA, PROB 11/1863.
49. I have heard this said at several lectures.
50. CWA, Baptism Registers of St Clement Danes, 27 November 1715.
51. He was baptised in Rochester, Kent in 1764 (SoG, unpublished transcript, KE/R 235, 'Registers of St Nicholas, Rochester, Kent'); married in the City of London on 3 March 1772 (GL, Ms 17,827/1, Registers of All Hallows, Staining); and came to Clapham around 1784. He was buried there on 1797 (LMA, Registers of Clapham). Perhaps members of the Clapham Sect, prominent in the movement to abolish the slave trade, were buying their fruit and vegetables from him.
52. LMA, MJ/SP/1795/10/032. I am grateful to Dr Caroline Bressey for drawing my attention to this case.
53. Adams, P.W.L., *Registers of Wolstanton* (Staffordshire Parish Register Society, np, nd [?1914]), p. 129. Entries of the marriages of the two John Millses, the baptisms and burials of their children, their wives and the men themselves do not distinguish between them.
54. *Proceedings* 1745–6, II, no. 100. The records of the Middlesex Sessions, where there was a preliminary hearing to commit the woman to the Old Bailey, reveal him to have been called Thomas Latham, although his race is not mentioned there. LMA, MJ/SP/2855 f. 21.
55. Rubenhold, H., *The Covent Garden Ladies: Pimp General Jack and the Extraordinary Story of Harris's List* (2005), p. 123. No reference is given.

56. Burford, E.J., *Royal St James* (1988), pp. 201-4
57. Rubenhold, *The Covent Garden Ladies*, p. 285. The years are 1761, 1764, 1773, 1779, 1788, 1789, 1790 and 1793.
58. *Harris's List* (1789), quoted in Rubenhold, *The Covent Garden Ladies*, p. 132. The name Love looks like a professional pseudonym.
59. *Harris's List* (1773), pp. 82-3.
60. *Ibid.*, 1773 and 1764.
61. *Proceedings* 1781-2, VI, no. 371.
62. *Proceedings* 1800-1, VIII, no. 646.
63. Under the name of Gustavus Vassa, Olaudah Equiano appears in various ships' musters, where his birthplace is given as Carolina, but there is no description of him. Without his autobiography it would be impossible to identify him as Black from these records.
64. Fowler, S., *Army Records for Family Historians* (1992), pp. 18-21.
65. Ellis, J.D., 'Drummers for the Devil? The Black Soldiers of the 29th (Worcestershire) Regiment of Foot, 1759-1843', *Journal of the Society for Army Historical Research* 80 (2002), pp. 186-202.
66. Wiltshire and Swindon RO, Microfiche, 9 February 1782. I am grateful to Sue Johnson for this reference.
67. His son Evan was baptised in Hereford St Peter on 14 September 1731. Herefordshire RO.
68. Ellis, J.D., 'Black Soldiers in British Army Regiments during the Early Nineteenth Century', *AAHGS News*, March/April 2001, pp. 12-15.
69. Rodger, N.A.M., *The Wooden World: an Anatomy of the Georgian Navy* (1986), pp. 159-61.
70. TNA PROB 6/125. The administration was granted in the Prerogative Court of Canterbury because it had jurisdiction over events which took place at sea on British ships, as well as being the highest court of probate for British colonies. Two other sailors surnamed Cato, which suggested they were Black, left standard wills, leaving their effects to friends: Joseph Cato, PROB 11/1116, and Robert Cato, PROB 11/1769.
71. Rodger, *The Wooden World*, p. 160.
72. NMM, LBK/38, *The Letters of Captain Edward Rotherham 1799-1930*, quoted in Cordingley, D., *Billy Ruffian: the Bellerophon and the Downfall of Napoleon, a Biography of a Ship of the Line, 1782-1836* (2003), pp. 208-12.
73. Lummis, T., *Life and Death in Eden: Pitcairn Island and the Bounty Mutineers* (1997), pp. 81-2. How many other mixed-race officers there were is not known: Young's background was of interest because of the mutiny. Edward Young called one of his sons, born on Pitcairn Island, George, suggesting a family connection with the Royal Navy captain (*ibid.*, p. 179) although Sir George's descendants deny this.
74. A photograph taken in 1854 by John Havers shows a group of aged Greenwich pensioners among whom are one person who is definitely of African

origin and another who might be. Reproduced in Marsh, J. (ed.), *Black Victorians: Black People in British Art 1800-1900*, p. 135. As Marsh notes, Andrew Morton's painting *United Services* (National Maritime Museum) shows Chelsea Pensioners visiting the Greenwich Hospital and among their numbers is a Black ex-soldier. The painting by Daniel Maclise, *The Death of Nelson* in the Walker Museum in Liverpool shows a Black sailor close to the dying admiral. At the Battle of Trafalgar there were 123 sailors whose birthplace was in the West Indies, and 20 born in India, although the records do not mention their colour or ethnicity, so it is not known how many were Black, <www.nationalarchives.gov.uk/nelson/>.

75. Bolster, W.J., *Black Jacks* (Cambridge, MA, 1997), pp. 23-5, 133.
76. *Sussex Weekly Advertiser or Lewes Journal*, 4 August 1760, p. 3. A snow was a two-masted merchant vessel.
77. I am grateful to Dr Jill Barber of Hertfordshire RO for these references.
78. Wiltshire RO, Registers of St Peter's Church, Marlborough, 9 May 1779. I am grateful to Sally M. Thomson for this reference.
79. Beckett, F.W., *The Buckinghamshire Posse Comitatis 1798* (Buckinghamshire Record Society, 1985) p. 152. The burial record of one of his children, Mary, is the only one to mention his colour (Hertfordshire RO, Registers of Penn, Buckinghamshire, 3 December 1788) but his own burial record simply notes that he was 'native of the Island of Cuba' (Hertfordshire RO, Registers of Penn, Buckinghamshire, 1813).
80. Beckett, *Buckinghamshire Posse Comitatis*, p. 152. I am grateful to Andrew Parker of New Zealand for drawing my attention to the Hanslope entries.
81. Francis Williams, the son of a free Black couple in Jamaica, was sent to Cambridge University under the patronage of the Duke of Montagu, who wanted to prove that Black people were as capable as white of benefiting from an education. On his return to Jamaica, he was refused a position on the governor's council, so ran a school in Spanish Town. Fryer, *Staying Power*, p. 241.
82. Evans, J.A.H., 'Nathaniel Wells of Piercefield and St Kitts: From Slave to Sheriff', *Monmouthshire Antiquary* (2000), pp. 91-106
83. His brother Nathaniel lived nearby, in East Knoyle, where his daughter Susanna was baptised in 1779. The register describes him as 'Esquire', a socially significant title. Nathaniel himself was baptised a year later, in 1780, where he is simply called 'a Negro man'. I am grateful to Jonathan Stevens for these references to both Richard and Nathaniel. Richard's legitimate half-brother, William Beckford, became an MP, first for Wells, then for Hindon. *Dictionary of National Biography* (Oxford, 1938).
84. *Alumni Oxonienses 1715-1886*, Vol. 3 (Oxford, 1891) p. 895; Ayres, J. (ed.), *Paupers and Pig Killers*, p. 106. He is the first known Black person to have been a minister who served in the Church of England in Britain.
85. Wedderburn, R., *The Horrors of Slavery and other Writings by Robert*

Wedderburn (1824), ed. MacCalman, I. (Edinburgh, 1991). Had he not been in prison at the time when the Cato Street conspirators were arrested for their plot to assassinate the Cabinet, he would probably have been executed for his involvement (p. 23).
86. Davidson's father seems to have demonstrated patience with a son who was so restless. He presumably paid the premiums to have him apprenticed twice, as well as for his school fees.
87. I am grateful to his great-great-grand-daughter, Lucy Richards, for information about him.
88. Thackeray, W. *Vanity Fair* (1847).
89. Dalrymple, W., *White Mughals* (2002), p. 478. She had attracted the attention of Thomas Carlyle when he was her brother's tutor, but he was considered too low-class for her.

Select bibliography

The place of publication is London, except where otherwise stated.

Unpublished primary sources

Public repositories

The database of Black people was compiled largely from transcripts from parish registers in the Society of Genealogists' library and county record offices, including:
Berkshire County Record Office, Reading
Bristol Record Office
Buckinghamshire County Record Office, Aylesbury
City of Westminster Archives Centre
Devon County Record Office, Exeter
Essex County Record Office, Chelmsford
Greenwich Heritage Centre
Guildhall Library, London
Herefordshire County Record Office, Hereford
Huntingdon Record Office, Huntingdon
Kent County Record Office
London Metropolitan Archives
The National Archives, Kew
Oxfordshire County Record Office, Oxford
Oxford Local Studies Library
Southwark Local Studies Library
Sussex County Record Office, Lewes
Surrey County Record Office, Woking

Online sources

Access to Archives <www.nationalarchives.gov.uk/a2a.org.uk>
Censuses of 1841, 1851, 1861, 1871, 1881, 1891 and 1901 on <www.ancestry.com>

Faculty Office Marriage Licence Allegations 1701–1812 on <www.ancestry.com>
National Library of Jamaica <www.nlj.org.jm>
Old Bailey on line <www.oldbaileyonline.org>
Rootsweb <www.rootsweb.com>

Published primary sources

Bills of Mortality for London 1660–1812

British Library

Microfilm copy of selected early newspapers in the Burney Collection

British Library Newspaper Library, Colindale

Canterbury Journal 1771
Chelmsford & Colchester Chronicle 1768–73
Derby Mercury 1773–78
Falmouth Packet (Index) 1770–74
Hampshire Chronicle 1772, 1796
Jackson's Oxford Journal (Index)
London Chronicle
London Evening Post 1744
London Gazette 1665–1712, 1715–19, 1722–36, 1738–41, 1743–48, 1750–51, 1753–64, July 1772–August 1773, 1774, 1776–79, 1781–88
Norwich Mercury (Index) 1770–79
Palmer's Index to The Times
Sherbourne Mercury (Index) 1737–40
Trewman's Exeter Flying Post 1804–9
Weekly Advertiser for Essex, etc., 1798
Western Flying Post 1749–90
Whitehall Evening Post October 1718–19, 1747–51, 1754–56, 1758–61, 1769, 1781–91, 1794–1800
York Herald 1801

Other published primary sources

City of Westminster Archives, *Sources for Black and Asian History at the City of Westminster Archives Centre* (2005).
A Complete Copy of the Poll for Electing Two Representatives in Parliament for the City and Liberty of Westminster (1774).
Coldham, P.W., *English Convicts in Colonial America*, 2 vols (New Orleans, 1976).

Coldham, P.W., *Emigrants from England to the American Colonies 1773–1776* (Baltimore, MD, 1988).
Coldham, P.W., *The Complete Book of Emigrants in Bondage* (Baltimore, MD, 1998).
Coldham, P.W., *More Emigrants in Bondage 1614–1775* (Baltimore, MD, 2002).
Edmonds, J.A., *Duke of Cornwall's Light Infantry & Cornwall & Devon RGA Militia Attestations*, CD-ROM (self-published, nd).
Garneray, L., *Mes Pontons* (1851), trans. Rose, R., published as *The Floating Prison: the Remarkable Account of Nine Years' Captivity on the British Prison Hulks during the Napoleonic Wars 1806 to 1814* (2003).
Herber, M., *Clandestine Marriages in the Chapel and Rules of the Fleet Prison 1680–1754*, 3 vols (1999–2001).
Horwood, R., *A Map of the Cities of London and Westminster, etc.* (1799), publ. as *The A–Z of Regency London* (1985).
Hotten, J.C., *Persons of Quality: People Who Went from Britain to the American Plantations 1600–1700* (nd) CD-ROM (Salisbury, 2003).
Ingram, A., *Patterns of Madness in the Eighteenth Century: a Reader* (Liverpool, 1998).
Jones, L., *Coroners' Inquisitions: an Index of Inquisitions in Dover & the Isle of Thanet 1802–1864*, CD-ROM (self-published, 2003).
The London 1768 Poll Book, CD-ROM (Salisbury, 2003).
The National Archives, *Board of Stamps Apprenticeship Books: IR1/1–19, IR1/41–51*, 5 CD-ROMs (Archive CD Books, nd).
The Ordinary of Newgate's *Account*, 22 March 1727; 3 March 1736/7; 19 July 1738; 12 July 1742; 7 November 1744; 24 December 1744; 18 October 1749.
Paley, R. (ed.), *Justice in 18th Century Hackney: the Justicing Notebook of Henry Norris* (1991).
Powell, D.L. (ed.), *Surrey Quarter Sessions Records: Order Book and Sessions Rolls 1666–1668* (Kingston, Surrey, 1951).
Roque, J., *Plan of the Cities of London and Westminster, etc.* (1747) publ. as *The A–Z of Georgian London* (1981).
Wyatt, R., *Deposition Book of Richard Wyatt, J.P. 1767–1776*, ed. Silverthorne, E. (Guildford, 1978).
Universal British Directory (1791) CD-ROM (Cinderford, Gloucs.,nd).

Published documents, correspondence and journals

Some of these do not specifically mention Black people, but they provide background information on everyday life between 1660 and 1812.

Baker, J., *The Diary of John Baker*, ed. Yorke, P. (1931).
Boswell, J., *London Journal 1762–1763* (1950).
Burney, F., *Fanny Burney's Diary: a Selection from the Diary and Letters*, ed. Wain, J. (1961).

Clifford, A., *The Diaries of Lady Anne Clifford*, ed. Clifford, D.J.H. (Stroud, 2nd edn, 1992).
Cook, J., *The Journals of Captain Cook*, ed. Edwards, P. (1999).
Evelyn, J., *Diary*, (1631–1705), selected and ed. Bédoyère, G. de la (Woodbridge, 1995).
Ham, E., *Elizabeth Ham by Herself 1783–1820*, ed. Gillett, E. (1945).
Hurst, S., *The Diaries of Sarah Hurst 1759–1762*, transcribed Hurst, B. & ed. Djabri, S.C. (Horsham, 2003).
Long, E. et al., *Records and Letters of the Family of the Longs of Longville, Jamaica, and Hampton Lodge, Surrey*, 2 vols, ed. Howard, R.M. (1925).
Newton, J., *The Journal of a Slave Trader 1750–1754*, ed. Martin, B. & Spurrell, M. (1962)
Pepys, S., *The Diary of Samuel Pepys*, 11 vols, ed. Latham, R. & Matthews, W. (1983).
Pepys, S., *Letters and the Second Diary of Samuel Pepys*, ed. Howarth, R.G. (1932).
Sheridan, E., *Betsy Sheridan's Journal*, ed. Lefanu, W. (1960).
Wilson, H., *Memoirs* (1825).
Winstanley, I. (ed.), *The Diary of Roger Lowe of Ashton-in-Makerfield, Lancashire 1663–1678* (2nd edn, Wigan, 2004).
Woodforde, D.H. (ed.), *Woodforde Papers and Diaries* (1932).
Woodforde, J., *The Diary of a Country Parson 1758–1802*, 5 vols (1924), selected and ed. Beresford, J. (Oxford, 1978).
Wordsworth, D., *The Grasmere Journals*, ed. Woof, P. (Oxford, 1991).
The Wynne Diaries 1789–1820, ed. Freemantle, A. (Oxford, 1952).

Other contemporary works

Anon., *The New Parish Officer* (1771).
Anon., *The Compleat Parish Officer* (7th edn, 1734, facsimile edition publ. 1990 by Wiltshire FHS).
Ashton, J. (ed.) *Chap-Books of the Eighteenth Century (repr., nd [?1980s])*.
Barnes, G.R. & Owen, J.H. (eds) *The Private Papers of John Earl of Sandwich, First Lord of the Admiralty 1771–1782*, Navy Records Society, vols 69, 71, 75 and 78 (1932–38).
Behn, A. *Oroonoko, The Rover and Other Works* (1688), ed. Todd, J. (1992).
Boswell, J. *The Life of Samuel Johnson*, ed. Canning, J. (1991).
Burn, R. *Justice of the Peace and Parish Officer*, 4 vols, ed. Burn, J. (18th edn, 1797).
Cobbett, W. *Rural Rides* (1830), ed. Woodcock, G. (1967).
Cugoano, Q.O., *Thoughts and Sentiments on the Evil of Slavery: or the Nature of Servitude as admitted by the Law of God, etc.* (1787), ed. Carretta, V. (NY, 1999).

Defoe, D., *The Complete English Tradesman* (1726, repr. Stroud, 1987).
Dibden, C., *Memoirs of Charles Dibdin the Younger*, ed. Speaight, G. (1956).
Egan, P., *Life in London* (1822).
Equiano, O., *The Interesting Narrative and Other Writings* (1789), ed. Carretta, V. (2nd edn, 2003).
Falconbridge, A.M. *Narrative of Two Voyages to the River Sierra Leone* (1784) with Falconbridge, A., *An Account of the Slave Trade on the Coast of Africa* (1788) ed. Fyfe, C. (Liverpool, 2000).
Fielding, J., *The Newgate Magazine or Malefactor's Monthly Chronicle*, Vol. I (1765).
Fielding, J., 'A Dictionary of Cant Words and Terms' , *The Newgate Magazine or Malefactors' Monthly Chronicle*, Vol. II (1766), pp. 834–44.
Fiennes, C., *The Journeys of Celia Fiennes*, ed. Morris, C. (1947).
Graunt, J., *Natural and Political Observations mentioned in a following Index, and made upon the Bills of Mortality* (1662).
Gronniosaw, J., *A Narrative of the Most Remarkable Particulars in the Life of James Albert Ukasaw Gronniosaw, an African Prince as related by Himself* (Bath, 1770?) on <www.etext.virginia.edu/readex/1311.html>
Grose, F., *The Vulgar Tongue* (1785, repr. Chichester, 2004).
Hammon, B., *Narrative of the Uncommon Sufferings and Surprizing Deliverance of Briton Hammon, a Negro Man, – Servant to General Winslow of Marshfield, in New-England; Who returned to Boston, after having been absent almost Thirteen Years, etc.* (Boston, MA, 1760) on <etext.virginia.edu/readex/8611.html>.
Hickey, W., *Memoirs*, ed. Quennell, P. (2nd edn, 1975).
Jacob, G. (?)., *The Complete Parish Officer* (1772).
Jea, J., *The Life, History, and Unparalleled Sufferings of John Jea, the African Preacher, Compiled and Written by Himself* (Portsea, c.1811) on <www.doc-souyh.unc.edu/neh/jeajohn/menu.html>.
King, B., 'Memoirs of the Life of Boston King, a Black Preacher, Written by Himself, during his Residence at Kingswood School', *Methodist Magazine*, March 1798 on <antislavery.eserver.org/narratives/boston_king/>.
Lewis, M. *Journal of a West Indian Proprietor Kept During a Residence in the Island of Jamaica* (1834), ed. Terry, J. (Oxford, 1997).
McDonald, J. *Travels*, ed. Beresford, J. (1927).
Mahomet, D. *The Travels of Dean Mahomet* (1794), ed. Fisher, M.H. (Berkeley, CA, 1997).
Marrant, J., *A Narrative of the Lord's Wonderful Dealings with John Marrant, a Black* (1785) on <blackloyalist.com/canadiandigitalcollection/documents/diaries/marrant_narrative.htm>.
Mountain, J., *Sketches in the Life of Joseph Mountain compiled by David Daggett* (New Haven, CT, 1790) on <www.docusouth.unc.edu/neh/mountain/menu.html>.
Nelson, W., *The Office and Authority of a Justice of Peace* (1718).

Nichol, J., *The Life and Adventures of John Nichol, Mariner* (1822), ed. Flannery, T. (Edinburgh, 2001)

Prince, M., *The History of Mary Prince, A West Indian Slave* (1831), ed. Ferguson, M. (revised edn, 1996).

Sancho, I., *Letters of the Late Ignatius Sancho, an African* (1782) ed. Carretta, V. (1998).

Shaw, J., *Parish Law* (1750).

Smith, W., *A Voyage to Guinea* (1774).

Snelgrave, W., *A New Account of Some Parts of Guinea* and *The Slave Trade* (1736).

Sprott, D., *1784* (1984).

Treleaven, S.A., *A Moretonhampstead Diary* on <www.moretonhampstead.org.uk>.

Uffenbach, Z.C. von, *London in 1710*, trans. Quarrel, W. & Moore, M. (1934).

Wadström, C.B., *An Essay on Colonisation* (1794, facsimile edn, Newton Abbott, 1968).

Wardroper, J. (ed.), *Lovers, Rakes and Rogues: a New Garner of Love-songs and Merry Verses, 1580–1830* (1995).

Wedderburn, R., *The Horrors of Slavery and other Writings by Robert Wedderburn*, ed. McCalman, I. (Edinburgh, 1991).

Whatman, S., *The Housekeeping Book of Susannah Whatman 1776–1800* (1956).

Wood, B. (ed.), 'The Letters of Simon Taylor of Jamaica to Chaloner Arcedekne, 1765–1775', in *Travel, Trade and Power in the Atlantic 1765–1884*, Camden Miscellany XXXV, Camden 5th Series, Vol. 19 (2002).

The Young Ladies' Pocket Library, or Parental Monitor (1727–1790) published as *For Her Own Good: a Series of Conduct Books*, ed. Jones, V. (Bristol, 1995).

Secondary works

On the subject of Black people in England and the colonies and slavery generally

Adams, G., 'Dido Elizabeth Belle: a Black Girl at Kenwood', *Camden History Review* 12 (1984), pp. 10–13.

Adolph, A., 'The Trial of John Ystumylln', *The Family and Local History Handbook* 10 (2006), pp. 140–3.

Ahmed, A. & Ibrahim A., *The Black Celts: an Ancient African Civilization in Ireland and Britain* (Cardiff, 1992).

Alexander, M., *Omai, 'Noble Savage'* (1977).

Anim-Adoo, J., *Longest Journey: the History of Black Lewisham* (1995).

Anim-Adoo, J., *Sugar, Spices and Human Cargo: an Early Black History of Greenwich* (1996).

Banton, M., *The Coloured Quarter* (1955).

Barber, J., *Celebrating the Black Presence in Westminster 1500–2000: Hidden Lives* (2000).
Birmingham Central Library, *Sources for the Study of Black People in Birmingham* (Birmingham, 2001).
Birmingham Future Group, *Making Connections* (Birmingham, nd).
BASA, *Newsletter*, issues 25–47.
Beckles, H. & Shepherd, V. (eds), *Caribbean Slave Society and Economy* (NY, 1991).
Behrendt, S., 'Counting the Slaves', *History Today* 51 (1) January 2001, pp. 4–5.
Black, C.V., *A New History of Jamaica* (Jamaica, 1973).
Bolster, W.J., *Black Jacks* (Cambridge, MA, 1997).
Boser, R., 'The Creation of a Legend', *History Today* 52 (10) October 2002, pp. 37–8.
Bourne, S., *Speak of Me As I Am: the Black Presence in Southwark since 1600* (2005).
Bowden-Dan, J., 'Mr Guy's Hospital and the Caribbean', *History Today* 56 (6) June 2006, pp. 50–6.
Bowen, H., '400 Years of the East India Company', *History Today* 50 (7) July 2000, pp. 47–53.
Braidwood, S.J., 'Initiatives and Organisation of the Black Poor 1786–1787', *Slavery & Abolition* 3 (1982), pp. 211–27.
Braidwood, S.J., *Black Poor and White Philanthropists: London's Blacks and the Foundation of the Sierra Leone Settlement 1786–1791* (Liverpool, 1994).
Bredin, M., *The Pale Abyssinian: a Life of James Bruce, African Explorer and Adventurer* (2000).
Bryant, M., *The Clapham Sect* (2004).
Bygott, D., *Black and British* (Oxford, 1992).
Carretta, V., 'Friends of Freedom: Three African-British Men of Letters in Eighteenth-Century Westminster', *Westminster History Review* 3 (1999), pp. 1–10.
Carretta, V., *Equiano, the African: Biography of a Self-Made Man* (Athens, GA, 2005).
Cashmore, E.E., *Dictionary of Race and Ethnic Relations* (2nd edn, 1988).
Chater, K., 'Where there's a Will', *History Today* 50 (4) April 2000, pp. 26–7.
Chater, K., 'Hidden from History: Black People in Parish Records', *Genealogists' Magazine* 26 (10), June 2000, pp. 381–4.
Chater, K., 'Black Ancestry', *Ancestors* 1, October/November 2001, pp. 19–23.
Coldham, P.W., *The King's Passengers to Maryland and Virginia* (Westminster, MD, 1997).
Collicott, S., *Connections: Haringey Local-National-World Links* (1986).
Cordingley, D., *Billy Ruffian: the Bellerophon and the Downfall of Napoleon, a Biography of a Ship of the Line, 1782–1836* (2003).
Costello, R., *Black Liverpool: the Early History of Britain's Oldest Black Community 1730–1918* (Liverpool, 2000).

Cottle, B., *The Penguin Dictionary of Surnames* (2nd edn, 1978).
Coules, V., *The Trade: Bristol and the Transatlantic Slave Trade* (Edinburgh, 2007).
Craton, M., *Empire, Enslavement and Freedom in the Caribbean* (Oxford, 1997).
Craton, M., Walvin, J. & Wright, D., *Slavery, Abolition and Emancipation* (1976).
Dabydeen, D., 'Hogarth – the Savage and the Civilised', *History Today* 31 (9) September 1981, pp. 48–51.
Dabydeen, D., *Hogarth's Blacks: Images of Blacks in Eighteenth Century English Art* (Kingston-upon-Thames, 1985).
Dabydeen, D., Gilmore, J. & Jones, C. (eds), *The Oxford Companion to Black British History* (Oxford, 2007).
Davis, D.B., *The Problem of Slavery in Western Culture* (Oxford, 1966).
Davis, D.B., *Slavery and Human Progress* (Oxford, 1984).
Drescher, S., 'Manumissions in a Society without Slave Law: Eighteenth Century England', *Slavery & Abolition* 10 (1989), pp. 85–101.
Dresser, M., *Slavery Obscured: the Social History of the Slave Trade in an English Provincial Port* (2001).
Duffield, I., 'History and the Historians', *History Today* 31 (9) September 1981, pp. 34–6.
Duffield, I., 'From Slave Colonies to Penal Colonies: the West Indian Convict Transportees to Australia', *Slavery & Abolition* 7 (1) 1986, pp. 25–45.
Dunn, R.S., *Sugar and Slaves: the Rise of the Planter Class in the English West Indies 1624–1713* (NY, 1973).
Edwards, P., 'Black Personalities in Georgian Britain', *History Today* 31 (9) September 1981, pp. 39–43.
Elder, M., *Lancaster and the Slave Trade* (Lancaster, nd).
Elkins, S.M., *Slavery: a Problem in American Institutional and Intellectual Life* (Chicago, 1959).
Ellis, J.D., 'Black Soldiers in British Army Regiments during the Early Nineteenth Century', *AAHGS News*, March/April 2001, pp. 12–15.
Ellis, J.D., 'Drummers for the Devil? The Black Soldiers of the 29th (Worcestershire) Regiment of Foot, 1759–1843', *Journal of the Society for Army Historical Research* 80, 2002, pp. 186–202.
Eltis, D., Behrendt, S.D., Richardson, D. & Klein, H.S. (eds), *The Trans-Atlantic Slave Trade on CD-ROM* (Cambridge, 1999).
Evans, J.A.H., 'Nathaniel Wells of Piercefield and St Kitts: From Slave to Sheriff', *Monmouthshire Antiquary* (2000), pp. 91–106.
Farrell, S., Unwin, M. & Walvin, J. (eds), *The British Slave Trade: Abolition, Parliament and People* (Edinburgh, 2007).
File, N. & Power, C., *Black Settlers in Britain 1555–1958* (1981).
Fisher, H.J., *Slavery in the History of Muslim Black Africa* (2001).
Fraser, P.D., 'The Contributions of Black People to London: Some Historical

Reflections', paper presented to the Conference on the History of Black People in London, London, 27-29 November 1984.

Fraser, P.D., *Before Windrush: the Early Black Presence in Hammersmith and Fulham* (2000).

Fryer, P., *Staying Power: the History of Black People in Britain* (1984).

Gerzina, G., *Black England* (1995).

Gerzina, G., *Black London* (1995).

Gilroy, P., *The Black Atlantic: Modernity and Double Consciousness* (1993).

GLC Ethnic Minorities Unit, *A History of the Black Presence in London* (1986).

Green, J., 'Before the Windrush', *History Today* 50 (10) October 2000, pp. 29-35.

Habib, I., *Black Lives in the British Archives, 1500-1677: Imprints of the Invisible* (Aldershot, 2008).

Harris, R., *The Diligent: a Voyage through the Worlds of the Slave Trade* (2002).

Heumann, G., 'The Response of the Slaves', *History Today* 34 (4) April 1984, p. 31.

Hochschild, A., *Bury the Chains* (NY, 2005).

Jagdish, G. & Duffield, I. (eds), *Essays on the History of Blacks in Britain: From Roman Times to the mid-Twentieth Century* (Avebury, 1992).

Jayasuriya, S. de S. & Pankhurst, R., *The African Diaspora in the Indian Ocean* (Lawrenceville, NJ, 2001).

Jones, P. & Youseph, R., *The Black Population of Bristol in the Eighteenth Century* (Bristol, 1994).

Jordan, M., *The Great Abolition Sham: the True Story of the End of the British Slave Trade* (Stroud, 2005).

Kaufman, M., '"the speedy transportation of Blackamoores", Caspar Van Senden's search for Africans and profit in Elizabethan England', *BASA Newsletter* 45.

Killingray, D. 'All Conditions of Life and Labour: the Presence of Black People in Essex before 1950', *Essex Archaeology and History* 35 (2004), pp. 114-22.

Killingray, D. & Edwards, J., *Black Voices: the Shaping of our Christian Experience* (Nottingham, 2007).

King, R., Sandhu, S., Walvin, J. & Girdham, J., *Ignatius Sancho an African Man of Letters* (1997).

Klein, H.S., *The Atlantic Slave Trade* (Cambridge, 1999).

Kolchin, P., *American Slavery 1619-1877* (Canada, 1993).

Kopytoff, I. & Meirs, S., *Slavery in Africa* (Wisconsin, 1977).

Liverpool and Slavery by a Genuine 'Dicky Sam' (Liverpool, 1884, reprinted Newcastle-upon-Tyne, 1969).

Little, K., *Negroes in Britain* (1948).

Locke, G., *Caribbeans in Wandsworth* (1998).

Lorimer, D., *Colour, Class and the Victorians* (1978).

Lotz, R. & Pegg, D. (eds), *Under the Imperial Carpet: Essays in Black History 1780-1950* (Crawley, 1986).

McGrady, R., *Music and Musicians in Early Nineteenth Century Cornwall: the World of Joseph Emidy – Slave, Violinist and Composer* (Exeter, 1991).

MacKeith, L., *Local Black History: a Beginning in Devon* (2003).

Marsh, J. (ed.), *Black Victorians: Black People in British Art 1800–1900* (2007)

Martin, S.I., *Britain's Slave Trade* (1999).

Merriman, N., *The Peopling of London* (1993).

Midgley, C., *Women Against Slavery: the British Campaigns 1780–1870* (1992).

Midgley, C., 'Feminist Historians and Challenges to Imperialist History', in *Re-presenting the Past*, ed. Gallagher, A.-M., Lubelska, C. & Ryan, L. (2001).

Millar, J. 'White Slaves with Black Faces: Scottish coalminers in the 17th and 18th centuries', *Family Tree Magazine* 18, April 2002, pp. 66–7.

Minney, S., 'The Search for Dido', *History Today* 55 (10) October 2005, pp. 2–3.

Morgan, P.D., & Hawkins, S. (eds) *Black Experience and the Empire* (Oxford, 2004).

Morris, D., 'Mile End Old Town Residents and the East India Company', *East London Record* 9, 1986, pp. 20–7.

Morris, D., 'Stepney Merchants and the Slave Trade', *Cockney Ancestor* 89, Winter 2000–1, pp. 20–5.

Morris, D., *Mile End Old Town Residents 1741–1790*, CD-ROM (2004).

Myers, N., *Reconstructing the Black Past: Blacks in Britain 1780–1830* (1996).

Paley, R., 'After Somerset: Mansfield, Slavery and the Law in England' in *Law, Crime and English Society 1660–1830*, ed. Landau, N. (Cambridge, 2002), pp. 165–84.

Pearl, S., 'Britain's Black African Ancestors', *Family Tree* 11, October 1995, pp. 11–12.

Pearson, M.P. & Godden, K., *In Search of the Red Slave* (Stroud, 2002).

Phillips, C., *The Atlantic Sound* (NY, 2000).

Phillips, C. & Redeker, M., *The Slave Ship: a Human History* (2007).

Pope-Hennessy, J., *Sins of the Fathers: a Study of the Atlantic Slave Traders 1441–1807* (1967).

Ramdin, R., *The Making of the Black Working Class in Britain* (Aldershot, 1987).

Ramdin, R., *Reimaging Britain: 500 Years of Black and Asian History* (1999).

Rawley, J.A., *London, Metropolis of the Slave Trade* (Colombia, MA, 2003).

Rigg, A.N., *Cumbria, Slavery and the Textile Revolution* (1994).

St Clair, W., *The Grand Slave Emporium: Cape Coast Castle and the British Slave Trade* (2006).

Salazar, L.E., *Love Child: a Genealogist's Guide to the Social History of Barbados* (Barbados, 2000).

Schama, S., *Rough Crossings* (2005).

Schwarz, S. (ed.), *Slave Captain: the Career of James Irving in the Liverpool Slave Trade* (Clywd, 1995).

Scobie, E., *Black Britannia* (Chicago, IL, 1972).

Sharpe, J., *Crime in Seventeenth Century England: a County Study* (Cambridge, 1983).
Sherwood, M., 'Blacks in the Gordon Riots', *History Today* 47 (12) December 1998, pp. 24-8.
Shirley, P., 'Tek Force Wid Force', *History Today* 54 (4) April 2004, pp. 30-5.
Shoemaker, R.B., *Prosecution and Punishment: Petty Crime and the Law in London and Rural Middlesex c.1660-1725* (Cambridge, 1991).
Shyllon, F.O., *Black Slaves in Britain* (Oxford, 1974).
Shyllon, F.O., *Black People in Britain 1555-1833* (Oxford, 1977).
Sparks, R.J., *The Two Princes of Calabar* (Cambridge, MA, 2004).
Spence, C., 'Seeing Some Black in the Union Jack', *History Today* 52 (10) October 2002, pp. 30-6.
Stead, D., 'Slaves to History', *BBC History* (October 2001), pp. 38-41.
Tattersfield, N., *The Forgotten Trade* (1991).
Taylor, S., *The Caliban Shore: the Fate of the Grosvenor Castaways* (2004).
Thomas, H., *The Slave Trade* (1997).
Tibbles, A., *Transatlantic Slavery: Against Human Dignity* (1994).
Tower Hamlets African Caribbean Mental Health Organisation, *Power Writers: Discovering and Celebrating Five African Writers who came to London in the Eighteenth Century* (2003).
Turley, D., *Slavery* (Oxford, 2000).
Vigne, R. & Littleton, C. (eds), *From Strangers to Citizens: the Integration of Immigrant Communities in Britain, Ireland and Colonial America, 1550-1750* (2001).
Visram. R., *Ayahs, Lascars and Princes* (1986).
Visram, R., *Asians in Britain: 400 Years of History* (2002).
Walker, C.E., *Deromanticizing Black History: Critical Essays and Reappraisals* (Knoxville, TN, 1991).
Walvin, J., *The Black Presence: a Documentary History of the Negro in England 1555-1860* (NY, 1971).
Walvin, J., *Black and White: the Negro and English Society 1555-1945* (1973).
Walvin, J., *Slavery, Abolition and Emancipation* (1976).
Walvin, J., 'The Eighteenth Century', *History Today* 31 (9) September 1981, pp. 37-9.
Walvin, J. (ed.), *Slavery and British Society 1776-1846* (1982).
Walvin, J., *Passage to Britain* (1984).
Walvin, J., *England, Slaves and Freedom 1776-1838* (Basingstoke, 1986).
Walvin, J., *Slaves and Slavery: the British Colonial Experience* (Manchester, 1992).
Walvin, J., *Black Ivory: a History of British Slavery* (1992).
Walvin, J., *Questioning Slavery* (1996).
Walvin, J., *The Slave Trade* (Stroud, 1999).
Walvin, J., *Britain's Slave Empire* (2000).
Walvin, J., *An African's Life: the Life and Times of Olaudah Equiano* (2000).

Walvin, J., *Making the Black Atlantic* (2000).
Walvin, J., 'Slavery and the British', *History Today* 52 (3) March 2002, pp. 48–54.
Walvin, J. *The Trader, the Owner, the Slave* (2007).
Walvin, J. & Heuman, G. (eds), *The Slavery Reader* (2003).
Walvin, J., Craton, M. & Wright, D. (eds), *Slavery and British Society 1776–1846* (1982).
Ward, W.E.F., *A History of the Gold Coast* (1948).
Waterson, M., *The Servants' Hall: a Domestic History of Erdigg* (1980).
Welch, P.L.V., 'The Urban Context of Slave Life: Views from Bridgetown, Barbados in the 18th and 19th Centuries', paper submitted to the 29th Annual Conference of the Association of Caribbean Historians, 7–12 April 1997, on <www.geocities.com/Athens/Ithaca/1834/document1.htm>.
Welch, P.L.V., 'Madams and Mariners: Expressions of Self-confidence among Free Coloured Women in Barbados 1750–1834' on <www.geocities.com/Athens/Ithaca/1834/documents..htm>.
Williams, E., *Capitalism and Slavery* (1964).
Williams, E., *From Columbus to Castro: the History of the Caribbean 1492–1969* (1970).
Wise, S.E., *Though the Heavens May Fall: the Landmark Trial that Led to the End of Human Slavery* (Cambridge, MA, 2005).

General works

Akyeampong, E. (ed.), *Themes in West Africa's History* (Oxford, 2006).
Attwater, D., *A Dictionary of Saints* (1965).
Barley, N., *The Innocent Anthropologist* (1983).
Barley, N., *A Plague of Caterpillars* (1986).
Bayne-Powell, R., *Eighteenth Century London Life* (1937).
Beames, T., *The Rookeries of London, Past, Present and Perspective* (1850).
Beattie, J.M., *Crime and the Courts in England 1660–1800* (Princeton, NJ, 1986).
Beattie, J.M., *Policing and Punishment in London 1660–1750* (Oxford, 2001).
Benton, T., *Irregular Marriage in London before 1754* (1993).
Black, J., *The English Press 1621–1861* (Stroud, 2001).
Bondeson, J., *The London Monster* (Philadelphia, PA, 2001).
Bryant, A., *Samuel Pepys: the Man in the Making* (1933).
Bryant, A., *Samuel Pepys: the Years of Peril* (1935).
Bryant, A., *Samuel Pepys: the Saviour of the Navy* (1938).
Cannadine, D., *Orientalism* (2001).
Carr, E.H., *What is History?* (1961).
Chamberlain, M.E., *The Scramble for Africa* (nd).
Cobley, J., *The Crimes of First Fleet Convicts* (1970).
Cockburn, J.S. (ed.), *Crime in England 1550–1800* (Princeton, NJ, 1977).
Coldham, P.W., *Emigrants in Chains: a Social History of Forced Emigration to the*

Americas of Felons, Destitute Children, Political and Religious Nonconformists, Vagabonds, and Other Undesirables 1607–1776 (Baltimore, MD, 1992).
Colley, L., *Britons: Forging the Nation 1707–1837* (1992).
Colley, L., *Captives: Britain, Empire and the World 1660–1850* (2002).
Dabydeen, D., *Hogarth, Walpole and Commercial Britain* (1987).
Davidson, B., *African Civilisation Revisited* (Trenton, NJ, 1991).
Dillon, P., *The Much-lamented Death of Madam Geneva: the Eighteenth Century Gin Craze* (2002).
Ditchfield, P.H., *The Parish Clerk* (1907).
Earle, P., *A City Full of People: Men and Women of London 1650–1750* (1994).
Ekirch, A.R., *Bound for America: the Transportation of British Convicts to the Colonies 1718–1775* (Oxford, 1987).
Emsley, C., *Crime and Society in England 1750–1900* (1987).
Faller, L.B., *Turned to Account* (Cambridge, 1987).
Findlay, R., *Population and Metropolis* (Cambridge, 1981).
Flinn, M.W., *British Population Growth 1700–1850* (1970).
Flynn, M., *The Second Fleet: Britain's Grim Convict Armada of 1790* (Sydney, NSW, 1993).
Foreman, A., *Georgiana, Duchess of Devonshire* (1998).
Friar, S., *A Companion to the English Parish Church* (Stroud, 1996).
Gage, J., 'The Rise and Fall of the St Giles Rookery', *Camden History Review* 12 (1984), pp. 17–23.
Gatrell, V.A.C., *The Hanging Tree: Execution and the English People, 1770–1868* (Oxford, 1994).
George, M.D., *London Life in the Eighteenth Century* (2nd edn, 1930).
Gérin, W., *Horatia Nelson* (Oxford, 1970).
Gillen, M., *The Founders of Australia: a Biographical Dictionary of the First Fleet* (Sydney, NSW, 1989).
Giraud, M. *Life in the English Country House* (Yale, 1978).
Glass, D.V. & Eversley, D.E.C., *Population in History* (1965).
Godfrey, R., *James Gillray: the Art of Caricature* (2001).
Goldsmith, N.M., *The Worst of Crimes: Homosexuality and the Law in Eighteenth-Century London* (Aldershot, 1998).
Gwynn, R.D., *Huguenot Heritage: the History and Contribution of the Huguenots in Britain* (1985).
Harding, A., *A Social History of English Law* (1966).
Harvey, A.D., *Sex in Georgian England* (1994).
Hawkings, D.T., *Bound for Australia* (Chichester, 1987).
Hay, D., Linebaugh, P., Rule, J.G., Thompson, E.P. & Winslow C., *Albion's Fatal Tree: Crime and Society in Eighteenth-Century England* (1975).
Hazelwood, N.J., *Savage: the Life and Times of Jemmy Button* (NY, 2001).
Hecht, J.J., *Continental and Colonial Servants in Eighteenth Century England* Smith College Studies in History, vol. XL, 1954 (Northampton, MA.).

Hecht, J.J., *The Domestic Servant Class in Eighteenth-Century England* (1956).
Henderson, T., *Disorderly Women in Eighteenth Century London* (1999).
HMSO, *Chronological Table of the Statutes* (published annually).
Hibbert, C., *King Mob: the London Riots of 1780* (1958).
Hill, C., *Reformation to Industrial Revolution* (2nd edn, 1969).
Horowitz, M.C. (ed.), *Race, Gender and Rank: Early Modern Ideas of Humanity* (NY, 1992).
Isichei, E., *A History of African Societies to 1870* (Cambridge, 1997).
James, P.S., *Introduction to English Law* (12th edn, 1989).
Jervis, J., *The Office and Duties of Coroners* (1829).
Johnson, N., *Eighteenth Century London* (1991).
King, P., *Crime, Justice, and Discretion in England 1740–1820* (Oxford, 2000).
Knight, B., *The History of the Coroner* on <www.britannia.com/history/coroner2.html>.
Langford, P., *A Polite and Commercial People: England 1727–1783* (Oxford, 1989).
Lasch-Quinn, E., *Race Experts: How Racial Etiquette, Sensitivity Training and New Age Therapy Hijacked the Civil Rights Revolution* (NY, 2001).
Laslett, P., Oosterveen, C. & Smith, R.M., *Bastardy and Its Comparative History* (1980).
Laslett, P., *The World We Have Lost Further Explored* (3rd edn, 1983).
Lewis, J., *Printed Ephemera* (1962).
Linebaugh, P., *The London Hanged* (1991).
Linebaugh, P. & Redeker, M., *The Many-Headed Hydra: the Hidden History of the Revolutionary Atlantic* (2000).
Lock, J., *Tales from Bow Street* (1982).
Lummis, T., *Life and Death in Eden: Pitcairn Island and the* Bounty *Mutineers* (1997).
Lummis, T. & Marsh, J., *The Woman's Domain: Women and the English Country House* (1990).
McEvedy, C. *The Penguin Atlas of African History* (rev. edn 1995).
McGrandle L.,*The Cost of Living in Britain* (1973).
McLynn, F., *Crime and Punishment in Eighteenth Century England* (1989).
McMullen, F., *The Canting Crew* (Rutgers, NJ, 1984).
Manwaring, G.E. and Dobree, B., *The Floating Republic* (1966).
Marshall, D.M., *Eighteenth Century England* (1962).
Marshall, D.M., *The English Poor in the Eighteenth Century* (1926).
Marshall, P.J. (ed.) *The Oxford History of the British Empire, Vol. II: the Eighteenth Century* (Oxford, 1998).
Martin, J., *Wives and Daughters: Women and Children in the Georgian Country House* (2004).
Milton, G., *White Gold: the Extraordinary Story of Thomas Pellow and North Africa's One Million European Slaves* (2004).

Minchinton, W.E. (ed.), *Wage Regulation in Pre-Industrial England* (Newton Abbot, 1972).
Mitchell, R.J. & Leys, M.D.R., *A History of London Life* (1958).
Morris, D., *Mile End Old Town 1740-1780: a Social History of an Early Modern London Suburb* (2002).
Mundy, G.B., *Life and Correspondence of the late Admiral Lord Rodney* (1830).
Neuberg, V., *Popular Literature: a History and Guide* (1977).
Nicholson, G. & Fawcett, J., *The Village in History* (1988).
Ogot, B. (ed.), *The UNESCO General History of Africa: Vol. V: Africa from the Sixteenth to the Eighteenth Century* (abridged edn, Oxford, 1999).
Oldham, W., *Britain's Convicts to the Colonies* (Sydney, NSW, 1990),
Peakman, J., *Mighty Lewd Books: the Development of Pornography in Eighteenth Century England* (Basingstoke, 2003).
Peakman, J., *Lascivious Bodies: a Sexual History of the Eighteenth Century* (2004).
Porter, R., *Madmen: a Social History of Madhouses, Mad-Doctors and Lunatics* (2004).
Prideaux, R.M., *Prideaux, A West Country Clan* (Chichester, 1989).
Pugh, R.B., 'Newgate between Two Fires', *Guildhall Studies in London History* 3 (3) October 1978, pp. 137-163.
Razzell, P., *Essays in English Population History* (1994).
Rees, S., *The Floating Brothel* (2001).
Rodger, N.A.M., *The Wooden World: an Anatomy of the Georgian Navy* (1986).
Rogers, B., *Beef and Liberty: Roast Beef, John Bull and the English Nation* (2003).
Rogers, N., 'Vagrancy, Impressment and the Regulation of Labour in Eighteenth-Century Britain', *Slavery & Abolition* 15 (1994) pp. 102-13.
Rose, M.E., *The English Poor Law 1780-1930* (Newton Abbott, 1971).
Rozbicki, M.J., 'To Save Them from Themselves: Proposals to Enslave the British Poor, 1698-1755', *Slavery & Abolition* 22 (2001), pp. 29-50.
Rubenhold, H., *The Covent Garden Ladies: Pimp General Jack and the Extraordinary Story of Harris's List* (2005).
Rumblew, D., *The Triple Tree* (1982).
Rutherford, J. (ed.), *Identity: Community, Culture, Difference* (NY, 1990).
Rudé, G., *The Crowd in History 1730-1848* (2nd edn, 1981).
Sambrook, G.A. (ed.), *English Life in the Eighteenth Century* (1960).
Samson, J. (ed.), *The British Empire* (Oxford, 2001).
Sawyer, P., *Christopher Rich of Drury Lane: the Biography of a Theatre Manager* (1986).
Schwarz, H., *The French Prophets: the History of a Millenarian Group in Eighteenth-Century England* (Los Angeles, CA, 1980).
Scouladi, I. *Returns of Strangers in the Metropolis 1593, 1627, 1635, 1639*, Huguenot Society of London, Quarto Series, Vol. LVII (1985).
Slack, P., *The English Poor Law 1531-1782* (Cambridge, 1995).
Smee, C.J., *First Fleet Families* (Artamon, NSW, 1991).

Smee, C.J., *Second Fleet Families* (Artamon, NSW, 1991).
Smee, C.J., *Third Fleet Families* (Artamon, NSW 1992).
Sprott, D., *1784* (1984).
Steedman, C., *Dust* (Manchester, 2001).
Stone, L., *Road to Divorce: England 1530–1987* (Oxford, 1990).
Stone, L., *Uncertain Unions: Marriage in England 1660–1753* (Oxford, 1992).
Stone, L., *Broken Lives: Separation and Divorce in England 1660–1857* (Oxford, 1993).
Stone, L., *The Family, Sex and Marriage in England 1500–1800* (1979).
Styles J., 'Crime in Eighteenth Century England', *History Today* 38 (3) March 1988, pp. 36–42.
Simond, L., *Journal of a Tour and Residence in Great Britain during the Years 1810 and 1811, etc.* (1815), republ. as *An American in Regency England*, ed. Hibbert, C. (1968).
Taylor, D., *Crime, Policing and Punishment in England, 1750–1914* (1998).
Tillyard, S., *Aristocrats: Caroline, Emily, Louisa and Sarah Lennox 1740–1832* (1994).
Tillyard, S., *Citizen Lord: Edward Fitzgerald 1763–1798* (1997).
Tosh, J., *The Pursuit of History: Aims, Methods and New Directions in the Study of Modern History* (2nd edn, 1991).
Vickery, A., *The Gentleman's Daughter: Women's Lives in Georgian England* (Yale, 1998).
Williams, E., *Capitalism and Slavery* (1944).
Williams, G., *The Prize of All the Oceans* (1999).
Williams, R.M., *British Population* (2nd edn, 1978).
Wrigley, E.A., *An Introduction to English Historical Demography* (1966).
Wrigley, E.A., *Population and History* (1969).
Wrigley, E.A. and Schofield, R.S., *The Population History of England 1541–1871* (1981).

Guides to records

Chater, K., *Tracing Your Family Tree in England, Ireland, Scotland and Wales* (2001).
CLRO, Research Guide 3: *Transportation and Emigration*.
CLRO, Information Sheet 14: *Sessions Records in CLRO*.
Colwell, S., *Family Roots* (1991).
Colwell, S., *Dictionary of Genealogical Sources in the Public Record Office* (1992).
Cox, J. & Padfield, T., *Tracing Your Ancestors in the Public Record Office*, ed. Bevan, A. & Duncan, A. (4th edn, 1990).
Guildhall Library, *City of London Parish Registers: Part I: City of London* (6th edn, 1990).

Grannum, G., *Tracing Your West Indian Ancestors* (2nd edn, 2002).
Hawkings, D.T., *Criminal Ancestors: a Guide to Historical Criminal Records in England and Wales* (Stroud, 1992).
Jones, P.E. & Smith, R., *A Guide to the Records in the Corporation of London Records Office and the Guildhall Library Muniment Room* (1951).
London Metropolitan Archives, Information Sheet: *Convicts Transported from Middlesex*.
Manross, W.W., *The Fulham Papers in the Lambeth Palace Library: American Colonial Section Calendars and Indexes* (Oxford, 1965).
Riden, P., *Record Sources for Local History* (1987).
Steel, D.J., *Sources for Nonconformist Genealogy and Family History* (1973).
Tate, W.E., *The Parish Chest* (3rd edn, Cambridge, 1969).
TNA (The National Archives), Legal Records Information 13: *Criminal Trials at the Assizes*.
TNA, Legal Records Information 27: *Old Bailey and the Central Criminal Courts: Criminal Trials*.
TNA, Legal Records Information 34: *the King's Bench (Crown Side) Records 1675-1875*.
TNA, Domestic Records Information 88: *Sources for Convicts and Prisoners 1100-1986*.
Walne, P. (ed.), *A Guide to the Manuscript Sources for the History of Latin America and the Caribbean in the British Isles* (Oxford, 1973).
Webb, C., *An Index of Wills Proved in the Archdeaconry Court of London 1700-1807* (1996).

Local and regional histories

Anon., *The Chronicles of the Parish of East Ham According to the Old Minute Books (1735-1867)*.
Burford, E.J., *Wits, Wenchers and Wantons* (1986).
Burford, E.J., *Royal St James* (1988).
Byrne, R., *Prisons and Punishments of London* (1989).
Chambers, J.D. *Nottinghamshire Life in the Eighteenth Century* (2nd edn, 1966).
Draper, W.H., *Hammersmith: a Study in Town History* (1913).
Hugues, E., *North Country Life in the Eighteenth Century*, 2 vols (Oxford, 1952 and 1965).
Landers, J., *Death and the Metropolis* (Cambridge, 1993).
Mitchell, R.J. & Leys, M.D.R., *A History of London Life* (1958).
Oliver, G., *History of the City of Exeter* (Exeter, 1861).
Picard, L., *Restoration London* (1997).
Picard, L., *Dr Johnson's London* (2000).
Rose, R., *Pembroke People* (2000).
Rudé, G., *Hanoverian London 1714-1808* (Los Angeles, CA, 1971).

Sykes, J. (comp.), *Local Records – Northumberland, Durham &c* (1866) CD-ROM (Cinderford, 2005).
Walford, E. and Thornbury, W., *Old and New London*, 3 vols (1872–78) reprinted as *London Recollected: Its History, Lore and Legends* (1986).
Waller, M., *1700: Scenes from London Life* (2000).
Weinreb, B. & Hibbert, C. (eds), *The London Encyclopaedia* (1983).
Whitting, P.D. (ed.), *A History of Fulham to 1965* (1970).
Wyld, P., *Stepney Story* (1952).

Index

Note: 'n' after a page references indicates the number of a note on that page. Page numbers in *italic* refer to illustrations

advertisements 3
   'Hue and Cry' 93
   places wanted 84
   for runaways 4, 82, 84, 92–4
   for sale 86–7, 197, 224
Africa, Sons of 39, 161, 180. 196
Africanus family of Nottingham 212–13, *213*
   George John Scipio 230, 233
Anglicans *see* England, Church of
apprentices and apprenticeships 4, 81, 85, 139, 229–32

baptisms 1, 55–61, 63, 108, 127–8, 176–82
   1812 Parochial Registers Act 138
   age at 58, 61–2, 67, 116
   of children 197–8
   and emancipation 84, 91
   motives for 181–2
   and settlement 136–7, 139
   sponsors/godparents 100n.60, 181–2
Barber, Francis 6, 192, 209–10
Barley, Nigel 163
bastardy *see* children, illegitimate
Batten, Sir William 87, 96n.9

Bedfordshire
   Bedford 207
Behn, Aphra *Oronooko or the Royal Slave* 46, 81
Belle, Dido Elizabeth 7, 100n.66, 184, 207, 212
Berkshire
   Windsor, Old 88
Bickerstaff, Isaac and Dibden, Charles *The Padlock* 46
'Black's Lamentation, The' 45
Boateng, Paul 175n.53
Braidwood, Stephen 7, 48
Burford, Edward 47
Buckinghamshire
   Aylesbury 221n.62
   Beaconsfield 237
   Hanslope 237
   Penn 245n.79
   Radnage 214
   Wycombe, High 226
   Wycombe, West 221n.54
burials 1, 21, 61, 63, 136, 178

Cambridgeshire
   Cambridge 150–7
Carr, E.H. 1–2
Carretta, Vincent 8, 210

Cashmore, E. Ellis 164
censuses 21, 149
Cheshire
   Altrincham 177
   Liscard 214
children 11, 95, 149–51, 211–12
   database of 11
   illegitimate 89, 139, 145–7, 207
   see also baptisms, of children
Chudleigh, Lady Mary 'To the Ladies' 81
Clarkson, Thomas 79
Collars 100n.61, 197–8
Committee for the Relief of the Black Poor 27, 136
Cornwall
   Calstock 89
   Falmouth 17n.26
   Fowey 136–7
   Launceston 228
   St Gluvias 33n.7, 205
   Truro 17n.26, 196
Cranbrook family 206, 214–15, *215*
   John 233
Craton, Michael 4, 5
courts 102–4
Cruikshank, George 46, *47*
Cuffay, William 5, 193–4
Cugoano, Ottobah 8, 161
Cumbria
   Whitehaven 27, 150

Dabydeen, David 82, 92, 222
databases of Black people 9–12
Davidson, William 5, 238, *239*
Davinier, Dido Elizabeth, *see* Belle, Dido Elizabeth
defining a 'Black' person 22–5, 107–9
Defoe, Daniel 45
Devon 216
   Exeter 200n.31
   Moretonhampstead 171
   Topsham 206

Dewjee, Audrey 30–1
Dickerson, Debra J. 163
discrimination *see* prejudice and discrimination
Dorset
   Poole 86
   Weymouth 27
Drescher, Seymour 83–5
Duck family 203
   Ann 25, 111–12, 116, 125, 128–9, 234
   John 225–6, 233

Earle, Peter 66, 233
East India Company 32, 54, 62
Edwards, Bryan 165
Edwards, Joel 9
Edward, Paul 8
Egan, Pierce *Life in London* 46–7, *47*
Ellis, John 26, 235
Emidy, Joseph 17n.26, 206
England, Church of 176–9
   1812 Parochial Registers Act 13, 138–9
   parish registers 10, 21
   role in local government 29, 137, 178–9, 232
Equiano, Olaudah 8, 39–40, 95, 161, 171–2, 179–80, 185–6, 195, 210–11, 235, 244n.63
Essex 67
   Birchanger 139–40
   Chigwell 143
   Earl's Colne 200n.31
   Ham, East 83
   Ham, West *80*, 99n.47, 202n.87
   Stratford 87
   Walthamstow 96n.9

Fielding, Henry 42, 45
Fielding, Sir John 42, 95, 115
Florida family 214, 214–17, *217*

Fraser, Peter 164
Fryer, Peter 7, 82, 93, 164, 197, 231

Gainsborough, Thomas 222
Garrick, David and Boyce, William 'Hearts of Oak' 81
Gates, Henry Louis 160
Gay, John *The Beggar's Opera* 46
George, M. Dorothy 2, 4, 6, 40, 50, 166, 199n.16
Gerzina, Gretchen 7, 47, 164
Gillray, James, 166
Gloucestershire 170
   Bristol 27, 29, 93, 148, 198n.6, 201n.66
   Coates 238
   Gloucester 134n.73
   Newnham on Severn 229
Gordon Riots (1780) 25, 68n.8, 112, 130, 133n.49, 170
Gronniosaw, Ukawsaw 8–9, 33n.2, 36, 95, 161, 171–2, 209

Habib, Imtiaz 195
Hammon, Briton 8, 235
Hampshire
   Lymington 151
   Portsmouth 115, 236
   Tichbourne House 240n.4
Harris's Lists 44
Hecht, J. Jean 2, 224
Herefordshire
   Donnington 214
   Hereford 199n.25, 244n.67
Hertfordshire 237
   Barnet, East 183
   Cheshunt 123
   Hunsdon 154n.24
   Mimms, North 202n.76
   Redbourne 207
   Thorley 86
   Watford 237
   Westmill 237
Heuman, Ged 6
Hogarth, William 44
Huntingdonshire
   Huntingdon 140–1

identity 179–80
Independence, American War of 7, 27, 32, 41, 53, 119, 136
inquests 1, 102, 121 *passim*
Ireland 139

Jackman, Isaac *The Divorce* 85
Jea, John 9, 95
Johnson, Dr 6, 192–209
Juba family of Leicester 206, 212–14
Juba family of Lowestoft
   John 137

Kaufman, Miranda 159
Kent 67
   Bromley 33n.4
   Chatham 192
   Cranbrook 196
   Deptford 134n.59, 136
   Faversham 101n.77
   Greenwich 140, 146, 149–50, 206, 244–5n.74
   Lewisham 232
   Rochester 199n.23, 201n.75, 243n.51
   Sandwich 196
   Sheppey 206
   Shoreham 196
   Woolwich 205
Keppel, Elizabeth *223*
Killingray, David 9
King, Boston 8–9, 235
King, Peter 94
King, Reyhahn 222
Knight v. Wedderburn 96n.5
Kolchin, Peter 38, 173n.23

Laing, Robert 238-9
Lancashire
  Ashton-under-Lyne 228
  Burnley 214
  Childwall 201n.66
Lasch-Quinn, Elizabeth 6-7
Liverpool 27, 29, 214, 238
Leicestershire
  Earl Shilton 212
  Leicester 207
Lewsham, Amelia 39
Lincolnshire
  Lincoln 147-8
Linebaugh, Peter 5
Little, Kenneth 2
London 6, 26-7, 29
  Black population of 59-66
  City of 59-60, 89, 231
  City Without the Walls 60, 63-6
  Places in
    All Hallows London Wall 68n.5
    All Hallows Staining 243n.51
    Christchurch Newgate 133n.38, 134n.60
    Farringdon Without, Ward of 99n.45
    Fleet Prison, Chapel and Rules of 205
    Holy Trinity Minories 55-6, 202n.79
    St Alphage London Wall 73n.81
    St Andrew Undershaft 155n.48
    St Ann & St Agnes 200n.29
    St Bene't and St Peter Paul's Wharf 73n.79
    St Botolph Aldersgate 73n.79
    St Bride Fleet Street 202n.86
    St Clement Eastcheap 73n.79
    St Dunstan in the West 193, 203
    St Edmund the King and Martyr 132n.22
    St Giles Cripplegate 48, 205
    St Helen's Bishopsgate 99n.45, 142, 200n.29
    St James Duke's Place 219n.23
    St Mary Aldermanbury 155n.47, 199n.21
    St Margaret Lothbury 73n.81
    St Margaret Moses 196
    St Olave Hart Street 73n.79, 99n.51, 142
    St Peter le Poer 190
    St Swithin London Stone 201n.66
    St Vedast Foster Lane 196
    Southwark 52, 60, 117, 178
    Temple Church 201n.70
Long, Edward 26, 47, 165, 170

Mackey, Brian 170-1, 238
Mansfield Judgment 3, 26, 40, 53, 57-8, 88-92, 94, 102, 137, 148-9, 159, 162, 235
Mansfield, Lord see Murray, William
Mansfield, Paul 94
Marrant, John 8-9, 235
marriage 208-11
  1753 Marriage Act 138, 204
  between Black and white people 151, 160, 203-4, 207-9
  between Black people 204-6
  irregular 55, 150, 219n.23
  motives for 208-11
  and settlement 136, *passim*
Marshall, M. Dorothy 144
Martin, S.I. 6
Mayo, Rev. Herbert 50-3, 178
Memoirs and Opinions of Mr Blenfield 45
Memorials 170, 228-9, 242n.24
Mercer, Kobena 179
Middlesex 67
  Barnet, East 183
  Bethnal Green 52
  Chelsea 123, 205
  Chiswick 146, 185
  Clerkenwell 105, 127, 145, 168, 233

Enfield 123
Hackney 106
Harmondsworth 88, 178
Harrow 140
Hillingdon 144-5, 228
Hounslow 226
Ickenham 70n.40
Kensington 205
Limehouse 196, 226
Mimms, South 70n.40, 195
Paddington 54-5
St Andrew Holborn 90, 201n.64
St George the Martyr Bloomsbury 42, 201n.62
St Giles in the Fields 40-50, *43*, 204,
   crime in 48-9
   St Giles's Black-birds 40-4
   Seven Dials 44,
St Katherine by the Tower 55-6, 60, 150
St Mary Moorfields 68n.8
St Marylebone 38, 55, 180
St Peter ad Vincula, 60
Smithfield, East 123-4, 162-3
Stanmore, Little 178
Stepney 205
   Mile End 50, 53-5
Stratford Bow 61, 73n.79
Teddington 89
Wapping 47, 50-3, 105, 148, 178, 207-8
Whitechapel 53 *passim*, 226
minorities, ethnic 36-8, 152, 231
   Dutch 37
   French 37, 44, 69n.27, 165, 169, 170-1
   Irish 40 *passim*, 121, 169
   Welsh 169-70
minorities, religious 21
   Catholics, Roman 37-8, 142, 152-3n.6, 159, 169, 177-8
   Huguenots 37, 45, 150 *passim*, 170, 180-1, 231
   Jews 37-8, 45, 107, 142, 160, 169, 231
   Muslims 37, 128, 136, 180

Nonconformists 29, 36, 151-2, 176, 203-4
Quakers (Society of Friends) 38, 77
Moors 24, 168, 195
Morris, Derek 54
Mortality, Bills of 35, *36*, 66
Murray, William (Lord Mansfield) 7, 26, 84, 184, 207 *see also* Mansfield Judgment
Myers, Norma 22, 29, 93, 110

Names 180-98
   African 193-5
   Christian 182-3
   classical 184-5
   generic 183-5
   heroic and whimsical 186
   place names 195-6
   standard 187-8
   surnames 189
   symbolic 190-1
   of women 187 *passim*
Nelson, Lord Horatio 193, 228, 244-5n.74
newspaper reports 1, 25, 105-6, 138, 161-2, 168 *passim*, 204
Norbrook/Northbrook family 216, 218
Nottinghamshire
Nottingham 212-13, 221, 230-3

occupations of Black people 10, 31, 39
   actress 46
   barrister 238
   beggars 26, 147-8, 153n.22, 161
   cabinet maker 230
   churchwarden 145, 233
   coal trader 233
   constable, parish 127, 145, 233
   drummer 183
   gardener 226
   groom 37
   market gardener 216
   militia 237

occupations of Black people (*cont.*)
  ministers of religion 238
  musicians 17n.26, 26, 206, 235
  prostitutes 129, 234
  sailors/seamen 30–1, 85, 116, 124, 235–7
  servants 31, 57, 83, 85, 88, 93, 95, 114–15, 129, 162, 170, 192–3, 204, 210, 222–5
    master-servant relationships 147, 226–9
    representations of Black servants 222
    and settlement 139–41
    wages and income 85–6, 139–40, 224–5
  sexton 145
  soldiers 26, 115, 130, 234–5
  teacher of sword fighting 225–6
  victuallers 226, 233
Old Bailey, Black people in trials at
  crimes 7
    arson 114–15
    assault 49, 112, 118
    committed against Black people 120–1
    committed by Black people 110–11
    database 11–2
    highwaymen 115
    manslaughter 97n.18, 123–4
    misdemeanours and felonies 103, 106
    murder 81, 82, 104, 116–18, 121–4
    perjury 204
    personation 109–10
    rape 110, 121, 129
    robbery and theft 48–9, 109, 121
  database of 11–12
  importance of character witnesses in 112 *passim*
  juries, exercise of 'discretion' by 103, 111–12
  pardons and commutations 103, 113
  sentences
    death 113–15
    imprisonment 124
    passed on Black people at the Old Bailey 115
    transportation 78–9, 113, 115–6, 119–20
    whipping 138
  roles of Black people in trials
    defendants 109–20
    prosecutors 120–1
    witnesses 81, 112, 127–8
  verdicts
    on crimes committed by Black people 111
    on crimes committed against Black people 124–7
Old Bailey, *Proceedings* of 40, 104–5, 107
Ordinary of Newgate's *Accounts* 114, 133n.38, n.40 and n.56, 134n.66, 241n.16
origins 8, 10–11, 24–5, 31–2, 41, 58–9, 62–6
  Africa 52, 83, 151, 178, 181, 228
  America, North 146, 187
  Canada 32
  Caribbean 187, 234
  Cuba 245n.79
  Barbados 83, 97n.24, 109, 194, 207
  Demerara 151
  Guadeloupe 148
  Jamaica 120, 141, 181, 194, 234, 237–8, 245n.81
  Martinique 228
  St Kitts 167, 194, 197, 236, 245n.82
  Tobago 151
  Asia
    China 32
    East Indies 117, 120, 128, 149, 183
    India 188, 238, 241n.16
Oxfordshire
  Oxford 226
  Wytham 178

Peakman, Julie 168
Pepys, Samuel 96n.9, 192, 225
Picton, Cesar 145, 233
Plague, Great of 1665 35, 61, 87
poor laws 137–43
   and illegitimate children 145–7
   and settlement 86, 103–4, 137–45
Pope-Hennessey, James 5
population, Black of England and Wales
   communities 38–55, 110, 160–3
   distribution of 26–30
   size of 25–30
prejudice and discrimination 127, 159–60
   class-based 5, 7
   cultural 112–13, 164
   racial 3, 118, 163–72
   segregation 1
Prince, Mary 171–2

racism *see* prejudice and discrimination
Ramdin, Ron 5
Redeker, Maurice 5
Richmond, Bill 230, *230*
runaways 84, 92–4
Royal Adventurers into Africa 12

Sancho, Ignatius 8–9, 39–40, 45, 161, 171–2, 179–80, 186–7, 197, 202n.89, 204, 211, 222, 233
Sandhu, Suhkdev 8
Schama, Simon 94
Scobie, Edward 3
Scotland 12, 78, 100n.61, 139, 147, 238
   Edinburgh 214
segregation *see* prejudice and discrimination
settlement *see* poor laws
sex ratio 30–1, 58, 61–2, 67, 128–9

Sharp, Granville 25–6, 79, 90, 171, 210
Shyllon, Folarian 4, 22, 29, 85, 92–3, 116, 161, 165 *passim*, 184, 197, 208
Sierra Leone project 7, 41, 50, 53, 210
slavery 3 *passim*, 77–8, 87, 91–5, 139
   abolition of 3, 77–9, 92
   in Africa 88
   definition of a slave 78
   in the colonies 94
   legality of 77, 88–9 *see also* Mansfield Judgment
   manumissions 83–5
   slave trades 5 *passim*, 24, *28*, 79
   slaves 1, 41
      sales of 86
      white 78–81, *80*
Smollett, Tobias 45
Snelgrave, William 54, 83
Somerset
   Bath 194
   Over Stowey 170–1
Somerset case *see* Mansfield Judgment
Soubise, Julius 197
Staffordshire
   Lichfield 98n.39
   Wolstanton 145, 233
stereotypes 167–70, 222
Stone, Lawrence 201n.54, 209
Stowe, Harriet Beecher *Uncle Tom's Cabin* 101n.75, 165
Suffolk
   Bury St Edmunds 27, 205
   Lowestoft 27, 137
   Tunstall 216
Surrey 67
   Ashtead 143
   Camberwell 48
   Cheam 203
   Clapham 214, 233

Surrey (*cont.*)
   Kingston-upon-Thames 233
   Lambeth 211
   Merton 193
   Putney 200n.42, 204–5
   Richmond 191–2
   Shalford 202n.87
   Surbiton 212
   Thames Ditton 154–5n.38
   Wimbledon 142
Sussex
   Battle 178
   Seaford 205

Thicknesse, Philip 47, 161, 165–6
Thomas, Hugh 5
Thomson, James 'Rule Britannia' 80
Tosh, John 2
Townley, James *High Life Below Stairs* 46

Vassa, Gustavus *see* Equiano, Olaudah

Wadström, Carl Bernard 40 *passim*
Wales 12–13, 77
   Caenarvonshire
     Ystumllyn 229
   Denbighshire
     Denbigh 28
   Glamorganshire
     Cardiff 3, 28, 34n.25, 38
   Monmouthshire 237
     Monmouth 221n.57
     Newport 28, 216
   Pembrokeshire
     Haverfordwest 28
     Monkton 205
Walvin, James 3 *passim*, 47, 208
Warwickshire
   Stratford-upon-Avon 214
   Wolverhampton 230
Wedderburn, Robert 5, 238
Wells, Nathaniel 237–8

Westminster 41–2, 48, 191
   Austria, Chapel of the Imperial Legation of 38
   Black population of 56–60 *passim*
   Dutch Chapel 37
   Queen's Chapel of the Savoy, The 56
   Royal Peculiars 56
   St Anne Soho 56
   St Clement Danes 45, 56 *passim*, 145, 153n.14, 203
   St George Hanover Square 56, 143, 200n.51 and n.52, 207
   St George's Chapel Mayfair 55
   St James Piccadilly 200n.45, 204, 218n.45
   St James's Park 168
   St John Smith Square 56
   St Margaret 72n.71, 145, 200n.39
   St Martin in the Fields 52, 56, 146, 153n.22
   St Mary le Strand 56, 72n.5, 66
   St Paul Covent Garden 47, 194, 201n.68, 230
   Venetian Chapel 38
Wheatley, Phyllis 172
Wheeler, Roxann 165
Wight, Isle of 236–7
wills
   of Black people 9, 85, 235
   Black people mentioned in 83, 88
Wiltshire
   Hindon 238
   Knoyle, East 245n.83
   Marlborough 237
   Trowbridge 235
Wise, Steven 100n.63, 152n.6
witchcraft 171

Yorkshire 31, 224
   Kirkby Ravensworth 145
   Hemsley Blackmoor 195
   Hull 169
   York 229

CPSIA information can be obtained
at www.ICGtesting.com
Printed in the USA
LVHW022327180720
661062LV00008B/283

9 780719 085970